This is a photograph of record album spines arranged vertically. The visible text on the spines (reading each spine):

- BTM 13949 — IRON BUTTERFLY
- LIVE IRON BUTTERFLY — IRON BUTTERFLY BALL
- IRON BUTTERFLY — IN-A-GADDA-DA-VIDA — No Muss...No Fuss — Donnie Iris
- THE BEST OF IRON BUTTERFLY — MCA-5111 — ATCO SD 33-318
- IRON MAIDEN · PIECE OF MIND — PRO-A-2265 — STAR COLLECTION IRON BUTTERFLY — EVOLUTION — HEAVY — IRON BUTTERFLY — ATCO SD 33-280
- 9 — 25156-1 — CHRIS ISAAK SILVERTONE — IRON CITY HOUSEROCKERS · HAVE A GOOD TIME (BUT GET OUT ALIVE) — ATCO SD 33-227
- 9 — 23686-1 — CHRIS ISAAK "DANCIN'"/"GONE RIDIN'" — WARNER BROS. RECORDS INC. PRINTED IN U.S.A.
- ROXY MUSIC · AVALON — FLESH AND BLOOD — WARNER BROS. RECORDS INC. PRINTED IN U.S.A.
- IRON MAIDEN · THE NUMBER OF THE BEAST — IRON MAIDEN · SEVENTH SON OF A SEVENTH SON
- IRON MAIDEN · MAIDEN JAPAN
- MS 2114 — ROXY MUSIC — ROXY MUSIC — GREATEST HITS
- SP-4744 — THE RETURN OF THE RED BARON — SNOOPY VS. THE RED BARON — THE ROYAL GUARDSMEN
- A&M SP 5234 — AMAZING GRACE—THE PIPES AND DRUMS AND MILITARY BAND OF THE ROYAL SCOTS DRAGOON GUARDS — POLYDOR DELUXE 2302 073
- 25914-1 — SNOOPY AND HIS FRIENDS · THE ROYAL GUARDSMEN — THE ROYAL GUARDSMEN — LAURIE RECORDS
- THE ROYAL COURT OF CHINA — GEARED & PRIMED — SIRE RECORDS
- ROYAL CRESCENT MOB · SPIN THE WORLD — ©1989 A&M RECORDS, INCORPORATED. PRINTED IN THE UNITED STA...
- 0598—WARNER BROS. RECORDS INC.—PRINTED IN U.S.
- BILLY JOE ROYAL · CHERRY HILL PARK — BILLY JOE ROYAL — MERCURY
- BILLY JOE ROYAL — GREATEST HITS — BILLY JOE ROYAL
- LET'S GONNA TAKE A BRIDGE — THE ROVLETTES
- 255592-1 — ROYALTY · RICH AND FAMOUS — 20th CENTURY-FOX RECORDS — WARNER BROS.
- WHERE'S MY HERO — ROZETTA — WARNER BROS. RECORDS INC.
- RPM — PHONOGENIC
- DEB CITY REBELS

Barcode labels:
- SO-CBP-951
- ART CENTER COLLEGE OF DESIGN
- 3 3220 00251 9390

# 1OOO
# RECORD
# COVERS

# 1OOO
# RECORD
# COVERS

Michael Ochs

# TASCHEN

KÖLN LONDON MADRID NEW YORK PARIS TOKYO

For Gertrude Ochs (1912–1994) who also loved Little Richard.

Front cover/Umschlag/Couverture:
Santana: *Abraxas* (p. 471)

Page/Seite 2:
Michael Ochs in the Michael Ochs Archives, Los Angeles, 1994
Photo: Jonathan Hyams

© 2002 TASCHEN GmbH
Hohenzollernring 53, D–50672 Köln
**www.taschen.com**

Original edition: © 1996 Benedikt Taschen Verlag GmbH

Text: Michael Ochs, Venice (CA), 1995
Design: Mark Thomson, London & Burkhard Riemschneider, Cologne
Edited by Burkhard Riemschneider, Cologne
French translation: Patrick Javault, Paris
German translation: Ulrike Wasel, Klaus Timmermann, Düsseldorf

Printed in Italy
ISBN 3–8228–1978–6
ISBN 2–7434–4333–2 (Edition réservée pour Maxi-Livres)

# Contents

# Inhalt

# Sommaire

## Introduction

When rock and roll and I were both very young, we started a friendship that has had its ups and downs, but has lasted many years. When first introduced to rock in the early fifties, I decided that I had to know everything about this new companion. My goal in life was to hear every rock record made. Now that my collection numbers well over 100,000 records, it gets increasingly difficult to see the trees for the forest. When I agreed to do this book, I looked forward to not only seeing the trees again, but also looking back at the roots of my record collecting mania.

The first records I remember seeing at home in the early fifties were my father's albums by such artists as Louis Armstrong, Louis Prima, Julie London and Doris Day. At the beginning of my teenage years, I wasn't hip enough to appreciate Prima and Armstrong, but the Doris Day and Julie London records definitely caught my eye, if not my ear. Actually, rock and roll did not introduce me to sex, the cleavage covers of the Day and London albums did.

In 1951, my parents bought us kids our own 78-rpm record player. The first record I remember playing till the grooves wore off was Frankie Laine's *Jezebel* backed by *Rose, Rose, I Love You*. Owning your own records sure beat the hell out of being at the mercy of the radio. Although Columbia Records introduced the 33 1/3-rpm album in 1948 and RCA announced the 45-rpm single the following year, the 78-pm disc reigned supreme until the mid-fifties when RCA literally gave away 45-rpm record players free to promote the 45-rpm record.

My record buying began with rock and roll 45s as they only cost 89 cents, albums were $3.98. On an allowance of 50 cents a week, purchasing records was not easy. The first 45 I bought was Bill Doggett's *Honky Tonk*, a safe investment, an instrumental with no words to get tired of. However, buying one record every two weeks could not sate my record collecting needs, so I soon turned to a life of crime. I made a box with a false bottom which I would take into the listening booth at my local record store. For every record they saw me take in to the booth, 3 or 4 more would magically disappear into the box.

I must have stolen hundreds of records before my greed got the better of me. I heard a new record called *Letter To An Angel* by the Five Shillings on the radio one week and knew I had to steal it from the store as soon as possible as it was a very black record that would quickly disappear as it was too ethnic for continued air play. There were no other customers in the record store when I got there, so there were no distractions for the clerks. In my head I knew that it was too dangerous, but my heart got the better of me. Sure enough I got caught and arrested. I swore it was my first time, and besides, they only caught me with one record, so they let me go – after informing my parents of my crime. After I was properly punished by my father, he felt sorry for me and told me that when he was a kid and couldn't afford new records, he used to buy them used from jukebox companies.

The next weekend, I raced downtown to check out all the jukebox companies I could find. Sure enough, they did sell used 45s for 25 cents each; however, I could still only afford two records a week. Then I found out that in the hospital where my father worked there was a terminally ill disc jockey. I went to visit him and asked if he'd like to do a radio show for the other patients through the hospital sound system. He said he'd love to if there were just some way to get the records. I told him I'd return next week with records.

I went back to all the jukebox companies and got them to donate records for the hospital. I didn't get to keep the records, but I soon had hundreds of records a week passing through my house. As a teenager I didn't care about ownership, I just had to hear as much music as possible, and now I knew I could get 45s for free legally.

The first L.P. I ever bought was the second Elvis Presley album, not because I didn't like the first one, but because I found the second one on sale at a hardware store for $1.98 rather than the standard $3.98 price. Getting my first album was very similar to getting my first girl-friend. Ah, the anticipation on the ride home. I stared at the beatific picture of Elvis on the cover, turned it over and read the liner notes, fondled the cover, peeked inside at the inner sleeve, looked at the vinyl, paused and then went back over every inch of the cover again. All that foreplay, before I even got home to lay the record on the turntable, was exquisite. Much to my surprise, it was all killer, no filler. Most rock albums I had heard at friends' houses contained just a hit or two and a lot of extraneous material. Soon I was collecting albums as well as singles.

For a number of reasons, albums seemed much more adult than singles. Albums were showcased on shelves and not kept in portable boxes, and albums expanded the aural experience with their visuals; albums were 5 inches bigger and 4 times more expensive, and you could hold the album cover while listening to the music and the music played for almost 20 minutes before you had to change records: no comparison, one was an affair while the other was a relationship.

However, the relationship most kids had with the music was through the radio, not through record collections. Early fifties' radio was dominated by the solo crooners like Perry Como, Doris Day, Nat "King" Cole, Joni James, Frank Sinatra, Tony Bennett and groups like The Chordettes, The Crew Cuts, The Four Lads, The Ames Brothers and The McGuire Sisters.

Soon, almost every town in the country had a local disc jockey who was, or at least sounded, black. In my hometown of Columbus, Ohio, our local station, W.C.O.L., hired Dr. Bop for the midnight to 6 a.m. shift. I used to lie in bed pretending to sleep while awaiting the good doin' doctor to come on the air and announce, "This is Dr. Bop on the scene, with a stack of shellac and his record machine". In the Buddy-Holly-movie tradition, Dr. Bop actually did lock himself in the studio one night so he could continuously play *It's Only Make Believe* all night long. Not only did this make Conway Twitty a star overnight, but he also played Columbus that week for free just to make sure the record sold through. Not long after that, Dr. Bop got fired for dedicating *It Only Hurts For A Little While* to all the virgins on Broad Street.

Having seen Twitty live, I soon started attending Alan Freed rock shows. In 1957 and 1958, I saw Clyde McPhatter, LaVern Baker, Frankie Lymon, the Everly Brothers, Chuck Berry, Jerry Lee Lewis, Joe Turner and Buddy Holly, just to name a few. Now my music mania was way out of control. I lived, breathed and even ate rock and roll – literally. I remember talking my mother into buying certain foods 'cause they had coupons you could redeem for free records. My final English paper in high school was a defense of rock and roll.

In 1960, I graduated high school and was off to college, leaving all my records at home, taking only the first three Bo Diddley albums with me. I got thrown out of more parties because of those Diddley records. At the college parties, everyone was interested in getting some, and I don't mean music, so the most played records were those of the make-out variety, especially Johnny Mathis' *Open Fire Two Guitars*. I kept trying to put Bo on the turntable and turn everyone on to the first feedback guitar on record. Needless to say, I did not exactly become a big man on campus with these tactics. Come to think of it, nor did I get any. All those tall tales about rock and roll driving women into sexual frenzies were not ringing true.

The best record store near the campus was run by an ex-associate of Sam Goody's record store chain. I soon became friends with the owner of the store and he confided to me how he got his store started. He and Sam got into an argument about money owed which Sam did not deal with to my friend's satisfaction. So, one night, my friend stole one of Sam's trucks full of records at gunpoint and drove it as far as it would go. He opened his record store where the truck finally died. Now it wasn't just the records that fascinated me, but the record industry too.

So, in 1966, fresh out of college, I headed out for western skies. Most of my friends were moving to San Francisco, so I went there first. Driving across the Golden Gate Bridge, *You're Gonna Miss Me* by the Thirteenth Floor Elevators came on the radio. If this was the kind of music coming out of Frisco, then this was my kinda town. After finding out that the Elevators were from Texas and the local bands were actually the Charlatans, Quicksilver and the Grateful Dead, I headed south to L.A., home of the Byrds, Love and the Buffalo Springfield.

I worked as a photographer, shooting such acts as the Chambers Brothers, the Raiders and Taj Mahal for their record companies. I got $50 per session and all the records I wanted for free. Then I started writing about music for the underground press. After my third article was published, I was offered a job as a publicist for Columbia Records – $200 a week but, once again, all the records I wanted for free.

When I left college, I had given all my records away except for a hundred of my favorites. True sixties hippie, I swore that I would never have more possessions than I could fit in the car I owned at the time, an oath I soon forsook. While at Columbia I told an associate about my teenage life of crime and how I was arrested for stealing that Five Shillings record and how I'd love to find it again. I found out that it was now a $40 record – if you could find it. I went into full panic mode as I realized that the music I'd grown up with might never be available to me again. I decided then and there to rebuild the collection no matter what, and it did end up taking every spare moment.

First I went through the Columbia catalog, ordering thousands of albums; then, there were all the trade deals with friends at the other record companies – "I'll send you the complete Miles Davis catalog in exchange for the complete Beatles and Beach Boys." You see, back then, every record company had hired at least one of us "house hippies" who loved music. The companies had no idea how we did our jobs so well, but they were willing to give us the perk of unlimited free records to keep us happy. Hell, it was cheaper than paying us a decent salary. Within a year, I had over 5,000 albums and it just kept increasing every year thereafter. Eventually, I even traded someone a rare Dylan single for a copy of *Letter To An Angel* by the Five Shillings.

Additionally, every weekend was spent at garage sales or in the garages of older record company executives. Then there were the incredible scores like getting into the Sun Records warehouse in Memphis (TN), finding the home of International Artists Records in Houston (TX) and getting first pick of the album finds in the Ace Records warehouse in Jackson (MS). One time in Tyler, Texas, I got attacked by both the blacks and the whites trying to find this rare record store. The whites got mad at me for wanting directions to "nigger town" and, once I got there, the blacks wanted to know what this white boy was doing there. Building the collection certainly did take a lot of time and trouble.

This book begins, as rock and roll did, with a total mixture of all the musical forms that predated it – pop, country and rhythm and blues. If rock and roll was the soundtrack to our lives, then these soundtrack albums had to encapsulate any of the teen topics of interest – automobiles, assorted fads, sexuality, rebellion, escape, energy, life, death, loneliness, dancing and dating.

The early covers were designed to capture teen America in all its innocence. Rock and roll was considered to be far too sexual for adult America at the time, so the album covers for the most part had to be one hundred per cent wholesome. Although most of the early rock artists were black, teenage America was a white world. So most of the record covers showed white teenagers in typical teen scenes. It's amazing how many black artists had pictures of white people on their record covers, while their own pictures were relegated to the back cover, if they were there at all. As an adult I found out that distributors in the South would not carry many records if there was a black on the cover.

Rock and roll came from blacks adding rhythm to the blues, but whites tried to usurp the music. Many black originals were covered by white artists such as Georgia Gibbs, Bill Haley, the McGuire Sisters and Pat Boone. Boone stole the hits from the black originals on *Ain't That A Shame*, *At My Front Door*, *I'll Be Home* and *I Almost Lost My Mind*. He and Little Richard hit the top ten with Richard's *Long Tall Sally*. Little Richard claimed Boone could never totally steal the song because he sang the words so fast that Boone couldn't cover it properly. Looking at the picture of the Little Richard album cover, his screaming, sweating face next to Boone's collegiate cover, white bucks and all, the teenage public finally saw their choices in vivid black and white, and black was finally becoming the color of choice.

But, just as rock and roll was hitting full stride in the late fifties, disaster struck. Little Richard saw God and gave up the devil's music; rock's most popular practitioner, Elvis Presley, got drafted; and Buddy Holly and Eddie Cochran got killed in plane and car crashes respectively.

On top of that, the payola scandals killed Alan Freed's career, one of the wildest disc jockeys in the country who put on the biggest and best rock concerts and even refused to play the white versions of the black hits. So, in the late fifties and early sixties, rock and roll was reduced to safe, manufactured teen idols like Frankie Avalon, Fabian, Bobby Vee, Johnny Tillotson, Bobby Darin, Ricky Nelson, Bobby Rydell. Besides their wholesome pictures on the album covers, the liner notes also attested to the fact that these stars were not just rockers – they aspired to improve themselves beyond rock and roll by studying acting and dancing.

As rock and roll was dying prematurely in the U.S., the seeds that Bill Haley, Eddie Cochran and Gene Vincent had planted in England took root with such British bands as the Beatles, the Stones, the Animals, the Yardbirds, the Who and Them, among others. Then, as the sixties really took off, the roots of rock and roll started sprouting branches in every direction simultaneously. Folk, Folk-Rock, Surf, San Francisco, Motown, Soul, Psychedelia, Garage Bands and the British Invasion combined to make a rock revolution that was unstoppable. The music of teenage America was now the sound of a generation, and the generation was more grown up and global. Now the record covers could truly reflect the times. The cover of Steve Miller's first album could not be deciphered unless you were stoned. The Barbarians' cover showed a drummer with a hook in place of a hand. David Bowie appeared in a dress on the cover of his first album, and Jimi Hendrix could have a bevy of nude women on his album cover, at least in England.

During the sixties, I went from record company to record company taking jobs for the free records, and finding free love as an additional bonus. For years, I had lived solely for the mania of this music, now the world was adopting the same lifestyle. The music and the musicians were accessible to everyone as the royal 'we' became the 'We' generation. The artists and the audiences seemed to have as much control of the music as the record industry did. There were even tribal gatherings called festivals that further united this musical movement. Pop music was so prevalent a part of pop culture that even the paramount pop artist, Andy Warhol, started designing album covers.

By the mid-seventies, music had grown from a business to an industry, forcing out people who favored the artists over the corporate concerns. In 1976, I was fired from my last record company job. I was national director of publicity for ABC Records and was told not to promote Freddy Fender's record, *Before The Next Teardrop Falls* as Freddy was over forty, a Chicano and an ex-convict. Against my boss' instructions, I helped make Freddy the biggest selling artist on the label, and was then fired for insubordination. I still have the gold record he sent me that said, "It wouldn't have been possible without you, brother".

So, in 1977, I started the Michael Ochs Archives, a company devoted to preserving the musical past I loved so much. I continued getting every record released, plus I started collecting photographs, sheet music, concert program books – everything that could effectively document the continuing story of rock and roll. The friendship that started in my teenage years had now blossomed into a marriage, in the traditional sense of the word – till death do us part.

I continued collecting records throughout the eighties. In the nineties, with the CD having effectively replaced the record album, I thought I had finally outgrown the record collection. I settled for the convenience of CDs, barely playing my albums, despite the fact that the sound of vinyl records is definitely better than CDs. Now the record industry is even talking about replacing the CDs with computer chips. All the artistic graphics that went on the covers of records will probably be replaced with live footage of the bands on the advanced CDs or on the computer chips.

I was interviewed recently for a television show, and I actually had trouble waxing nostalgic about the record collection. For the first time, I felt a distance between the collection and me, like a kid who wasted his youth collecting stamps or some such. Right after that, a rare records dealer told me that he could probably sell the record collection for close to a million dollars. Then I was approached to do this book.

It was all so synchronistic. It was as though God was telling me that now that I was a married adult with a family of my own, I could finally forsake the first and foremost love of my life. When I started this book, I told myself that when I finished, I would sell the collection. In the eleventh hour of finishing this book, I found the original Little Willie John *Fever* album cover with the white nurse on the cover in a collectors' record store. I borrowed the record and photographed it for the book and returned it to the store to be sold. This was a record I had been looking for since the fifties. Today I called the store and purchased the album, rekindling the collecting passion I thought I'd lost.

I finally realized that you cannot put a price on love – my record collection is only for sale through this book.

This compilation of the many faces of rock and roll was designed to be as enjoyable as the music itself. This is neither a studious anthology of album cover art nor a complete history. These are just the one thousand or so album covers from my collection that I felt would give a comprehensive picture of rock and roll from its infancy to the present. When I first went through my record collection, I only picked the albums that I would enjoy seeing repeatedly in a book. The only criterion I used in this selection process was what caught my eye as being unique and memorable for its time. After taking out the first couple of thousand covers, I tried to put them in some order other than just chronological. Besides the coupling of musical genres I started to see obvious patterns, such as different depictions of blacks and of women over the decades. I realize that there are serious omissions in my selection, but that is the only serious part of the book. Due to clearance problems or the peculiarity of my taste, I am sure there are a number of album covers that should have been included but were not. The method to my madness should be obvious from the layout of the covers – and my apologies to all the great artists who did not survive the final cut.

I hope you enjoy this representative sampling of my favorite album covers as much as I've enjoyed collecting them.

Michael Ochs
Venice (CA)
December, 1995

## Einleitung

Als der Rock 'n' Roll und ich noch sehr jung waren, schlossen wir eine Freundschaft, die sich trotz vieler Höhen und Tiefen bis heute gehalten hat. Gleich nachdem ich ihn kennengelernt hatte, war ich wild entschlossen, alles über meinen neuen Gefährten zu erfahren. Ich machte es mir zum Lebensziel, jede Platte zu hören, die je aufgenommen wurde. Heute beläuft sich meine Sammlung auf weit über 100.000 Platten, und es wird zunehmend schwieriger, vor lauter Wald noch die Bäume zu sehen. Als ich einwilligte, das vorliegende Buch über Cover-Kunst zu machen, freute ich mich nicht nur darauf, wieder die Bäume zu sehen, sondern auch, auf die Wurzeln meiner Schallplattenmanie zurückzuschauen.

Die ersten Schallplatten, die ich in meinem Elternhaus Anfang der fünfziger Jahre kennenlernte, waren die Alben meines Vaters von Louis Armstrong, Louis Prima, Julie London und Doris Day. Ich hatte gerade erst das Teenageralter erreicht und kannte mich noch nicht so gut aus, aber die Platten von Doris Day und Julie London fielen mir ins Auge, auch wenn sie mir nicht unbedingt ins Ohr gingen. Nicht der Rock 'n' Roll war meine erste Begegnung mit Erotik, sondern die Fotos der Dekolletés von Doris Day und Julie London auf ihren Alben.

Im Jahre 1951 kauften meine Eltern für uns Kinder einen eigenen Plattenspieler mit 78 Umdrehungen pro Minute. Die erste Schallplatte, die ich so oft abgespielt habe, daß sie hinterher keine Rillen mehr hatte, war Frankie Laines *Jezebel*, mit *Rose, Rose, I Love You* auf der Rückseite. Obwohl Columbia Records 1948 die 33 1/3 Langspielplatten einführte und RCA für das folgende Jahr die Single ankündigte, blieb die 78er Platte bis Mitte der fünfziger Jahre vorherrschend, als RCA Plattenspieler mit 45 Umdrehungen praktisch verschenkte, um die 45er Platten zu promoten.

Mein erstes Geld für Platten gab ich für Rock 'n' Roll-Singles aus, da sie nur 89 Cent kosteten, Alben dagegen 3,98 Dollar. Mit 50 Cent Taschengeld die Woche war der Kauf von Schallplatten nicht einfach. Meine allererste, selbst gekaufte Single war *Honky Tonk* von Bill Doggett, ein Instrumentalstück, *an dem man sich kaum satt hören konnte.* Doch eine Platte alle zwei Wochen reichte einfach nicht aus, um meine Sammelleidenschaft zu befriedigen, und so nahm meine kriminelle Karriere ihren Anfang. Ich baute einen kleinen Kasten mit doppeltem Boden, den ich mit in die Hörkabine im Plattenladen nahm. Auf jede Schallplatte, die ich vor den Augen der Verkäufer mit in die Kabine nahm, kamen drei bis vier, die wie von Zauberhand in dem Kasten verschwanden.

Ich hatte wohl schon Hunderte von Platten gestohlen, als meine Gier einfach zu groß wurde. Eines Tages hörte ich im Radio ein neues Stück mit dem Titel *Letter To An Angel* von den Five Shillings, und mir war sofort klar, daß ich die Platte so bald wie möglich im Laden stehlen mußte. Es handelte sich um echte schwarze Musik, und deshalb war nicht damit zu rechnen, daß sie lange im Radio gespielt oder auf dem Markt angeboten werden würde. Als ich den Laden betrat, waren sonst keine Kunden da, die die Verkäufer hätten ablenken können. Mein Verstand sagte mir, daß es zu gefährlich war, aber mein Herz gewann die Oberhand. Natürlich wurde ich erwischt, und die Verkäufer holten die Polizei. Ich schwor, es sei das erste Mal gewesen, und außerdem hatten sie mich mit nur einer Platte erwischt. Also ließ man mich laufen, nicht ohne zuvor meine Eltern über meinen Diebstahl informiert zu haben. Nachdem mein Vater mich gehörig bestraft hatte, erzählte er mir, daß er sich in seiner Jugend gebrauchte Platten bei Jukebox-Firmen gekauft hatte.

In der Woche darauf fuhr ich in die Stadt und ging zu allen Jukebox-Firmen, die ich finden konnte. Und tatsächlich, sie verkauften Singles für 25 Cent das Stück. Aber noch immer konnte ich mir nicht mehr als zwei Platten pro Woche leisten. Dann erfuhr ich, daß in dem Krankenhaus, in dem mein Vater arbeitete, ein Diskjockey lag, der unheilbar krank war. Ich besuchte ihn und fragte, ob er Lust habe, für die anderen Patienten über die Lautsprecheranlage des Krankenhauses eine Musiksendung zu machen. Er war begeistert und erklärte sich bereit, falls ich ihm ausreichend Schallplatten besorgen könnte.

Ich ging erneut zu den Jukebox-Firmen und brachte sie dazu, Schallplatten für das Krankenhaus zu spenden. Ich durfte sie zwar nicht behalten, aber schon bald hatte ich Woche für Woche vorübergehend einige hundert Platten zu Hause. Jetzt wußte ich, wie ich Singles umsonst bekam, und noch dazu legal.

Die allererste LP, die ich mir kaufte, war das zweite Album von Elvis Presley, nicht etwa, weil mir die erste Elvis-LP nicht gefiel, sondern weil ich die zweite in einem Haushaltswarengeschäft zum Angebotspreis von 1,98 Dollar statt der üblichen 3,98 Dollar entdeckte. Als ich mein erstes Album erstand, hatte ich in etwa das gleiche Gefühl wie beim ersten richtigen Kuß. Ich starrte auf das Coverfoto eines strahlend lächelnden Elvis, klappte das Album auf und las die Titel auf der Hülle, streichelte das Cover, spähte in die Hülle, blickte auf die Platte, hielt inne und studierte dann wieder jeden Quadratzentimeter des Covers. Zu meiner großen Überraschung war die ganze Platte eine Wucht, ohne einen einzigen Flop. Auf den meisten Rockalben, die ich bei Freunden gehört hatte, waren ein bis zwei Hits und ansonsten keine besonderen Songs. Schon bald sammelte ich Alben ebenso wie Singles.

Aus mehreren Gründen kamen mir LPs „erwachsener" vor als Singles. Sie waren nicht nur ein Hörerlebnis, sondern auch etwas fürs Auge; sie waren etwa 13 Zentimeter größer und viermal so teuer wie Singles. Man konnte das Plattencover in der Hand halten, während man die Musik hörte, und man mußte erst nach 20 Minuten die Platte umdrehen oder eine neue auflegen. Alben waren unvergleichlich, zu ihnen hatte man eine Beziehung, mit Singles eine Affäre.

Aber bei den meisten Jugendlichen lief die Beziehung zur Musik über das Radio, nicht über die Plattensammlung. Anfang der fünfziger Jahre hörte man im Radio überwiegend Schnulzen von Solisten wie Perry Como, Doris Day, Nat „King" Cole, Joni James, Frank Sinatra, Tony Bennett und von Gruppen wie den Chordettes, den Crew Cuts, den Four Lads, den Ames Brothers und die McGuire Sisters.

Es dauerte nicht lange, und jede Provinzstadt im Lande hatte einen eigenen Lokalsender mit Diskjockey, der schwarz war oder sich zumindest so anhörte. In meiner Heimatstadt Columbus, Ohio, engagierte unser Lokalsender W.C.O.L. Dr. Bop für die Nachtschicht von Mitternacht bis morgens um sechs. Ich lag im Bett und stellte mich schlafend, während ich darauf wartete, daß der gute Dr. Bop sich über den Äther mit den Worten ankündigte: „This is Dr. Bop on the scene, with a stack of shellac and his record machine." In der Tradition der Buddy-Holly-Filme schloß sich Dr. Bop sogar einmal im Studio ein, damit er die ganze Nacht hindurch ununterbrochen *It's Only Make Believe* spielen konnte. Dadurch wurde Conway Twitty über Nacht zum Star und gab in derselben Woche in Columbus ein kostenloses Konzert. Wenig später wurde Dr. Bop gefeuert, weil er die Platte *It Only Hurts For A Little While* allen Jungfrauen auf der „Broad Street" gewidmet hatte.

Nachdem ich Twitty live gesehen hatte, ging ich regelmäßig in die Rockshows von Alan Freed. Zwischen 1957 und 1958 sah ich Clyde McPhatter, LaVern Baker, Frankie Lymon & The Teenagers, die Everly Brothers, Chuck Berry, Jerry Lee Lewis, Joe Turner und Buddy Holly, um nur einige zu nennen. Ich lebte, atmete und aß sogar Rock 'n' Roll – im wahrsten Sinne des Wortes. Ich weiß noch, wie ich meine Mutter dazu überredete, solche Lebensmittel zu kaufen, bei denen es Coupons gab, für die man dann Gratis-Schallplatten bekam. Das Thema meiner Abschlußarbeit an der High-School war eine Verteidigung des Rock 'n' Roll.

Diesen Abschluß machte ich 1960 und ging dann aufs College. Die einzigen Schallplatten, die ich mitnahm, waren die ersten drei Alben von Bo Diddley. Wegen dieser Platten wurde ich auf so mancher Party vor die Tür gesetzt. Auf College-Partys wollte jeder seinen Spaß haben, und zwar nicht unbedingt den musikalischer Art. Deshalb wurden überwiegend Schmuseplatten gespielt, vor allem *Open Fire Two Guitars* von Johnny Mathis. Ich versuchte immer wieder, Bo aufzulegen und alle für die erste Aufnahme einer elektrischen Gitarre mit Rückkoppelung zu begeistern. Es erübrigt sich wohl zu sagen, daß ich mit solchen Taktiken nicht gerade der Campus-Star wurde. Ehrlich gesagt, ich hatte bei keiner Frau Erfolg. All die tollen Geschichten darüber, wie der Rock 'n' Roll Frauen wild vor Leidenschaft machte, waren pure Übertreibung.

Der beste Plattenladen in der Nähe des Campus gehörte einem ehemaligen Mitarbeiter von Sam Goodys Plattenladenkette. Nach kurzer Zeit freundete ich mich mit dem Besitzer an, und er erzählte mir, wie er dazu gekommen war, sein eigenes Geschäft aufzumachen. Er und Sam hatten sich wegen Geld gestritten, das Sam ihm schuldete und nicht zahlen wollte. Also hatte mein Freund eines Nachts mit vorgehaltener Waffe einen von Sams LKW voller Platten gestohlen und war damit so weit gefahren, wie der Wagen durchhielt. Er hatte seinen Plattenladen genau dort aufgemacht, wo der LKW schließlich den Geist aufgab.

1966, direkt nach dem College, fuhr ich in den Westen der USA, zunächst nach San Francisco. Als ich über die Golden Gate Bridge fuhr, kam im Radio *You're Gonna Miss Me* von den Thirteenth Floor Elevators. Wenn in Frisco solche Musik gespielt wurde, dann war das meine Stadt. Als ich dann jedoch erfuhr, daß die Elevators aus Texas stammten und daß die Charlatans, Quicksilver und die Grateful Dead die eigentlichen Bands der Stadt waren, fuhr ich weiter gen Süden nach L. A., der Heimat von den Byrds, Love und Buffalo Springfield.

Ich arbeitete als Fotograf und machte Aufnahmen von Gruppen wie den Chambers Brothers, den Raiders und Taj Mahal für deren Plattenfirmen. Ich bekam 50 Dollar pro Fototermin und so viele Platten wie ich wollte. Dann fing ich an, für die Underground-Presse über Musik zu schreiben, und nachdem mein dritter Artikel erschienen war, bot man mir einen Job als Publizist bei Columbia Records an – für 200 Dollar die Woche; und erneut bekam ich alle Platten umsonst.

Als ich das College verließ, hatte ich alle meine Platten verschenkt, bis auf etwa Hundert meiner Lieblingsplatten. Wie ein richtiger Hippie der sechziger Jahre schwor ich, niemals mehr besitzen zu wollen, als in den Kofferraum meines damaligen Wagens paßten, ein Schwur, von dem ich mich bald wieder distanzierte. Bei Columbia erzählte ich einem Kollegen von meinen Diebstählen als Teenager, daß ich verhaftet worden war, weil ich eine Platte von den Five Shillings gestohlen hatte, und daß ich genau diese Platte gern wieder ausfindig machen würde. Ich fand heraus, daß sie inzwischen 40 Dollar kostete – wenn man sie überhaupt auftreiben konnte. Ich bekam richtig Panik, als mir klar wurde, daß ich an die Musik, mit der ich groß geworden war, vielleicht nie wieder herankommen würde. Ich beschloß daher, meine alte Plattensammlung wiederaufzubauen, um jeden Preis.

Zunächst durchforstete ich den Columbia-Katalog und bestellte Tausende von Alben; dann ließ ich meine Geschäftskontakte zu Freunden in anderen Plattenfirmen spielen. Damals hatte jede Plattenfirma mindestens einen von uns musikvernarrten „Haus-Hippies" engagiert. Um uns bei Laune zu halten, bekamen wir als Sondervergütung so viele Platten kostenlos, wie wir wollten. Das war billiger, als uns ein anständiges Gehalt zu zahlen. Innerhalb eines Jahres hatte ich über 5.000 LPs. Schließlich konnte ich eine seltene Dylan-Single gegen eine *Letter To An Angel* von den Five Shillings tauschen.

Außerdem verbrachte ich jedes Wochenende bei Garagenverkäufen. Und dann waren da noch die unverschämten Glücksfälle, wie beispielsweise in das Lager von Sun Records in Memphis, Tennessee, reinzukommen oder bei International Artists Records in Houston, Texas, oder wenn man zu den ersten gehörte, die sich im Lager von Ace Records in Jackson, Mississippi, etwas aus den Beständen aussuchen konnte. Einmal wurde ich in Tyler, Texas, von Schwarzen und Weißen angegriffen, als ich versuchte, einen bestimmten Plattenladen zu finden. Die Weißen wurden wütend, weil ich nach dem Weg zur „Nigger Town" fragte, und als ich schließlich dort war, wollten die Schwarzen wissen, was ein Weißer da zu suchen hatte. Der Aufbau meiner Sammlung kostete nicht nur Zeit, sondern brachte mir auch einigen Ärger ein.

Wie damals der Rock 'n' Roll so beginnt auch das vorliegende Buch mit einer Mischung sämtlicher Musikrichtungen, die ihm vorausgingen, Pop, Country und Rhythm & Blues. Wenn der Rock 'n' Roll der Soundtrack unseres Lebens war, dann ist es unumgänglich, daß diese Soundtrack-Alben sämtliche Themen behandeln, die damals die Teens faszinierten – Autos, Mode, Sexualität, Rebellion, Flucht, Leben, Tod, Einsamkeit, Tanzen und Liebe.

Die frühen Cover thematisierten das Amerika der unschuldigen Teenagerzeit. Der Rock 'n' Roll galt damals im Amerika der Erwachsenen als viel zu stark sexuell aufgeladen, daher mußten die Cover absolut unverfänglich sein. Obwohl die frühen Musiker überwiegend schwarz waren, war das Amerika der Teenager eine weiße Welt. Die meisten Plattencover zeigten weiße Teenager in typischen Teenagerszenen. Erstaunlich ist, wie viele schwarze Künstler auf ihren Covern Fotos von Weißen hatten, während Fotos von Schwarzen, falls überhaupt vorhanden, auf die Rückseite verbannt wurden. Später erfuhr ich, daß Großhändler in den Südstaaten nicht viele Platten in ihren Bestand aufnahmen, wenn auf dem Cover ein Schwarzer abgebildet war.

Obwohl der Rock 'n' Roll von schwarzen Musikern stammte, die dem Blues seinen Rhythmus verliehen hatten, versuchten Weiße, die Musik für sich zu vereinnahmen. Hinter vielen Songs von „unverfänglichen" weißen Künstlern wie Georgia Gibbs, Bill Haley, den McGuire Sisters und Pat Boone versteckten sich Originale von Schwarzen. Boone stahl seine Hits *Ain't That A Shame*, *At My Front Door*, *I'll Be Home* und *I Almost Lost My Mind* von schwarzen Sängern. Boone und Little Richard landeten beide mit Richards Song *Long Tall Sally* unter den Top Ten der Hitparade. Little Richard behauptete, daß Boone den Song unmöglich gestohlen haben konnte, da er, Richard, so schnell gesungen habe, daß Boone den Text gar nicht richtig mitkriegen konnte. Beim Vergleich des Fotos auf dem Cover des Little-Richard-Albums, auf dem sein schreiendes, schwitzendes Gesicht zu sehen ist, mit dem aseptischen Cover von Boone (ganz der adrette Collegejunge) sah die Käuferschicht der Teenager endlich ihre Wahlmöglichkeiten in lebendigem Schwarzweiß, und Schwarz wurde die bevorzugte Farbe.

Doch gerade als der Rock 'n' Roll Ende der fünfziger Jahre so richtig in Schwung kam, schlug das Unglück zu. Little Richard sah sich von Gott berufen und kehrte der Teufelsmusik den Rücken zu, der populärste Rocker, Elvis Presley, wurde zur Armee eingezogen, und Buddy Holly und Eddie Cochran kamen bei einem Flugzeugabsturz bzw. Autounfall ums Leben. Obendrein kostete eine Schmiergeldaffäre Alan Freed die Karriere, einen der wildesten Diskjockeys im Lande, der die größten und besten Rockkonzerte organisiert und sich sogar geweigert hatte, die weißen Coverversionen von schwarzen Hits zu spielen. Somit verkümmerte der Rock 'n' Roll zum Ende der fünfziger und Anfang der sechziger Jahre zu harmlosen, maßgeschneiderten Teenageridolen wie Frankie Avalon, Fabian, Bobby Vee, Johnny Tillotson, Bobby Darin, Ricky Nelson, Bobby Rydell und so weiter. Abgesehen von ihren „sauberen" Fotos auf den Covern, bescheinigte der Umschlagtext außerdem, daß diese Stars nicht bloß Rockmusiker waren – nein, sie waren auch bestrebt, über den Rock 'n' Roll hinauszuwachsen, und studierten Schauspiel und Tanz.

Als der Rock 'n' Roll in den USA viel zu jung starb, ging die Saat auf, die Bill Haley, Eddie Cochran und Gene Vincent in England gestreut hatten, mit britischen Bands wie den Beatles, Stones, Animals, Yardbirds, Who und Them. Und dann, als die sechziger Jahre so richtig loslegten, verzweigten sich die Wurzeln des Rock 'n' Roll in alle Richtungen. Folk, Folk Rock, Surf, San Francisco, Motown, Soul, Psychedelic, Garage und die britische Invasion, all diese Elemente führten zusammen zu einer Rock-Revolution. Die Musik der amerikanischen Teenager war nun der Sound einer ganzen Generation, und diese Generation war erwachsener und globaler. Die Plattencover spiegelten nun den Zeitgeist wider. Das Cover von Steve Millers erstem Album ließ sich nur entschlüsseln, wenn man bekifft war. Auf dem Barbarian-Cover hatte der Drummer statt einer Hand einen Haken. David Bowie ließ sich für das Cover seines ersten Albums in einem Kleid ablichten, und Jimi Hendrix wurde auf dem Cover (zumindest in England) von nackten Frauen umschwärmt.

In den sechziger Jahren jobbte ich in verschiedenen Plattenfirmen, um Gratis-Schallplatten zu bekommen; als Dreingabe entdeckte ich die freie Liebe. Über Jahre hatte ich nur für meine Musikbesessenheit gelebt. Die Musik und die Musiker waren jedem zugänglich, während aus dem „Wir" des Pluralis majestatis die demokratische Wir-Generation wurde. Die Künstler und ihr Publikum schienen die Musik ebensosehr zu bestimmen wie die Plattenindustrie. Es fanden sogar Stammesfeste statt, genannt Festivals, auf denen die Musikbewegung noch stärker zusammengeschweißt wurde. Die Popmusik war ein so wesentlicher Teil der Popkultur, daß sogar der tonangebende Popkünstler Andy Warhol Plattencover gestaltete.

Mitte der siebziger Jahre jedoch hatte sich die Musik von einem

Geschäft in eine Industrie verwandelt, was dazu führte, daß solche Leute hinausgedrängt wurden, die die Interessen der Künstler über die der Konzerne stellten. 1976 verlor ich meinen letzten Job in einer Plattenfirma. Ich war Leiter der PR-Abteilung bei ABC Records und hatte Anweisung, die Platte *Before The Next Teardrop Falls* von Freddy Fender nicht zu promoten, da Freddy über vierzig, mexikanischer Abstammung und im Gefängnis gewesen war. Gegen die Anordnung meines Chefs half ich mit, aus Freddy den meistverkauften Künstler des Labels zu machen und wurde daraufhin wegen Insubordination gefeuert. Ich habe noch immer die goldene Schallplatte, die Freddy mir mit den Worten zuschickte: „Bruder, ohne Dich wäre sie nicht zustande gekommen."

1977 eröffnete ich die „Michael Ochs Archives", eine Firma, die sich der Bewahrung der von mir über alles geliebten Musikvergangenheit verschrieben hat. Ich verschaffte mir weiterhin jede Platte, die auf den Markt kam, und sammelte darüber hinaus Fotos, Noten, Konzertprogramme – einfach alles, was die Geschichte des Rock 'n' Roll anschaulich dokumentierte. Aus der Freundschaft, die in meiner Jugend begonnen hatte, war inzwischen eine Ehe geworden, im herkömmlichen Sinne des Wortes – bis daß der Tod uns scheidet.

Auch die achtziger Jahre hindurch sammelte ich weiter Schallplatten. In den neunziger Jahren dann, nachdem die CD die LP erfolgreich verdrängt hatte, bekam ich allmählich das Gefühl, aus meiner Plattensammlung herausgewachsen zu sein. Ich verlegte mich auf die praktischen CDs, spielte meine LPs so gut wie gar nicht mehr, obwohl Vinylscheiben eindeutig besser klingen als CDs. Jetzt denkt die Plattenindustrie sogar daran, die CDs durch Computerchips zu ersetzen.

Vor kurzem wurde ich im Fernsehen interviewt, und es fiel mir regelrecht schwer, mich wie sonst wehmütig über meine Plattensammlung auszulassen. Zum erstenmal spürte ich zwischen der Sammlung und mir eine Distanz, wie jemand, der seine ganze Jugend mit Briefmarkensammeln oder ähnlichem vergeudet hat. Direkt danach sagte mir ein Plattenhändler, er könne meine Sammlung wahrscheinlich für knapp eine Million Dollar verkaufen. Dann wurde ich gebeten, dieses Buch über meine tausend Lieblingscover zu machen.

Es paßte zeitlich gut zusammen. Als ich mit dem Buch anfing, sagte ich mir, daß ich die Sammlung verkaufen würde, sobald es fertig sein würde. Kurz bevor es soweit war, fand ich im Plattenladen eines Sammlers das Original von Little Willie Johns *Fever*. Ich lieh mir die

Platte aus, fotografierte sie für mein Buch und brachte sie wieder in den Laden zurück, damit sie verkauft werden konnte. Es war eine Platte, nach der ich seit den fünfziger Jahren gesucht hatte. Heute habe ich in dem Laden angerufen und die Platte gekauft; meine Sammelleidenschaft, die ich erloschen geglaubt hatte, ist wieder entflammt. Mir ist letztlich klargeworden, daß man Liebe für keinen Preis der Welt verkaufen kann – meine Plattensammlung ist nur über dieses Buch zu erwerben.

Diese Zusammenstellung der vielen Gesichter des Rock 'n' Roll soll so unterhaltsam sein wie die Musik selbst. Es will weder eine wissenschaftliche Anthologie der Kunst des Coverdesigns noch ein vollständiger Überblick über dessen Geschichte sein. In diesem Buch stelle ich Ihnen lediglich die tausend Plattencover aus meiner Sammlung vor, von denen ich glaube, daß sie einen Überblick über die Geschichte des Rocks von seinen Anfängen bis zur Gegenwart vermitteln. Als ich zum ersten Mal meine Plattensammlung durchging, habe ich zuerst nur die Alben ausgesucht, die ich selbst gerne in einem Buch gesehen hätte. Meine Auswahl basiert auf dem, was mir persönlich als einzigartig und stellvertretend für seine Zeit ins Auge stach. Nachdem ich so die ersten Tausend LPs zusammenhatte, versuchte ich sie in eine Reihenfolge zu bringen, die über die bloße Chronologie hinausging. Neben der Zusammenstellung nach Musikrichtungen begann ich, so offensichtliche Kriterien zu erkennen wie den Wandel über die Jahrzehnte hinweg in der Darstellung von schwarzen Musikern oder Frauen. Ich stellte fest, daß in meiner Auswahl wichtige Platten fehlten, aber das ist der einzig ernsthafte Teil dieses Buches. Aufgrund der Abwegigkeiten meines Musikgeschmacks wird sicherlich das eine oder andere Plattencover hier nicht abgebildet sein, das es verdient hätte. Die Methodik meiner Verrücktheit schlägt sich nieder im Layout der Cover, und meine Entschuldigungen gelten all den großen Künstlern, die die endgültige Auswahl nicht überlebt haben.

Ich hoffe, Sie werden an dieser repräsentativen Auswahl aus meinen Lieblingscovern ebensoviel Freude haben wie ich, als ich sie sammelte.

Michael Ochs
Venice (CA)
Dezember, 1995

## Introduction

Lorsque nous étions très jeunes le rock 'n' roll et moi nous avons en-
tamé une amitié qui a connu des hauts et des bas mais qui a duré de
longues années. Quand j'ai découvert le rock au début des années cinquante, j'ai décidé qu'il me fallait tout en connaître. Mon but dans la vie
était d'écouter chaque disque de rock. Aujourd'hui que ma collection
comprend bien plus de 100 000 disques, il devient de plus en plus
difficile de distinguer les arbres dans la forêt. Lorsque j'ai accepté de
faire ce livre sur l'art des pochettes de disque, j'ai regardé en avant pour
ne pas seulement revoir les arbres, mais j'ai aussi regardé en arrière
vers les racines de ma folie de collectionneur de disques.

Les premiers disques que je me souviens d'avoir vus à la maison au
début des années cinquante étaient des albums de Louis Armstrong,
Louis Prima, Julie London et Doris Day appartenant à mon père. Adolescent, je n'étais pas suffisamment dans le coup pour apprécier Prima
et Armstrong, mais les disques de Doris Day et de Julie London avaient
franchement excité mon regard à défaut d'avoir séduit mon oreille. A
vrai dire, je n'ai pas découvert le sexe avec le rock 'n' roll mais avec les
pochettes très décolletées des albums de Day et de London.

En 1951, mes parents nous ont acheté à nous les enfants notre
propre tourne-disques pour 78 tours. Le premier disque que je me souviens d'avoir écouté jusqu'à effacement du sillon était le *Jezebel* de Frankie Laine avec *Rose, Rose, I Love You* sur l'autre face. Celui qui possède
ses propres disques n'a plus besoin de la radio. Quoique Columbia
Records ait introduit l'album 33 tours en 1948 et que RCA ait annoncé le
45 tours l'année suivante, le disque 78 tours a régné jusqu'au milieu des
années cinquante, jusqu'à ce que RCA bazarde littéralement ses électro-
phones pour 45 tours pour promouvoir la vente des disques.

Mes achats de disques ont commencé avec les 45 tours de rock 'n'
roll qui ne coûtaient que 89 cents, alors que les albums se vendaient
3$98. Avec 50 cents d'argent de poche par semaine, acquérir des
disques n'était pas facile. Le tout premier disque que j'ai acheté fut le
*Honky Tonk* de Bill Doggett, un placement sûr puisque, s'agissant d'un
morceau instrumental, on ne risquait pas de se lasser des paroles. Quoi
qu'il en soit, acheter un disque tous les quinze jours ne suffisait pas à
assouvir mon besoin de collectionner. Très vite, j'ai plongé dans l'uni-
vers du crime. J'ai confectionné une petite boîte à double-fond que

j'emportais dans la cabine d'écoute de mon magasin de quartier. Pour chaque disque qu'ils me voyaient emporter dans la cabine, trois ou quatre autres disparaissaient magiquement dans la boîte.

J'ai bien dû voler des centaines de disques avant d'être victime de mon avidité. Un jour, j'ai entendu à la radio un nouveau disque intitulé *Letter To An Angel* par les Five Shillings et j'ai su que je devais le voler aussitôt que possible; s'agissant d'un morceau de vraie musique noire, il serait jugé trop ethnique et ne resterait pas longtemps programmé sur les ondes. Il n'y avait pas d'autres clients lorsque j'entrai dans la boutique et donc aucun motif de distraction pour les vendeurs.Ma raison savait que c'était trop dangereux, mais c'est mon cœur qui a décidé pour moi. Bien entendu, j'ai été attrapé et arrêté. J'ai juré que c'était la première fois, et comme ils n'avaient trouvé qu'un seul disque sur moi, ils m'ont laissé partir, non sans avoir informé mes parents. Après m'avoir puni, mon père se déclara désolé pour moi et me dit que lorsqu'il était gosse et ne pouvait s'offrir de disques, il avait l'habitude d'en acheter d'occasion à des compagnies de juke-boxes.

Le week-end suivant, je me précipitai en ville pour faire le tour de tous les loueurs de juke-boxes que j'avais pu trouver. Ils vendaient bien des 45 tours d'occasion à 25 cents pièce, mais cela voulait dire que je ne pouvais toujours pas m'en offrir plus de deux par semaine. C'est alors que j'ai appris que dans l'hôpital où travaillait mon père se trouvait un disc jockey atteint d'une maladie incurable. Je vins lui rendre visite et lui demandai s'il aimerait faire une émission de radio pour les autres malades en utilisant le circuit de sonorisation de l'hôpital. Il me dit qu'il adorerait le faire s'il y avait un moyen d'obtenir les disques. Je lui répondis que je reviendrais la semaine suivante avec tout ce qu'il fallait.

Je retournai voir tous les loueurs de juke-boxes et obtins d'eux qu'ils me donnent des disques pour l'hôpital. Bientôt des centaines de 45 tours transitèrent chaque semaine par ma maison. Adolescent, je ne pensais pas à l'avenir, ni à la possession, il me fallait simplement écouter le plus de musique possible, et à présent je savais que je pouvais avoir des disques pour rien; et cela en toute légalité.

Le premier L.P. que j'ai acheté était le deuxième album d'Elvis Presley, non que je n'aie pas aimé le premier album, mais simplement parce que j'ai trouvé le deuxième soldé dans un bazar à 1$98 au lieu des 3$98 habituels. Avoir mon premier album était une expérience très voisine de celle d'avoir ma première copine. Ah, cette anticipation sur le chemin du retour! J'ai contemplé la magnifique photo d'Elvis sur la pochette, ai retourné celle-ci pour lire les notes, l'ai caressée, ai glissé mon regard à l'intérieur pour regarder le vinyle, me suis arrêté et ai recommencé à en examiner chaque centimètre. Ce long préambule avant même de rentrer pour poser le disque sur le plateau était délicieux. A ma grande surprise, il n'y avait dans ce disque que du solide, aucune sorte de remplissage, alors que la plupart des albums que j'avais écoutés chez des amis contenaient seulement un tube ou deux et un tas de choses qu'il valait mieux oublier. Bientôt, je me mis à collectionner aussi les albums.

Pour un tas de raisons, les albums paraissaient plus adultes que les «simples». Ils étaient exposés sur des présentoirs et non pas conservés dans des bacs transportables, et de plus ils ajoutaient à l'expérience auditive une expérience visuelle. Les albums étaient plus larges d'une douzaine de centimètres et quatre fois plus chers, on pouvait tenir la pochette en écoutant la musique, et celle-ci durait presque vingt minutes par face. Aucune comparaison possible, dans un cas, il s'agissait d'une liaison amoureuse; dans l'autre, d'une simple relation.

Quoi qu'il en soit, la relation que la plupart des gamins entretenaient avec la musique passait par la radio, pas par des collections de disques. La radio du début des années cinquante était dominée par des crooners tels que Perry Como, Doris Day, Nat King Cole, Joni James, Frank Sinatra, Tony Bennett et des groupes tels que les Chordettes, les Crew Cuts, les Four Lads, les Ames Brothers et les McGuire Sisters.

Très vite, presque chaque ville du pays eut un disc jockey local qui était, ou en tout cas sonnait, noir. Dans ma ville de Columbus, Ohio, notre station locale, W.C.O.L., recruta Dr. Bop pour la tranche horaire de minuit à six heures. J'avais l'habitude de m'allonger sur mon lit en faisant semblant de dormir, et j'attendais l'arrivée du bon docteur sur les ondes et son annonce: «Voici le Dr. Bop, avec sa machine à disques et de quoi secouer.» Dans le style du film sur Buddy Holly, Dr. Bop s'enferma une fois dans le studio afin de pouvoir passer toute la nuit en boucle It's Only Make Believe. Non seulement Conway Twitty devint une star en une nuit, mais il donna la même semaine un concert gratuit à Columbus pour assurer la vente du disque. Peu de temps après, Dr. Bop fut viré pour avoir dédié It Only Hurts For A Little While (Ça ne fait pas mal très longtemps) à toutes les vierges de Broad Street.

Après avoir vu Twitty sur scène, je me mis à suivre les spectacles de rock de Alan Freed. En 1957 et 1958, j'ai vu Clyde McPhatter, LaVern

Baker, Frankie Lymon, the Everly Brothers, Chuck Berry, Jerry Lee Lewis, Joe Turner et Buddy Holly, pour n'en citer que quelques-uns. Ma discomanie était devenue incontrôlable. Je vivais, respirais et mangeais littéralement le rock 'n' roll. J'ai même incité ma mère à acheter certains aliments parce qu'ils offraient des bons à échanger contre des disques. Mon dernier devoir d'anglais fut une défense du rock 'n' roll.

En 1960, j'obtins mon diplôme de fin d'études au lycée et allai à l'université, laissant tous mes disques à la maison à l'exception des trois premiers albums de Bo Diddley. Je fus jeté de la plupart des surprises-parties à cause de ces disques de Diddley. Aux surprises-parties de l'université, tout le monde cherchait à tomber une fille, aussi jouait-on le plus souvent des morceaux pour emballer, en particulier *Open Fire Two Guitars* de Johnny Mathis. Je persistais à essayer de mettre Bo sur la platine et de brancher tout le monde sur le premier feedback de guitare jamais enregistré sur disque. Inutile d'ajouter que je ne suis pas exactement devenu l'homme fort du campus. En y repensant, je n'ai pas fait de conquête non plus. Toutes ces grandes histoires sur le rock 'n' roll qui entraîne les femmes dans des frénésies sexuelles sonnaient faux.

La meilleure boutique de disques près du campus était tenue par un ex-associé de Sam Goody, propriétaire de la chaîne de magasins de disques qui porte son nom. Lui et Sam s'étaient querellé pour une histoire d'argent. Une nuit, mon ami s'était emparé sous la menace d'une arme d'un camion de Sam bourré de disques et l'avait conduit aussi loin que possible. Il avait ouvert sa boutique à l'endroit où le moteur avait fini par mourir. Je n'étais plus seulement fasciné par les disques eux-mêmes, mais également par les histoires de cette industrie.

En 1966, à peine sorti de l'université, j'ai mis le cap sur la côte ouest. La plupart de mes amis partaient pour San Francisco, et je fis comme eux. Alors que je roulais sur le Golden Gate Bridge, la radio a diffusé *You're Gonna Miss Me* par les Thirteenth Floor Elevators. Si c'était ça le genre de musique de Frisco, alors j'étais fait pour Frisco. Après avoir découvert que les Elevators étaient en fait du Texas et que les groupes locaux s'appelaient Charlatans, Quicksilver et Grateful Dead, je mis le cap sur L.A., pays des Byrds, de Love et du Buffalo Springfield.

J'ai travaillé pour les maisons de disques, photographiant des musiciens comme les Chambers Brothers, les Raiders ou Taj Mahal. Je recevais 50 $ par séance et j'avais tous les disques que je voulais gratuitement. Puis, j'ai commencé à écrire sur la musique pour la presse underground. Après la publication de mon troisième article, on m'offrit un poste de publiciste chez Columbia – 200 $ par semaine mais, une fois encore avec tous les disques que je voulais.

En quittant l'université, j'avais bazardé tous mes disques, à l'exception d'une centaine de mes préférés. Dans le plus pur style hippie des années soixante, j'avais juré de ne rien posséder de plus que ce qui tiendrait dans la voiture que j'avais à cette époque. J'ai très vite rompu mon serment. Après avoir raconté à l'un de mes collègues de Columbia ma vie d'adolescent criminel, comment j'avais été arrêté pour avoir volé ce disque des Five Shillings et combien j'aimerais le retrouver aujourd'hui, j'ai découvert qu'il coûtait à présent 40 $; à condition, bien entendu, d'avoir la chance de mettre la main dessus. Je fus saisi de panique à l'idée que la musique avec laquelle j'avais grandi pourrait un jour ne plus m'être accessible. Je résolus de rebâtir la collection quoi qu'il m'en pût coûter, et cela finit par me prendre chaque moment libre.

Je commençai par éplucher le catalogue Columbia, et commandai des milliers d'albums. Ensuite, il y eut tous les arrangements avec les amis travaillant dans d'autres maisons de disques – «Je t'enverrai tous les disques de Miles Davis en échange de tous les Beatles et de tous les Beach Boys». Il faut dire que chaque compagnie avait recruté au moins l'un d'entre nous, ces «hippies d'intérieur» qui adoraient la musique. Les compagnies ne s'expliquaient pas comment nous faisions si bien notre travail, mais elles voulaient nous offrir ce bonus des disques gratuits pour que nous soyons contents. Cela leur revenait sacrément moins cher que si elles avaient dû nous payer un salaire décent. La première année, j'ai récolté 5000 albums, et je n'ai cessé d'améliorer ce chiffre les années suivantes. J'ai fini par échanger un 45 tours rare de Dylan contre un exemplaire du *Letter To An Angel* des Five Shillings.

En plus de tout cela, je passais toutes mes fins de semaine dans des ventes de garage ou dans les garages de responsables de maisons de disques plus âgés. Et puis, il y eut ensuite ces aventures incroyables comme celles qui ont consisté à me rendre dans les entrepôts de Sun Records à Memphis, Tennessee, à trouver le siège d'International Artists Records à Houston, Texas, et à mettre la main sur le meilleur choix d'albums dans l'entrepôt d'Ace Records à Jackson, Massachusetts.Un jour à Tyler, Texas, je fus agressé à la fois par les blancs et par les noirs en cherchant une boutique de disques rares. Les blancs se sont mis en rogne parce que je demandais une direction dans les quartiers noirs et, lorsque je fus arrivé à destination, les noirs voulurent savoir ce que ce type blanc venait faire dans le secteur. Réunir la collection m'a assurément pris beaucoup de temps et causé beaucoup d'ennuis.

Ce livre commence comme le rock 'n' roll, avec un mélange des formes musicales qui ont nourri celui-ci: pop, country et rythm and blues. Si le rock était la bande-son de nos vies, alors les albums dans lesquels se trouvait cette bande-son devaient contenir chacun des thèmes d'intérêts de l'adolescence – automobiles, lubies diverses, sexualité, révolte, évasion, énergie, vie, mort, solitude, danse et sorties.

Les premières pochettes étaient conçues pour capturer l'Amérique adolescente dans toute son innocence. Le rock était considéré comme trop sexualisé pour l'Amérique adulte, aussi les pochettes devaient-elles être pour la plupart cent pour cent anodines. Quoique la majorité des premiers musiciens rock aient été noirs, l'Amérique adolescente était un monde blanc. C'est pourquoi la plupart des pochettes de disques montrent des adolescents blancs dans des scènes typiques de ce tâge. C'est incroyable combien d'artistes noirs ont eu des photographies d'individus blancs sur leurs pochettes de disques, alors que leurs propres portraits étaient dans le meilleur des cas relégués au verso. Une fois adulte, j'ai appris que dans le Sud, les distributeurs refusaient beaucoup de disques parce qu'un noir figurait sur la pochette.

Quoique le rock soit venu des noirs qui ajoutèrent le rythme au blues, les blancs se sont donné un mal de chien pour usurper cette musique. Beaucoup de morceaux de musique noire étaient repris par des artistes aussi rassurants que Georgia Gibbs, Bill Haley, les McGuire Sisters et Pat Boone. Boone a décroché des hits avec des morceaux noirs tels que *Ain't That A Shame, At My Front Door, I'll Be Home* et *I Almost Lost My Mind*. Boone et Little Richard ont tous deux atteint la liste des dix meilleures ventes avec le *Long Tall Sally* du deuxième cité. Little Richard a prétendu que Boone n'avait jamais pu lui voler sa chanson parce qu'il ne pouvait l'imiter de manière convaincante. En comparant la photo de pochette de Little Richard, qui le présente le visage en sueur et hurlant, avec celle de Boone, entouré de camarades blancs, le public adolescent voyait son choix en noir et blanc, et il a finalement préféré le noir.

Mais, juste au moment où le rock atteignait sa pleine vitesse à la fin des années cinquante, le désastre survint. Little Richard vit Dieu et renonça à la musique du diable. Le praticien le plus populaire du rock, Elvis Presley, fut appelé sous les drapeaux. Buddy Holly et Eddie

Cochran se tuèrent respectivement en avion et en voiture. Pour couronner le tout, le scandale des pots-de-vin ruina la carrière d'Alan Freed, l'un des disc jockeys les plus fous de ce pays, qui avait organisé les plus grands et les meilleurs concerts de rock et qui refusait même de passer les reprises blanches des succès noirs. Finalement, à la fin des années cinquante et au début des années soixante, le rock se réduisit à des idoles adolescentes inoffensives et manufacturées comme Frankie Avalon, Fabian, Bobby Vee, Johnny Tillotson, Bobby Darin, Ricky Nelson, Bobby Rydell et consorts. En plus de leurs photos innocentes sur les pochettes, les notes au verso insistaient sur le fait que ces stars n'étaient pas uniquement des rockers mais qu'elles voulaient s'améliorer au-delà du rock en étudiant le jeu d'acteur et la danse.

Tandis que le rock mourait prématurément aux Etats-Unis, les graines que Bill Haley, Eddie Cochran et Gene Vincent avaient plantées en Angleterre prenaient racine avec des groupes comme les Beatles, les Rolling Stones, les Animals, les Yardbirds, les Who, les Them. Ensuite, quand les années soixante prirent réellement leur élan, les racines du rock firent pousser des branches dans toutes les directions en même temps. Le Folk, le Folk-Rock, le Surf, San Francisco, Motown, la Soul, le Psychédélisme, les Garage Bands et l'Invasion Britannique s'unirent pour produire une irrésistible révolution. La musique de l'Amérique adolescente était à présent le son d'une génération, et la génération était plus mûre et plus universelle. Désormais, les pochettes de disques pouvaient vraiment refléter l'époque. La pochette du premier album de Steve Miller ne pouvait être déchiffrée à moins d'être défoncé. David Bowie apparaissait en robe sur la pochette de son premier album, et Jimi Hendrix pouvait avoir une troupe de femmes nues sur sa pochette d'album; du moins en Angleterre.

Pendant les années soixante, je passai d'une maison de disques à l'autre, acceptant des boulots à cause des disques gratuits et trouvant l'amour libre comme extra-bonus. Durant des années, j'avais vécu pour la folie de cette musique, et c'était le monde qui adoptait maintenant ce style de vie. La musique et les musiciens devinrent accessibles à tous. Les musiciens et les publics semblaient avoir autant de contrôle sur la musique que l'industrie du disque. Il y eut même des réunions tribales appelées festivals qui plus tard unifièrent ce mouvement musical. La musique pop était si prédominante dans la culture pop que même Andy Warhol, se mit à réaliser des pochettes d'albums.

Au milieu des années soixante-dix, la musique était devenue une industrie, et les intérêts de l'entreprise primaient sur ceux des artistes. En 1976, je fus viré de mon ultime boulot dans une compagnie. J'étais le directeur national de la publicité pour ABC Records et on me demanda de ne pas promouvoir le disque de Freddy Fender, *Before The Next Teardrop Falls*, parce que Freddy avait plus de quarante ans, était chicano et ancien taulard. Contre les instructions de mon chef, j'ai aidé Freddy à devenir l'artiste le plus vendu de cette compagnie, et je fus donc licencié pour insubordination. J'ai toujours le disque d'or que Freddy m'a envoyé avec écrit dessus «Ce n'aurait pas été possible sans toi, frère».

En 1977, j'ai commencé à constituer les Michael Ochs Archives, une compagnie ayant pour vocation la conservation du passé musical que j'aime tant. J'ai continué à me procurer chaque nouveau disque et j'ai commencé à collectionner des photos, des partitions, des programmes de concerts – tout ce qui pouvait documenter l'histoire pas encore terminée du rock. L'amitié qui avait commencé dans mes années d'adolescence s'était maintenant épanouie en un mariage, au sens traditionnel du terme – jusqu'à ce que la mort nous sépare.

J'ai continué à collectionner des disques tout au long des années quatre-vingt. Au cours des années quatre-vingt-dix, avec le remplacement du microsillon par le CD, j'ai pensé que la collection était devenue trop grande. J'ai opté pour le côté pratique des CD, en dépit du fait que le son des disques vinyle est incomparablement meilleur. A présent, l'industrie du disque envisage même de remplacer les CD par des puces informatiques. Toutes les œuvres graphiques qui ornaient les pochettes de disques seront probablement remplacées par des bandes filmées des groupes transférées sur CD vidéo ou sur puce informatique.

Récemment interviewé dans une émission de télévision, j'ai ressenti une difficulté à parler avec nostalgie de ma collection. Pour la première fois, j'ai éprouvé une distance entre elle et moi, un peu comme un gamin qui a gaspillé sa jeunesse à collectionner des timbres ou quelque chose du même ordre. Après l'émission, un marchand de disques rares m'a appelé pour me dire qu'il pourrait probablement vendre la collection de disques près d'un million de dollars. Ensuite, j'ai été contacté pour réaliser ce livre.

Tous ces signes me parvinrent en même temps. C'était comme si Dieu était en train de me dire que maintenant que j'étais marié et père de famille, je pouvais renoncer au premier et plus grand amour de ma vie. Quand j'ai commencé ce livre, je me suis dis que lorsque je l'aurais fini, je vendrais ma collection. Dans la onzième heure qui suivit son achèvement, je suis tombé dans un magasin de disques rares sur la pochette originale de l'album *Fever* de Little Willie John, celle avec l'infirmière blanche. J'ai emprunté le disque, l'ai photographié pour le livre et rendu à la boutique. C'était un disque que je recherchais depuis les années cinquante. Aujourd'hui, j'ai appelé la boutique et acheté l'album, ranimant ainsi la passion que je croyais avoir perdue.

J'ai enfin compris que l'amour n'a pas de prix – ma collection de disques n'est à vendre qu'à travers ce livre.

Cette compilation des différents visages du rock'n roll voudrait être aussi délectable que la musique elle-même. Il ne s'agit ni d'une anthologie critique de l'art des pochettes, ni d'une histoire exhaustive. Il s'agit seulement des mille pochettes d'albums de ma collection dont j'ai pensé qu'elles donneraient une vue d'ensemble du rock 'n' roll depuis sa plus tendre enfance jusqu'à son âge actuel.

Lorsque j'ai commencé à sélectionner les disques, je n'ai pris que les albums que j'aurais eu plaisir à voir reproduits dans un livre. Le seul critère retenu était ce qui m'avait frappé comme étant unique et mémorable pour son époque. Après en avoir extrait quelques milliers, j'ai essayé de déterminer un ordre autre que simplement chronologique. A côté de l'assemblage par genres musicaux, j'ai commencé à voir certains fils conducteurs évidents tels que les différentes représentations des noirs et des femmes à travers les décennies.

Je me rends compte que ma méthode de sélection a entraîné de sérieuses omissions, mais c'est bien la seule chose qui soit sérieuse dans ce livre. En raison des difficultés de sélection ou de la particularité de mes goûts, je suis convaincu que de nombreuses pochettes qui auraient dû figurer dans ce livre n'y figurent pas. La logique de ma folie devrait être évidente au vu des illustrations de pochettes. Toutes mes excuses à tous les grands artistes qui n'ont pas survécu au montage final.

J'espère que vous aimerez ce choix significatif de mes pochettes de disques préférées autant que j'ai aimé les collectionner.

Michael Ochs
Venice (CA).
Décembre 1995.

# 1950s

The fifties was the decade when all the war babies entered their teenage years. This new generation needed a new form of music to make their own. The big bands of the forties were downsized into combos, as solo singers and vocal groups became the new stars. While crooners and quartets dominated the charts, black "race" records were becoming so popular that in the early fifties *Billboard Magazine* had to start a separate rhythm and blues chart; and soon thereafter, rock and roll was born.

Rock and roll's birth certificate has never been found, so there is no definitive date for its birthday. Some say it all started in 1951 with Jackie Brenston's *Rocket 88* and The Dominoes *Sixty-Minute Man*, while others cite 1954 because of The Chords' *Sh-Boom* and The Crows' *Gee*. To confuse the birth date further, Johnny Otis, Joe Turner, Little Esther, Fats Domino and Ivory Joe Hunter all started recording before 1951. The early fifties was a magical musical-merging that created rock and roll by mixing gospel, rhythm, blues, pop and country.

In the beginning the major record companies tried to ignore rock and roll thinking it was a temporary aberration and would soon disappear. This gave rise to a number of independent record labels like

Atlantic, Chess, King and Specialty that got their start by recording these new rhythm-and-blues and rock and roll artists. The two most important emerging forms of rock were "doo-wop" and "rock-a-billy", although neither became national crazes. By the mid-fifties, though, rock and roll swept the nation as Bill Haley's *Rock Around The Clock*, featured in the hit film *Blackboard Jungle*, quickly became the biggest rock hit to date, associating rock with juvenile delinquency. And Elvis Presley was discovered by Sun Records.

Rock and roll was often accused as being a plot to lower the white man to the level of the Negro – but Elvis showed us that rock actually raised us to that level. Although Elvis started recording for Sun in 1954, he didn't explode on to the national scene until 1956 when he switched to RCA. In that year alone, Elvis had five number-one records, starred in his first feature film, *Love Me Tender* and appeared on national television eleven times. The following year, rock and roll was seen regularly on television as many local dance shows made their appearance, and Dick Clark's *American Bandstand* show, live from Philadelphia, was broadcast nationally every afternoon. Even the *Ozzie and Harriet* show started to feature songs by Ricky Nelson every week.

By 1960, rock music had grown way beyond a teenage fad, as *Bye Bye Birdie* became the first rock musical on Broadway. Rock and roll was now becoming safe and sanitized with a preponderance of teen idols like Frankie Avalon and Fabian, and dance crazes like "The Twist" and the "Hully Gully". In rebellion, many kids turned to the more basic sounds of folk music. Although The Kingston Trio and The Limeliters brought folk back into popularity in the late fifties, it wasn't until Bob Dylan started recording that the folk revival really took off.

The other great musical movement that dominated the charts at the end of the first decade of rock was the "girl group" sound. The greatest records of that genre were created by the first teenage millionaire, Phil Spector, who changed the production sound of all future recordings with his "wall of sound" technique. At a time when most pop music was becoming simpler and saner, Spector took rock to Wagnerian heights with groups like The Crystals and The Ronettes.

The biggest selling artists of the fifties such, as Pat Boone, Little Richard, Perry Como, Bill Haley, Chuck Berry, and The Platters, were all disappearing from the hit parade charts as the war babies grew out of their teens and the fifties came to a close.

Die fünfziger Jahre waren das Jahrzehnt, in dem die während des Krieges geborenen Kinder ins Teenageralter kamen. Die neue Generation verlangte nach einer neuen, eigenen Musikrichtung. Die Big Bands der vierziger Jahre waren zu Combos verkümmert, während Solosänger und Gesangsgruppen zu den neuen Stars wurden. Während einerseits Schnulzensänger und Quartette die Hitlisten anführten, gewannen die sogenannten „Race" Records der Schwarzen auf der anderen Seite eine derartige Popularität, daß das *Billboard Magazine* Anfang der fünfziger Jahre eigens eine Rhythm & Blues-Hitparade einrichtete, und bald darauf wurde der Rock 'n' Roll geboren.

Die Geburtsurkunde des Rock 'n' Roll ist bis heute verschollen, so daß sich nicht eindeutig bestimmen läßt, wann genau er seinen Anfang nahm. Einige meinen, daß alles im Jahre 1951 mit Jackie Brenstons *Rocket 88* und dem *Sixty-Minute-Man* von den Dominoes begann, andere hingegen verweisen auf *Sh-Boom* von den Chords und *Gee* von den Crows aus dem Jahre 1954. Für weitere Verwirrung sorgt die Tatsache, daß Johnny Otis, Joe Turner, Little Esther, Fats Domino und Ivory Joe Hunter allesamt schon vor 1951 ihre ersten Schallplattenaufnahmen machten. Die frühen fünfziger Jahre wurden zu einem musikalischen Schmelztiegel, in dem so verschiedene Musikrichtungen wie Gospel, Rhythm, Blues, Pop und Country sich vermischten, so daß schließlich der Rock 'n' Roll daraus hervorging.

Zunächst schenkten die großen Plattenfirmen dem Rock 'n' Roll keine Beachtung, da sie ihn für eine kurzlebige Verirrung hielten, die sich bald wieder legen würde. So entstanden etliche unabhängige Labels wie Atlantic, Chess, King Records und Specialty Records, die sich mit Platten der führenden Rhythm & Blues- und Rock 'n' Roll-Künstler auf dem Markt etablierten. Der Doo-Wop und der Rockabilly waren anfangs die beiden bedeutendsten Formen des Rock. Doch schon Mitte der fünfziger Jahre löste der Rock 'n' Roll im ganzen Land Begeisterungsstürme aus, als Elvis Presley von Sun Records entdeckt wurde und Bill Haleys Platte *Rock Around The Clock*, die als Filmmusik in dem Riesenerfolg „The Blackboard Jungle" („Die Saat der Gewalt") ganz groß rauskam, in Windeseile zum bis dahin erfolgreichsten Rock-Hit avancierte – wobei der Song gleichzeitig dafür sorgte, daß Rock 'n' Roll und Jugendkriminalität von nun an in einem Atemzug genannt wurden.

Man hat dem Rock 'n' Roll oft vorgeworfen, er würde die Weißen auf die Ebene der Schwarzen herabziehen, doch Elvis trat den Beweis dafür an, daß der Rock 'n' Roll die Weißen vielmehr auf ebendiese Ebene emporhob. Obwohl Elvis schon 1954 seine erste Platte bei Sun herausgebracht hatte, wurde er erst 1956 mit seinem Wechsel zu RCA der Superstar schlechthin. Allein in diesem einen Jahr landete Elvis fünf Hits, spielte die Hauptrolle in seinem ersten Kinofilm „Love Me Tender" und trat elfmal im Fernsehen auf. Schon im Jahr darauf war Rock 'n' Roll aus dem Fernsehen nicht mehr wegzudenken. Viele regionale Tanzshows wurden ins Leben gerufen, und Dick Clarks *American Bandstand-Show* wurde jeden Nachmittag live aus Philadelphia in die ganzen USA ausgestrahlt. Sogar die *Ozzie-and-Harriet-Show* hatte jede Woche Songs von Ricky Nelson im Programm.

1960 war der Rock 'n' Roll längst über das Image der belanglosen Teenagermarotte hinausgewachsen, und „Bye Bye Birdie" wurde als erstes Rock 'n' Roll-Musical am Broadway aufgeführt. Allmählich etablierte sich der Rock 'n' Roll und war dank so freier Teenageridole wie Frankie Avalon und Fabian und so ausgelassener Tanzformen wie Twist und Hully Gully gesellschaftsfähig geworden. Viele Jugendliche der rebellischen Sechziger wandten sich wieder den einfacheren Klängen des Folk zu. Zwar hatten das Kingston Trio und die Limeliters den Folk Ende der fünfziger Jahre wieder populär gemacht, doch von einer Renaissance des Folk konnte man erst nach den ersten Schallplattenaufnahmen von Bob Dylan sprechen.

Die andere große Musikrichtung, die die Charts gegen Ende der ersten Rock-Dekade beherrschte, war der Sound der Girl Groups. Die erfolgreichsten Schallplatten dieses Genres produzierte der erste Jung-Millionär Phil Spector, der mit seiner orchestralen Tontechnik, den sogenannten »Soundmauern«, den Produktionsstil aller zukünftigen Studioaufnahmen veränderte. Während die Popmusik ansonsten meist einfacher und gemäßigter wurde, schwang Spector den Rock mit Gruppen wie den Crystals und den Ronettes zu wagnerischen Höhen auf.

Die Hitparadenmusik der fünfziger Jahre mit Musikern wie Pat Boone, Little Richard, Perry Como, Bill Haley, Chuck Berry und den Platters verschwand vollends aus den Charts, als die „Kriegskinder" aus dem Teenageral ließen.

Les années cinquante furent la décennie au cours de laquelle les enfants de la guerre entrèrent dans l'adolescence. Cette nouvelle génération avait besoin d'une nouvelle forme de musique qui lui appartienne. Les grands orchestres des années quarante furent dans les années cinquante réduits à la taille de combos, tandis que les chanteurs et les groupes vocaux devenaient les nouvelles stars. Alors que les crooners et les quatuors vocaux dominaient les listes des meilleures ventes, les disques de «race» noire devinrent si populaires que *Billboard Magazine* dut, au début des années cinquante, créer parallèlement une liste des meilleures ventes de rythm and blues. Et presque aussitôt après, le rock 'n' roll vit le jour.

On n'a jamais trouvé l'acte de naissance du rock 'n' roll, c'est pourquoi il n'est pas possible de dater avec exactitude ses débuts. Certains disent que tout a commencé en 1951 avec *Rocket 88* de Jackie Brenston et *Sixty-Minute Man* des Dominoes, alors que d'autres parlent de 1954 à cause du *Sh-Boom* des Chords et du *Gee* des Crows. Pour compliquer encore cette datation, Johnny Otis, Joe Turner, Little Esther, Fats Domino et Ivory Joe Hunter ont tous commencé à enregistrer avant 1951. Le début des années cinquante fut une fusion magique qui créa le rock 'n' roll en mélangeant le gospel, le rythme, le blues, la pop et la country.

Les plus grandes maisons de disques ont au début essayé d'ignorer le rock 'n' roll en pensant qu'il s'agissait d'une complète aberration vouée à une disparition prochaine. C'est ce qui a donné naissance à de nombreuses maisons de disques indépendantes tels qu'Atlantic, Chess, King et Specialty, qui toutes ont commencé en enregistrant des artistes de blues et de rock 'n' roll. Les deux formes de rock les plus importantes qui sont apparues étaient le doo-wop et le rock-a-billy, quoiqu'aucune d'elles ne soit devenue une folie nationale. Pourtant, au milieu des années cinquante, le rock 'n' roll déferla sur l'Amérique lorsque le *Rock Around The Clock* de Bill Haley, entendu dans le film à succès *Blackboard Jungle* («Graine de Violence»), devint le plus grand hit de rock en associant celui-ci à la délinquance juvénile, et qu'Elvis Presley fut découvert par Sun Records.

Le rock fut souvent accusé d'être un complot visant à abaisser l'homme blanc au niveau de la musique nègre, mais Elvis a prouvé que le rock nous a en fait élevés jusqu'à ce niveau. Quoiqu'Elvis ait commencé à enregistrer pour Sun en 1954, il n'explosa véritablement à l'échelon national qu'en 1956 lorsqu'il passa chez RCA. Pendant cette seule année, Elvis eut cinq disques numéro un, joua son premier film en vedette, *Love Me Tender* («Le Cavalier du Crépuscule»), et parut onze fois sur les écrans de la télévision nationale. L'année suivante, le rock passait régulièrement à la télévision tandis que débutaient de nombreuses émissions de danse locales et que le Dick Clark's *American Bandstand* Show, en direct de Philadelphie, était diffusé chaque après-midi à travers l'ensemble du pays. Même le *Ozzie and Harriet* Show se mit à présenter chaque semaine des chansons de Ricky Nelson.

En 1960, la musique rock était devenue autre chose qu'une lubie d'adolescent et *Bye Bye Birdie* devint la première comédie musicale rock de Broadway. Le rock 'n' roll était désormais en train de devenir sûr et aseptisé avec une majorité d'idoles adolescentes telles que Frankie Avalon et Fabian et un engouement frénétique pour des danses comme le Twist et le Hully Gully. En réaction, de nombreux gamins se tournèrent vers les sonorités plus élémentaires de la musique folk. Quoique le Kingston Trio et les Limeliters aient rendu le folk à nouveau populaire à la fin des années cinquante, le genre ne se renouvela vraiment qu'avec les premiers enregistrements de Bob Dylan.

L'autre grande tendance musicale qui marqua le hit-parade à la fin de la première décennie rock fut le son des groupes féminins. Les plus grands disques du genre furent créés par le premier adolescent milliardaire, Phil Spector, qui a transformé la production de tous les disques à venir avec sa technique du mur de son. Alors que la majeure partie de la musique pop devenait de plus en plus simple et de plus en plus anodine, Spector entraîna le rock jusqu'à des sommets wagnériens avec des groupes tels que les Crystals et les Ronettes.

Les plus gros vendeurs de disques des années cinquante, tels que Pat Boone, Little Richard, Perry Como, Bill Haley, Chuck Berry et les Platters disparaissaient du hit-parade à mesure que les enfants de la guerre laissaient derrière eux leur adolescence.

**Hen Gates And His Gaters**
*Let's Go Dancing To Rock And Roll*
Masterseal, 1957

Design: Unknown

**Various Artists**
*Dance The Rock & Roll*
Atlantic, 1957

Design: Unknown
*Courtesy Atlantic Recording Corp.*

**The Robins**
*Rock & Roll With The Robins*
Whippet, 1958

Design: Unknown

**Frank Sinatra**
*No One Cares*
Capitol, 1959

Design: Unknown

**Nat "King" Cole**
*Just One Of Those Things*
Capitol, 1957

Design: Unknown

**Bing Crosby**
*Bing With A Beat*
RCA Victor, 1957

Photo: Gene Lester

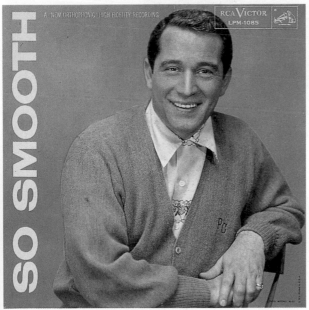

**Perry Como**
*So Smooth*
RCA Victor, 1955

Photo: Mitchell Bliss

**Peggy Lee**
*Olé Ala Lee!*
Capitol, 1960

Design: Unknown

MERCURY SR 60010 • PATTI PAGE • LET'S GET AWAY FROM IT ALL

# STEREO
HI-FI

## Patti Page Sings

"Let's get away from it all"

Printed in U.S.A.

Patti Page
*Let's Get Away From It All*
Mercury, 1957

Design: Unknown

**Frankie Laine**
*Rockin'*
Columbia, 1957

Photo: John Engstead

**Julie London**
*Julie Is Her Name*
Liberty, 1956

Photo: Phil Howard

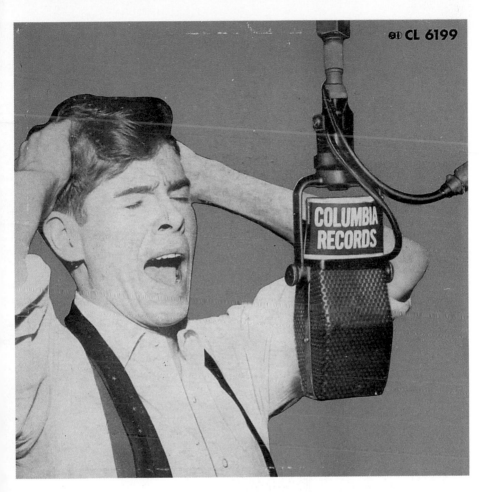

CL 6199

**Johnnie Ray**
*Johnnie Ray*
Columbia, 1951

Design: Unknown

**Julie London**
*Calendar Girl*
Liberty, 1956

Photos: Gene Lester

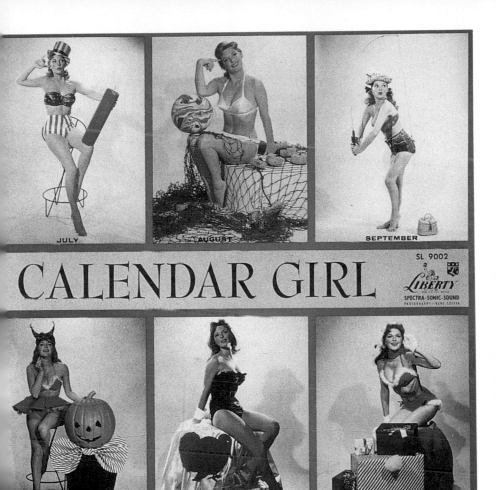

JULY AUGUST SEPTEMBER

# CALENDAR GIRL

SL 9002

*Liberty*

SPECTRA-SONIC-SOUND

OCTOBER NOVEMBER DECEMBER

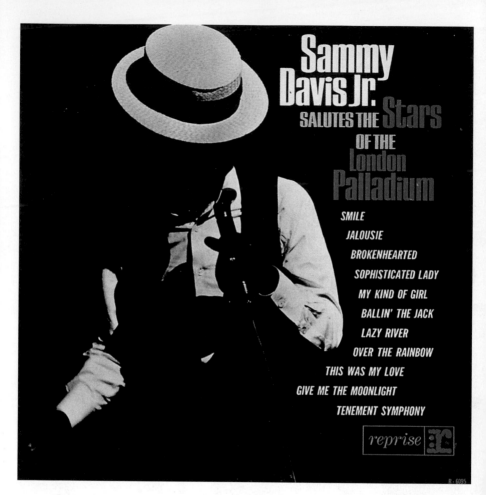

**Sammy Davis Jr.**
*Sammy Davis Jr. Salutes The Stars Of
The London Palladium*
Reprise, 1963

Design: Unknown

**Les Paul & Mary Ford**
*Les And Mary*
Capitol, 1955

Design: Unknown

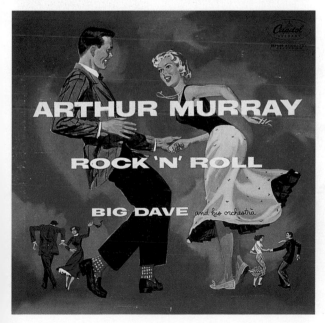

**Big Dave Cavenaugh**
*Arthur Murray Rock 'N' Roll*
Capitol, 1950s

Design: Unknown

**The McGuire Sisters**
*Sugartime*
Coral, 1958

Photo: Garrett-Howard

**The Four Coins**
*The Four Coins In Shangri-La*
Epic, 1958

Design: Unknown

**The Four Lads**
*The Four Lads Swing Along*
Columbia, 1959

Design: Unknown

**The Four Aces**
*The Swingin' Aces*
Decca, 1958

Design: Unknown

**Earl Bostic**
*For You*
King, 1956

Design: Unknown

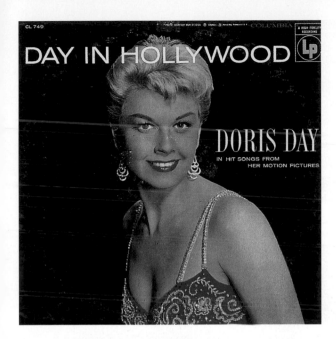

**Doris Day**
*Day In Hollywood*
Columbia, 1955

Photo: Courtesy MGM Studios

**Teresa Brewer**
*Miss Music*
Coral, 1958

Photo: Hobart Baker

**The Crew Cuts**
*Capers*
Mercury, 1957

Design: Unknown

**The Diamonds**
*All New Songs*
Mercury, 1950s

Design: Unknown

earl
bostic

songs
of the

FANTASTIC

50'S

Vol. 2

KING
838

I CAN DREAM CAN'T I

IT'S A SIN

BAUBLES BANGLES & BEADS

CHERRY PINK

VAYA CON DIOS

YOUR CHEATING HEART

TAMMY

TOO YOUNG

MISTER SANDMAN

HIGH AND THE MIGHTY

OH MY PAPA

LOVE LETTERS IN THE SAND

OFFICIAL U.S. NAVY PHOTO

ViViD SOUND

**Earl Bostic**
*Songs of the Fantastic 50's, Vol. 2*
King, 1963

Photo: Garrett-Howard

**Johnny "Scat" Davis**
*Here's Lookin At'cha*
King, 1959

Design: Unknown

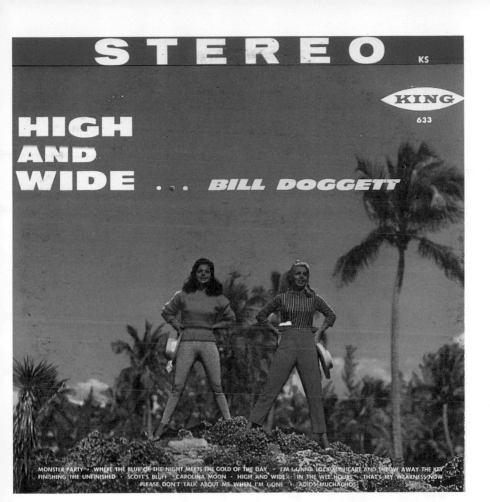

**Bill Doggett**
*High And Wide …*
King, 1959

Design: Unknown

**Various Artists**
*Rock All Night!*
Mercury, 1958

Design: Unknown

**Various Artists**
*Jamboree!*
Warner Bros., 1955

Design: Unknown

**The Crew Cuts**
*Rock And Roll Bash*
Mercury, 1957

Design: Unknown

**Various Artists**
*Rock, Rock, Rock*
Chess, 1958

Design: Chuck Stewart

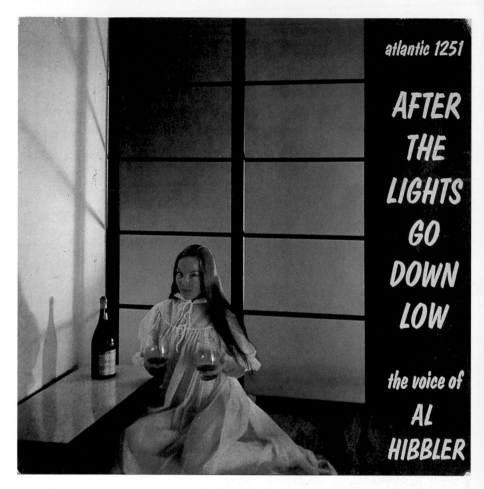

atlantic 1251

AFTER
THE
LIGHTS
GO
DOWN
LOW

the voice of
AL
HIBBLER

**Al Hibbler**
*After The Lights Go Down Low*
Atlantic, 1957

Design: Unknown
*Courtesy Atlantic Recording Corp.*

**Earl Bostic**
*By Popular Demand*
King, 1962

Design: Unknown

**Ivory Joe Hunter**
*Ivory Joe Hunter Sings Sixteen Of His Greatest Hits*
King, 1958

Design: Unknown

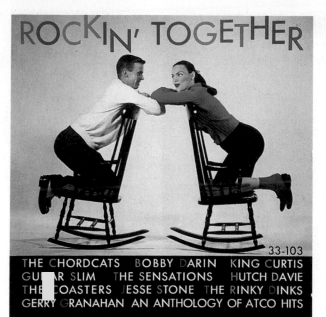

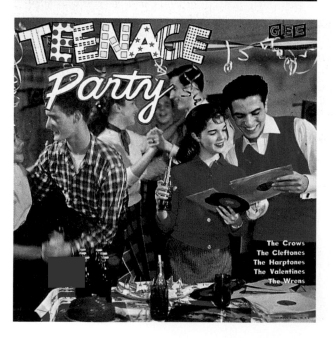

**Various Artists**
*Rockin' Together*
Atco, 1958

Design: Marvin Israel
Photo: Jules
*Courtesy Atlantic Recording Corp.*

**Various Artists**
*Teenage Party*
Gee, 1958

Design: Lee-Miles Associates,
New York City

These compilations are of primarily black recording artists, yet, once again, only white people are shown on the covers.

Obwohl diese Alben überwiegend von schwarzen Musikern aufgenommen wurden, werden auf den Covern nur Weiße abgebildet.

Ces compilations contiennent essentiellement de la musique noire, même si, une fois encore, seuls des blancs apparaissent sur les photos de pochettes.

**Various Artists**
*Herald The Beat*
Herald, 1960

Design: Unknown

**Various Artists**
*Rock 'N' Roll Dance Party*
King, 1958

Design: Unknown

**Chet Atkins**
*Chet Atkins' Workshop*
RCA Victor, 1961

Design: Unknown

# "THEY'RE RIDING HIGH," SAYS ARCHIE
# THE CHORDETTES

**They loved them in Sheboygan,** but the Chordettes weren't long for Wisconsin. Faster than you can say "Mr. Sandman," they took the whole country by storm. Archie, too. That's why he brings you all their happy, hummable hits on this Cadence record.

a high-fidelity recording by **CADENCE CLP-3001**

**The Chordettes**
*The Chordettes*
Cadence, 1957

Design: Unknown

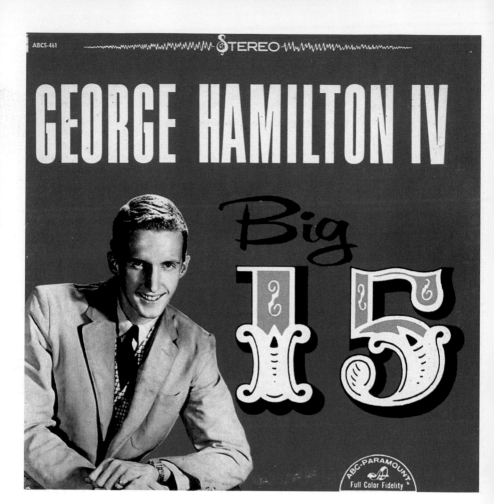

**George Hamilton IV**
*Big 15*
ABC-Paramount, 1963

Design: Joe Lebow

**Cadillacs/Orioles**
*Cadillacs Meet The Orioles*
Jubilee, 1961

Design: Sy Leichman
Photo: Charles Varron

jubilee **LP**

1098

THE
PARAGONS
MEET
THE
JESTERS

**The Paragons/The Jesters**
*The Paragons Meet The Jesters*
Jubilee, 1959

Design: Sy Leichman
Photo: Charles Varron

Not only do these compilations of black artists have white people on the covers, but they also add to rock's dangerous image by tying the music to juvenile delinquency.

Nicht nur, daß diese Alben schwarzer Künstler Weiße auf den Covern zeigen, sie tragen außerdem zu dem schlechten Image von Rockmusik bei, indem sie Jugendkriminalität mit Rockmusik in Verbindung bringen.

Non seulement ces compilations de musique noire montrent des blancs sur la pochette, mais elles contribuent à la mauvaise image du rock en associant cette musique à la délinquance juvénile.

**Various Artists**
*Whoppers!*
Jubilee, 1960

Design: Sy Leichman
Photo: Charles Varron

**Various Artists**
*Boppin'!*
Jubilee, 1961

Design: Sy Leichman/
Charles Varron

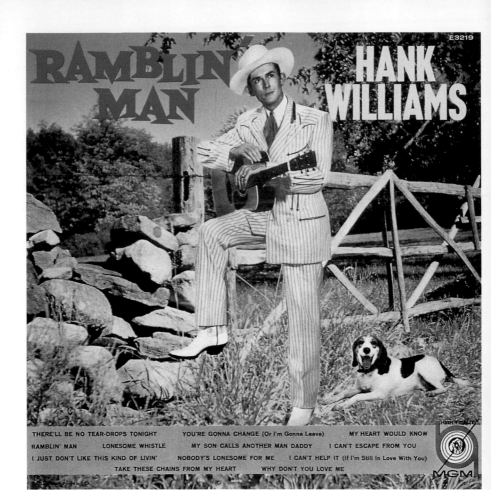

E3219

# RAMBLIN' MAN

# HANK WILLIAMS

| THERE'LL BE NO TEAR-DROPS TONIGHT | YOU'RE GONNA CHANGE (Or I'm Gonna Leave) | MY HEART WOULD KNOW |
| RAMBLIN' MAN | LONESOME WHISTLE | MY SON CALLS ANOTHER MAN DADDY | I CAN'T ESCAPE FROM YOU |
| I JUST DON'T LIKE THIS KIND OF LIVIN' | NOBODY'S LONESOME FOR ME | I CAN'T HELP IT (If I'm Still In Love With You) |
| TAKE THESE CHAINS FROM MY HEART | WHY DON'T YOU LOVE ME |

HIGH FIDELITY

MGM

**Hank Williams**
*Ramblin' Man*
MGM, 1954

Design: Unknown

A fine example of great early paste-up "art". Note Hank's free floating foot and dog.

Ein schönes Beispiel für die „gelungenen" Fotomontagen der Fünfziger. Beachtung verdienen Hanks freischwebender Fuß und der Hund.

Un bon exemple du «grand art» du photomontage des débuts. Notez le pied et le chien d'Hank flottant librement.

**Hank Williams**
*Moanin' The Blues*
MGM, 1952

Design: Unknown

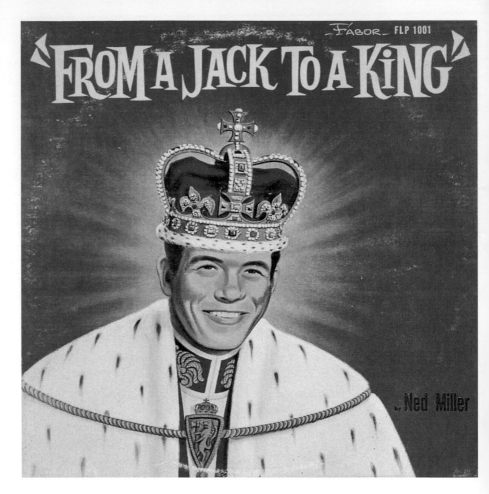

**Ned Miller**
*From A Jack To A King*
Fabor, 1963

Design: Unknown

**Johnny Cash**
*Johnny Cash With His Hot And Blue Guitar!*
Sun, 1956

Design: Unknown
*Courtesy Sun Entertainment Corporation*

**Jimmy Dean**
*A Thing Called Love*
RCA Victor, 1968

Design: Unknown

**Rusty Draper**
*Rusty Meets Hoagy*
Mercury, 1957

Design: Unknown

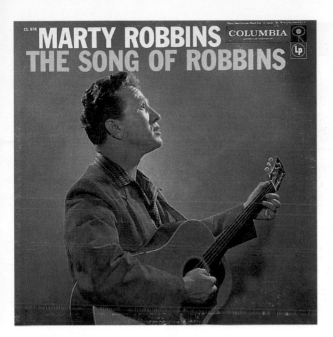

**Marty Robbins**
*The Song Of Robbins*
Columbia, 1957

Design: Unknown

**Don Gibson**
*All My Love*
RCA Victor, 1967

Design: Unknown

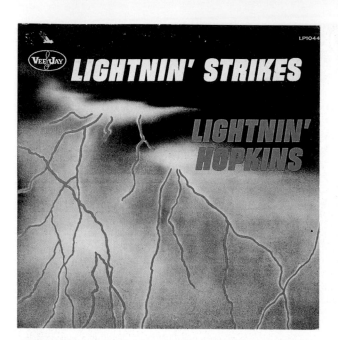

**Lightnin' Hopkins**
*Lightnin' Strikes*
Vee-Jay, 1962

Design: Unknown

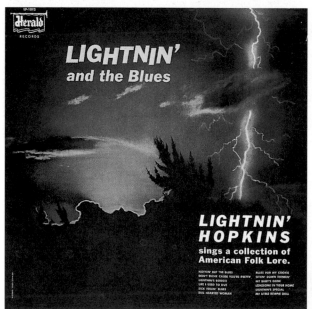

**Lightnin' Hopkins**
*Lightnin' And The Blues*
Herald, 1959

Design: Unknown

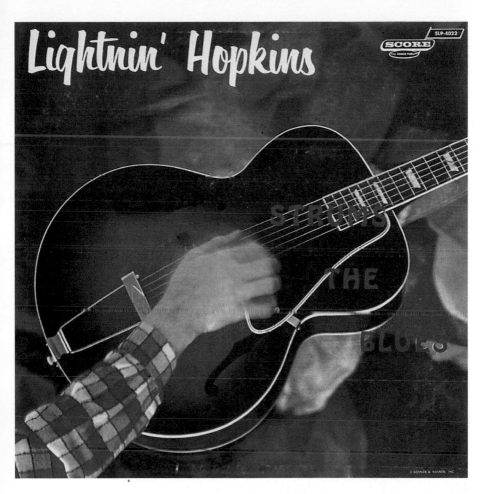

**Lightnin' Hopkins**
*Lightnin' Hopkins Strums The Blues*
Score, 1958

Artwork: Sharon Pose
Photo: Ovid Neal

**Lightnin' Hopkins**
*Lightnin' Hopkins*
Folkways, 1962

Design: Ronald Clyne
Photo: Samul B. Charters

**Reverend Gary Davis**
*Pure Religion!*
Prestige, 1964

Design: Unknown

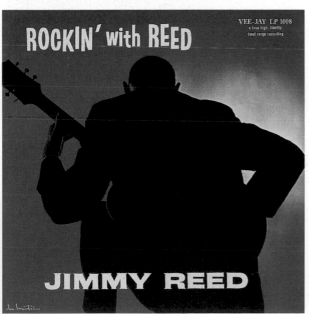

**Jimmy Reed**
*Rockin' With Reed*
Vee-Jay, 1959

Design: Don Bronstein

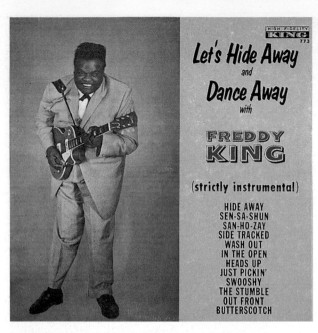

**Freddy King**
*Let's Hide Away And Dance Away
With Freddy King*
King, 1961

Design: Unknown

**Muddy Waters**
*Muddy Waters Sings 'Big Bill'*
Chess, 1960

Design: Don Bronstein

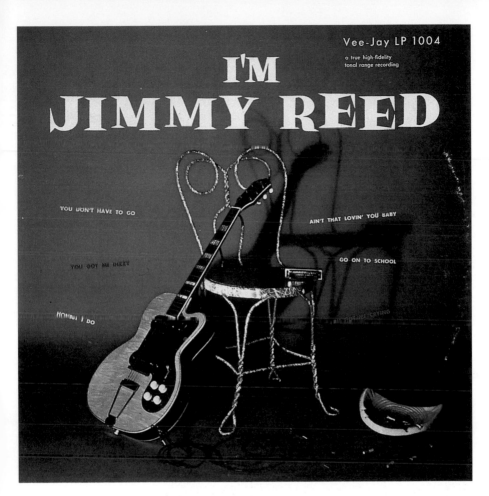

**Jimmy Reed**
*I'm Jimmy Reed*
Vee-Jay, 1958

Design: Leroy Winbush

**Earl Hooker**
*Sweet Black Angel*
Blue Thumb, 1970s

Art Direction: Michangelo Linguini
Photo: John Hayes

**Arthur "Big Boy" Crudup**
*Mean Ol' Frisco*
Fire, 1960

Design: Unknown

**The Five Keys**
*The Five Keys*
King, 1960

Photo: Bernard Gray

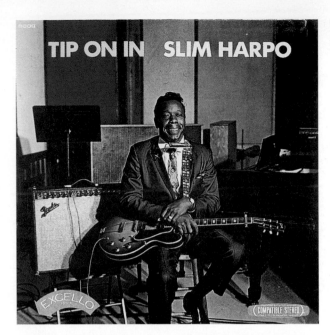

**Slim Harpo**
*Tip On In*
Excello, 1968

Design: Dan Quest Art Studios
*Courtesy AVI Record Production Corp.,
a division of AVI Entertainment
Group, Inc.*

**Rare Earth**
*Willie Remembers …*
Motown, 1972

Design: David Larkham/
Tepee Graphics
Photo: Ed Caraeff

**Sonny Boy Williamson**
*Sonny Boy Williamson Sings Down and Out Blues*
Checker, 1959

Design: Unknown

**Jimmy Rushing**
*Five Feet Of Soul*
Colpix, 1963

Design: Unknown

**Various Artists**
*Symposium In Blues*
RCA Victor, 1966

Design: Unknown

therapy often helpful in DEPRESSION

# ELAVIL HCl

ELAVIL is indicated in moderate to severe depression. It has a mild tranquilizing component
to its action which makes it of special value in depressed patients with associated mild anxiety or agitation.

When the depressed patient is treated with ELAVIL the following target symptoms may be
anticipated to respond well to the drug: Depressed Mood, Anxiety, Insomnia, Psychomotor Retardation,
Functional Somatic Complaints, Loss of Interest, Feelings of Guilt, Anorexia, Headache.

ELAVIL is particularly useful in ambulatory patients because it is generally well tolerated. Patients
usually do not show startling changes in their attitudes or behavior, but gradually develop
more interest in their surroundings and show a slowly increasing elevation of mood. As with other
psychotherapeutic agents, all patients do not respond to the same degree. Some patients respond promptly,
while others may require four to six weeks to obtain benefit, and lack of response sometimes occurs.

This MONAURAL record should be played at 33⅓ RPM

This is the only album ever found that uses the blues to
promote a mood-elevating drug.

Dieses Album ist das einzige überhaupt, bei dem mit Blues-
Musik für eine stimmungsaufhellende Droge geworben wird.

C'est l'unique album au monde à utiliser le blues pour promouvoir un antidépresseur.

(Back cover)
*Symposium In Blues*

**Ruth Brown**
*Miss Rhythm*
Atlantic, 1959

Design: Marvin Israel
Photo: Bill Fotiades
*Courtesy Atlantic Recording Corp.*

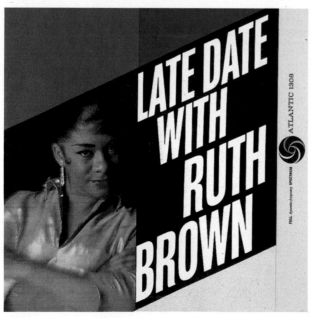

**Ruth Brown**
*Late Date with Ruth Brown*
Atlantic, 1959

Design: Marvin Israel
Photo: Bill Fotiades
*Courtesy Atlantic Recording Corp.*

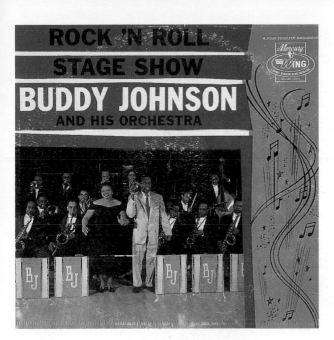

**Buddy Johnson and His Orchestra**
*Rock 'N' Roll Stage Show*
Mercury-Wing, 1956

Design: Unknown

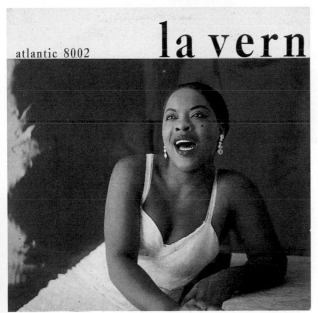

**LaVern Baker**
*La Vern*
Atlantic, 1956

Design: Marvin Israel
Photo: Jerry Schatzberg
*Courtesy Atlantic Recording Corp.*

**The Dells**
*Oh, What A Nite*
Vee-Jay, 1959

Design: Unknown

HERALD
HLP 1014

# STAY

with **MAURICE WILLIAMS**
and the **ZODIACS**

Another example of rock racism as black artists again had white people on their album covers.

Ein weiteres Beispiel für den Rassismus im Rock-Business, denn wieder einmal sind auf den Plattencovern von schwarzen Künstlern Weiße zu sehen.

Un autre exemple du racisme rock avec à nouveau des photos de blancs sur les pochettes d'artistes noirs.

**Maurice Williams And The Zodiacs**
*Stay With Maurice Williams And The Zodiacs*
Herald, 1961

Design: Unknown

# BILLY WARD AND HIS

## DOMINOES

*Featuring —*

## Clyde McPhatter and Jackie Wilson

HIGH FIDELITY
**KING**
733

### A SELECTED GROUP OF STANDARD SONGS

TENDERLY

OVER THE RAINBOW

LEARNIN' THE BLUES

WHEN THE SWALLOWS COME BACK TO CAPISTRANO

HARBOR LIGHTS

THESE FOOLISH THINGS

THREE COINS IN THE FOUNTAIN

LITTLE THINGS MEAN A LOT

RAGS TO RICHES

MAY I NEVER LOVE AGAIN

LONESOME ROAD

UNTIL THE REAL THING COMES ALONG

---

**Billy Ward And The Dominoes**
*Billy Ward And The Dominoes Featuring –*
*Clyde McPhatter And Jackie Wilson*
King, 1960

Design: Unknown

Note that Clyde McPhatter and Jackie Wilson (both pictured on the cover) got their start in this group.

Sowohl Clyde McPhatter als auch Jackie Wilson, die beide auf dem Cover abgebildet sind, begannen mit dieser Gruppe ihre Karriere.

Notez que Clyde McPhatter et Jackie Wilson ont tous deux débuté avec ce groupe, et qu'ils sont représentés sur la pochette.

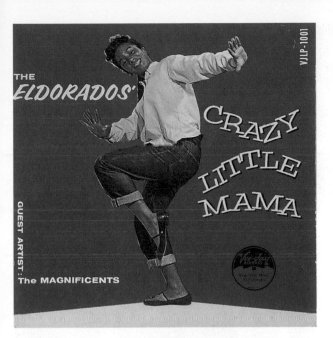

**The Eldorados'**
*Crazy Little Mama*
Vee-Jay, 1959

Design: Herbert Temple
Photo: David Jackson

**The Dubs/The Shells**
*The Dubs Meet The Shells*
Josie, 1962

Design: Unknown

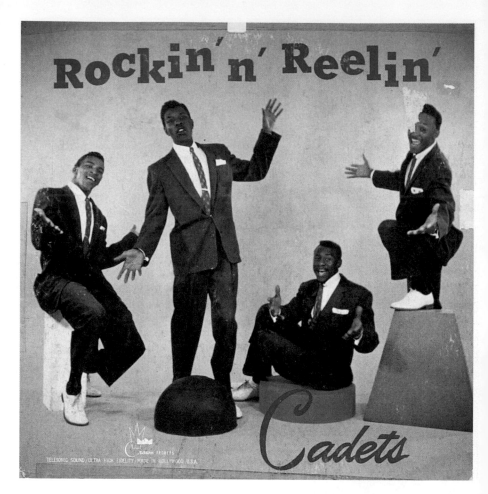

**Cadets**
*Rockin' n' Reelin'*
Crown, 1957

Art Direction: Florette Bihari
Photo: Gene Lesser, Hollywood

ULTRA HIGH FIDELITY

Two very rare picture covers soon replaced by covers with just drawings of the groups. Crown Records decided that photos were too costly for a budget label.

Diese beiden Cover sind eine Rarität. Crown Records fand, daß Fotos für ein Low-Budget-Label einfach zu teuer seien, und auf allen folgenden Alben fanden sich ausschließlich Zeichnungen von den Musikern.

Ces deux pochettes sont très rares car elles furent très vite remplacées par d'autres où ces groupes étaient représentés par des dessins. Crown Records estima que les photos étaient trop coûteuses et par la suite n'employa que ce type d'illustrations.

**The Jacks**
*Jumpin' With The Jacks*
Crown, 1956

Design: Unknown

**The Flamingos**
*Flamingo Serenade*
End, 1959

Design: Unknown

**The Flamingos**
*Requestfully Yours*
End, 1960

Design: Unknown

**Nolan Strong And The Diablos**
*Fortune Of Hits*
Fortune, 1961

Design: Unknown

**The Spaniels**
*Goodnite, It's Time To Go*
Vee-Jay, 1958

Design: Leroy Winbush
Photo: David Jackson

**Big Mama Thornton**
*Jail*
Vanguard, 1975

Design: Jules Halfant
Photo: Marv Lyons

**Big Bill Broonzy**
*Big Bill's Blues*
Columbia, 1958

Design: Unknown

The Flamingos
*Flamingo Favorites*
End, 1960

Design: Unknown

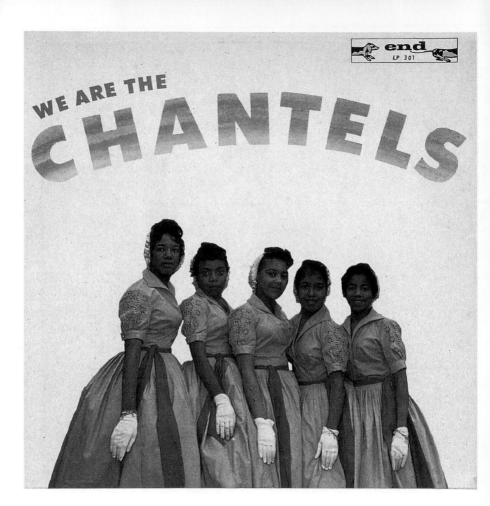

**The Chantels**
*We Are The Chantels*
End, 1958

Design: Unknown

This original cover was changed soon after release and a white couple was put on the cover to get the record carried in the South. The original album is one of the rarest rock albums.

Das Foto der Mädchen auf dem Originalcover wurde rasch gegen die Abbildung eines weißen Pärchens ausgetauscht, um den Absatz im Süden der USA zu fördern. Das Original-Album zählt zu den größten Raritäten der Rockmusik.

Le dessin des filles sur la pochette originale fut très vite remplacé après la sortie par un couple de blancs pour permettre au disque d'être distribué dans le Sud. La pochette originale avec les filles est l'un des albums de rock les plus rares.

**The Chantels**
*The Chantels*
End, 1950s

Design: Unknown

**The Penguins**
*The Cool, Cool Penguins*
Dooto, 1959

Design: Unknown

**The Clovers**
*The Clovers*
Atlantic, 1956

Design: Burt Goldblatt
*Courtesy Atlantic Recording Corp.*

**The Spaniels**
*The Spaniels*
Vee-Jay, 1950s

Design: Unknown

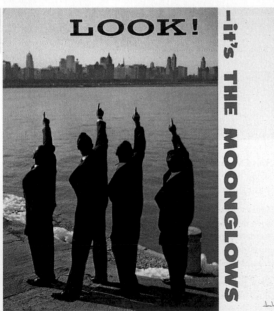

**The Moonglows**
*Look! – It's The Moonglows*
Chess, 1959

Design: Don Bronstein

**The Five Keys**
*The Five Keys On Stage*
Capitol, 1957

Design: Unknown

This Five Keys cover is rare, because the thumb on the far left might have been misunderstood as an exposed penis. The cover was banned and most copies have the thumb airbrushed out.

Dieses Cover der Five Keys ist außergewöhnlich, weil der Daumen des Sängers links außen als entblößter Penis mißdeutet werden kann. Das Cover wurde daher verboten, und auf den meisten Exemplaren dieser Schallplatte wurde der Daumen retuschiert.

Cette pochette des Five Keys est rare parce que le pouce du chanteur aurait pu être confondu avec un pénis. Elle fut donc interdite et sur la plupart des exemplaires le pouce a été supprimé.

**Otis Williams And His Charms**
*Otis Williams And His Charms Sing
Their All Time Hits*
King, 1957

Design: Unknown

**The "5" Royales**
*Dedicated To You*
King, 1957

Design: Unknown

**The Platters**
*The Flying Platters Around The World*
Mercury, 1959

Photo: Herman Leonard

**Little Anthony & The Imperials**
*We Are The Imperials Featuring Little Anthony*
End, 1959

Design: Unknown

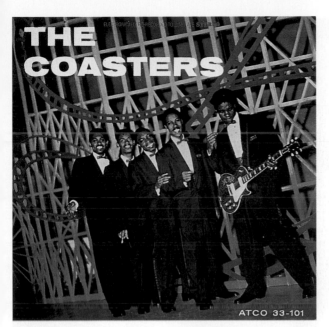

**The Coasters**
*The Coasters*
Atco, 1962

Design: Charles Varron
*Courtesy Atlantic Recording Corp.*

**The Cadillacs**
*The Fabulous Cadillacs*
Jubilee, 1957

Photo: Varron

**Buck Ram And His Orchestra**
*The Magic Touch Of Buck Ram And His Orchestra*
Mercury, 1960

Design: Unknown

Managing the Platters, Buck got some extra royalties by releasing this instrumental album, a practice continued by George Martin with the Beatles and Andrew Loog Oldham with the Stones.

Als Manager der Platters verdiente sich Buck Ram zusätzliche Tantiemen durch dieses Instrumentalalbum ihrer Hits – genau wie George Martin bei den Beatles und Andrew Loog Oldham bei den Stones.

Buck, le manager des Platters, obtint quelques royalties supplémentaires en publiant cet album instrumental, une pratique poursuivie par George Martin avec les Beatles et Andrew Loog Oldham avec les Rolling Stones.

**The Drifters**
*Under The Boardwalk*
Atlantic, 1964

Design: Loring Eutemey
Photo: Garrett-Howard
*Courtesy Atlantic Recording Corp.*

**The Cleftones**
*Heart And Soul*
Gee, 1961

Design: Unknown

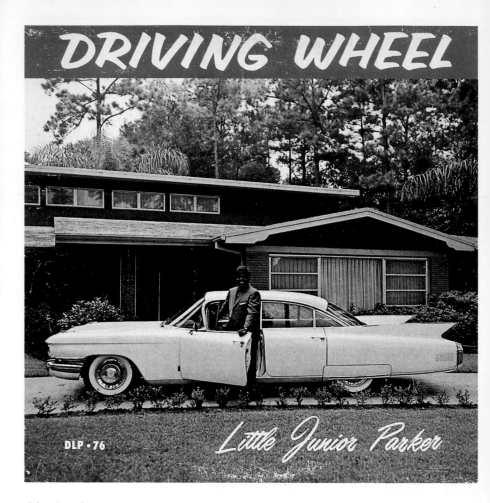

**Little Junior Parker**
*Driving Wheel*
Duke, 1962

Design: Unknown

**The Platters**
*The Flying Platters*
Mercury, 1957

Photo: Garrett-Howard

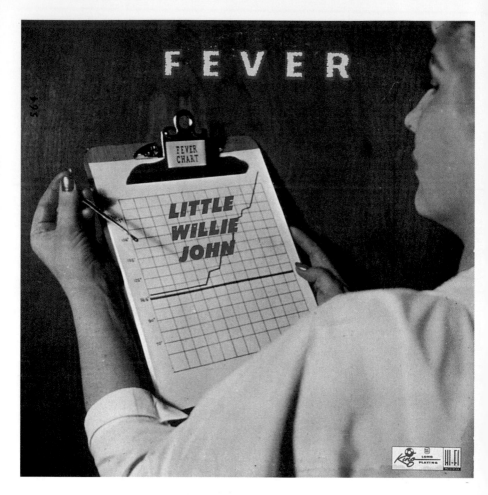

**Little Willie John**
*Fever*
King, 1956

Design: Unknown

This is the super rare original cover with the white nurse. All other copies of this album just had the word "Fever" in big block type on the cover.

Hier handelt es sich um eine echte Rarität: das Originalcover mit der weißen Krankenschwester. Auf allen anderen Ausgaben dieses Albums steht bloß das Wort „Fever" in großen Blockbuchstaben auf dem Cover.

Ceci est la rarissime pochette originale avec l'infirmière blanche. Tous les autres exemplaires de ce disque portaient le mot «Fever» en très grosses lettres sur la pochette.

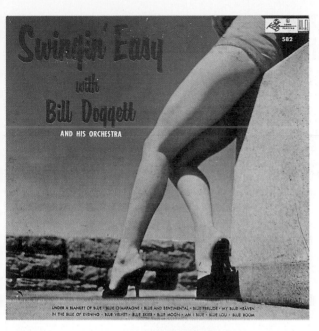

**Bill Doggett And His Orchestra**
*Swingin' Easy*
King, 1959

Design: Unknown

**James Brown And His Famous Flames**
*Please, Please, Please*
King, 1958

Design: Record Design Studio

**Hank Ballard And The Midnighters**
*Their Greatest Juke Box Hits*
King, 1958

Design: Unknown

**Chuck Berry**
*New Juke Box Hits*
Chess, 1961

Design: Unknown

**Little Willie John**
*The Sweet, The Hot, The Teen-Age Beat*
King, 1961

Design: Unknown

**Shep & The Limelites**
*Our Anniversary*
Hull, 1962

Design: Unknown

**Fats Domino**
*This Is Fats*
Imperial, 1957

Design: Unknown

**Fats Domino**
*Here Stands Fats Domino*
Imperial, 1957

Design: Unknown

**Little Richard**
*Here's Little Richard*
Specialty Records, 1957

Design: Thadd Roark
Photo: Globe

**Johnny Olenn**
*Just Rollin' with Johnny Olenn*
Liberty, 1957

Color Lithography: Phil Howard

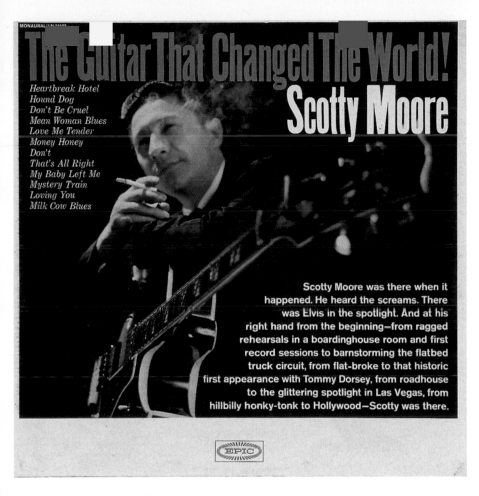

MONAURAL

# The Guitar That Changed The World!

## Scotty Moore

Heartbreak Hotel
Hound Dog
Don't Be Cruel
Mean Woman Blues
Love Me Tender
Money Honey
Don't
That's All Right
My Baby Left Me
Mystery Train
Loving You
Milk Cow Blues

Scotty Moore was there when it happened. He heard the screams. There was Elvis in the spotlight. And at his right hand from the beginning—from ragged rehearsals in a boardinghouse room and first record sessions to barnstorming the flatbed truck circuit, from flat-broke to that historic first appearance with Tommy Dorsey, from roadhouse to the glittering spotlight in Las Vegas, from hillbilly honky-tonk to Hollywood—Scotty was there.

EPIC

Scotty never got the money he deserved as Elvis' guitarist, but he tried to get recognition with this solo. The Presley phenomenon carried no passengers and the album is rare.

Scotty Moore verdiente als Gitarrist von Elvis eigentlich nie besonders viel Geld. Mit diesem Album versuchte er als Solo-Künstler Anerkennung zu finden, aber das Elvis Phänomen duldete keine Trittbrettfahrer, und dieses Album ist eine Rarität.

Scotty était méconnu en tant que guitariste d'Elvis, il tenta de se faire apprécier avec cette sortie en solo. Malheureusement, le phénomène Presley ne lui amena aucun client et la rareté de l'album est due à son échec commercial.

**Scotty Moore**
*The Guitar That Changed The World!*
Epic, 1964

Photo: Bill Forshee

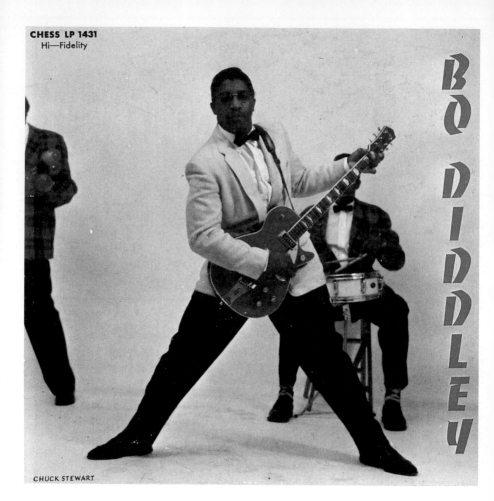

**Bo Diddley**
*Bo Diddley*
Chess, 1958

Design: Unknown

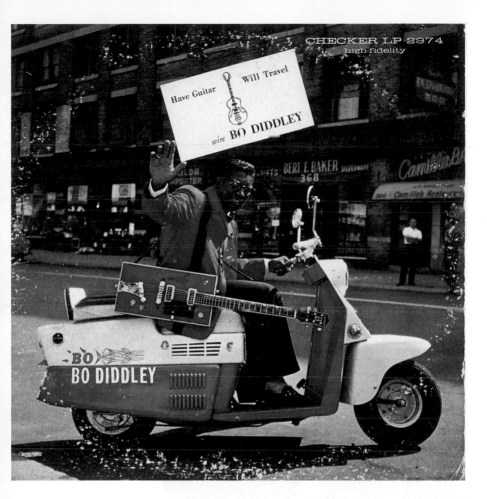

**Bo Diddley**
*Have Guitar Will Travel*
Checker, 1960

Design: Unknown

**Joe Turner**
*Big Joe Rides Again*
Atlantic, 1960

Photo: Lee Friedlander
*Courtesy Atlantic Recording Corp.*

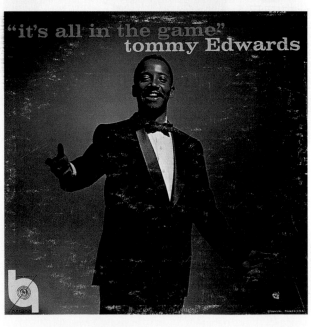

**Tommy Edwards**
*It's All In The Game*
MGM, 1958

Photo: Lester Kraus

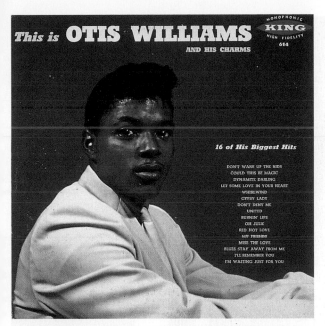

**Otis Williams And His Charms**
*This Is Otis Williams And His Charms*
King, 1959

Design: Record Design Studio

**Clyde McPhatter**
*Clyde*
Atlantic, 1959

Design: Unknown
*Courtesy Atlantic Recording Corp.*

**Chuck Berry**
*After School Session With Chuck Berry*
Chess, 1958

Design: Unknown

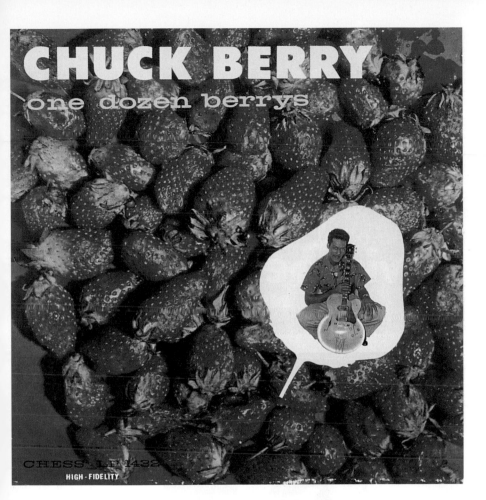

**Chuck Berry**
*One Dozen Berrys*
Chess, 1958

Design: Unknown

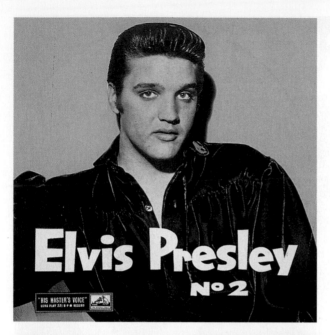

**Elvis Presley**
*Elvis Presley N° 2*
RCA/EMI International, 1956

Photo: Courtesy of The Daily Sketch
© Elvis Presley Enterprises, Inc.

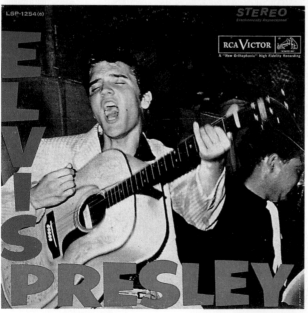

**Elvis Presley**
*Elvis Presley*
RCA Victor, 1956

Photo: Popsie
© Elvis Presley Enterprises, Inc.

**Elvis Presley**
*50,000,000 Elvis Fans Can't Be Wrong*
*Elvis' Gold Records – Vol. 2*
RCA Victor, 1960

Design: Unknown
© Elvis Presley Enterprises, Inc.

**Elvis Presley**
*Elvis*
RCA Victor, 1956

Design: Unknown
© Elvis Presley Enterprises, Inc.

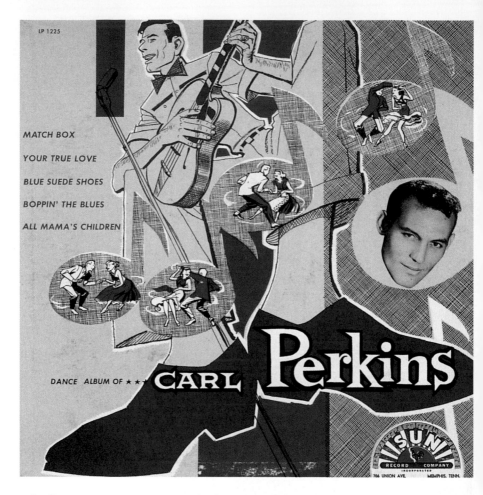

**Carl Perkins**
*Dance Album Of Carl Perkins*
Sun, 1957

Design: Unknown
*Courtesy Sun Entertainment Corporation*

This is the rare first cover of Carl's *Teen Beat* Sun Records album.

Das seltene erste Cover von Carls Sun-Records-Album *Teen Beat*.

Ceci est la très rare première pochette de l'album de Carl *Teen Beat* pour Sun Records.

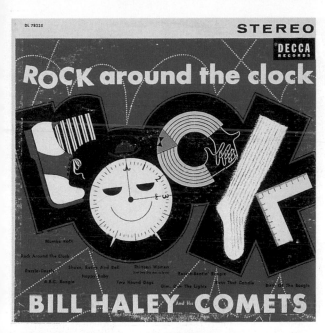

**Bill Haley And His Comets**
*Rock Around The Clock*
Decca, 1956

Design: Unknown

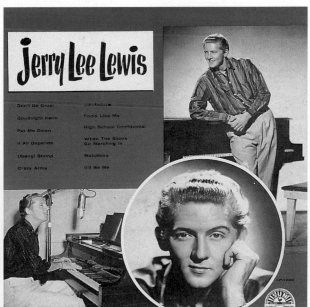

**Jerry Lee Lewis**
*Jerry Lee Lewis*
Sun, 1958

Design: Unknown
*Courtesy Sun Entertainment
Corporation*

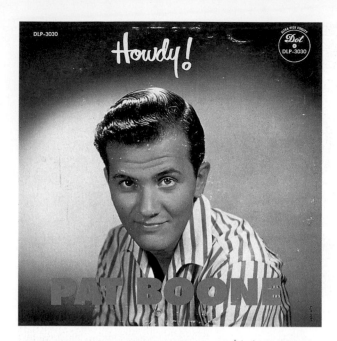

**Pat Boone**
*Howdy!*
Dot, 1956

Photo: Lebowitz

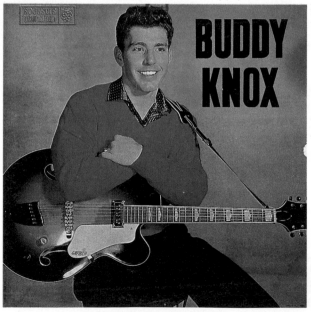

**Buddy Knox**
*Buddy Knox*
Roulette, 1957

Photo: Chuck Stewart

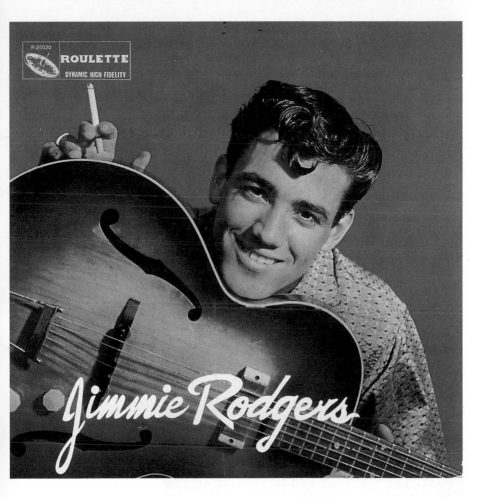

**Jimmie Rodgers**
*Jimmie Rodgers*
Roulette, 1958

Photo: Chuck Stewart

**Various Artists**
*Favorite Calypsos From The West Indies*
Monogram, 1950s

Design: Unknown

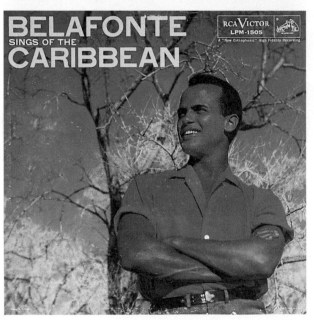

**Harry Belafonte**
*Belafonte Sings Of The Caribbean*
RCA Victor, 1957

Design: Unknown

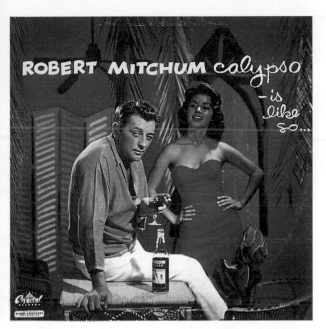

**Robert Mitchum**
*Calypso – Is Like So …*
Capitol, 1957

Design: Unknown

**Various Artists**
*Calypsos From Jamaica*
Ritmo, 1950s

Design: Unknown

BL 5403B

**Brunswick** RECORDS

The "CHIRPING" CRICKETS

Printed in U.S.A.

**The Crickets**
*The "Chirping" Crickets*
Brunswick, 1957

Design: Unknown

Look at the top of the heads of the group members to see yet another example of great paste-up "art".

Ein Blick auf die Köpfe der Musiker dieser Gruppe offenbart ein weiteres Beispiel für eine „gelungene" Fotomontage.

Regardez les têtes des membres du groupe pour découvrir un autre exemple du «grand art» du photomontage.

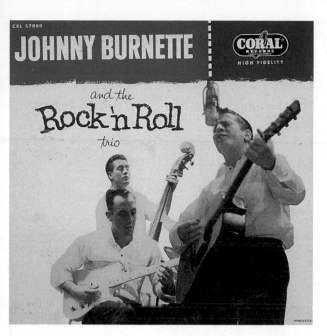

**Johnny Burnette And The Rock 'N Roll Trio**
*Johnny Burnette And The Rock 'N Roll Trio*
Coral, 1956

Design: Unknown

**Buddy Holly**
*The Buddy Holly Story*
Coral, 1959

Design: Unknown

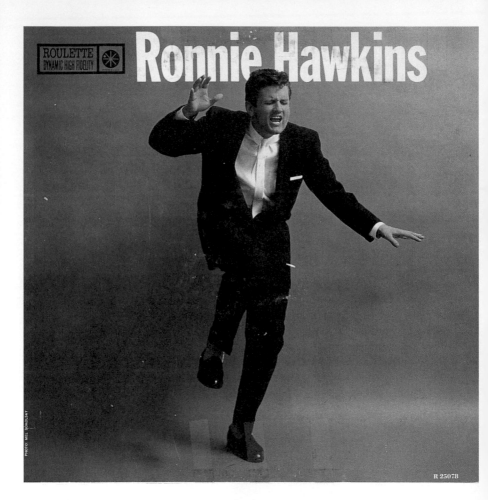

**Ronnie Hawkins**
*Ronnie Hawkins*
Roulette, 1959

Photo: Mel Sokolsky

Note that this artist had the same shot used for two different covers.

Hier wurde ein und dasselbe Foto von Ronnie Hawkins für zwei verschiedene Cover verwendet.

Notez que cet artiste eut la même photo utilisée pour deux pochettes différentes.

**Ronnie Hawkins And The Hawks**
*Mr. Dynamo*
Roulette, 1960

Photo: Mel Sokolsky

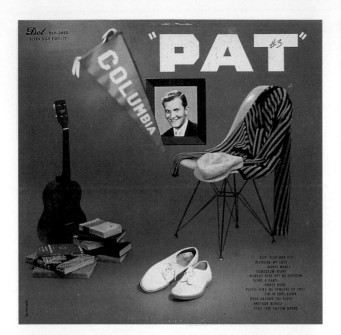

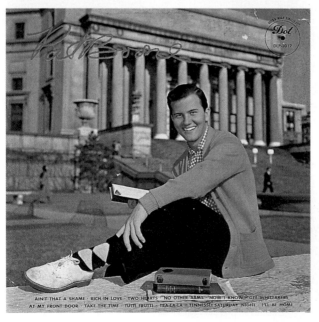

**Pat Boone**
*Pat*
Dot, 1957

Design: Unknown

**Pat Boone**
*Pat Boone*
Dot, 1956

Design: Unknown

"they're off and rolling," says Archie

# THE EVERLY BROTHERS

The minute *Bye-Bye Love* hit, the Everlys were in. Frails sent mail by the bale. The same thing happened with *Wake Up Little Susie* —only more so. Their pickin' and singin' won everybody with an ear to hear. The whole country woke up and spoke up for the Everlys. That's why Archie brings you more of the kind of music that made them famous on this Cadence LP.

a high-fidelity recording by
CADENCE CLP-3003

**The Everly Brothers**
*The Everly Brothers*
Cadence, 1959

Design: Unknown
*Courtesy Atlantic Recording Corp.*

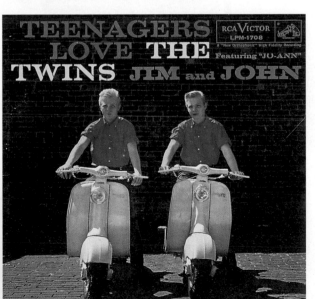

**The Twins**
*Teenagers Love The Twins*
*Jim And John*
RCA Victor, 1958

Design: Unknown

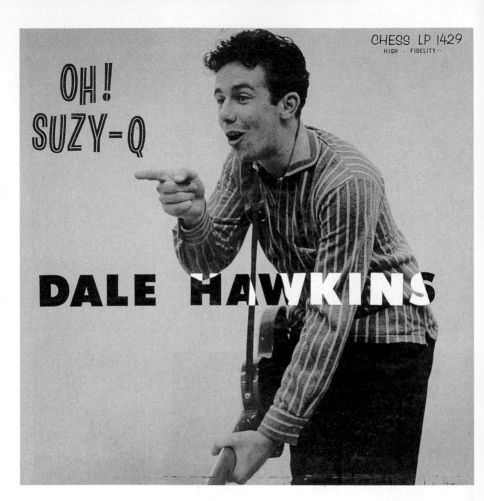

**Dale Hawkins**
*Oh! Suzy-Q*
Chess, 1958

Design: Unknown

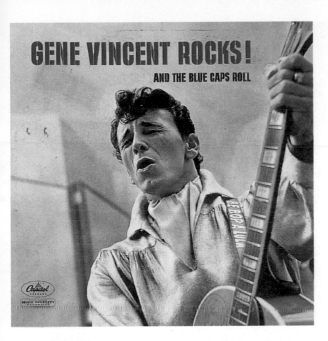

**Gene Vincent And The Blue Caps**
*Gene Vincent Rocks! And The Blue Caps Roll*
Capitol, 1958

Design: Unknown

**Gene Vincent And The Blue Caps**
*Gene Vincent And The Blue Caps*
Capitol, 1957

Design: Unknown

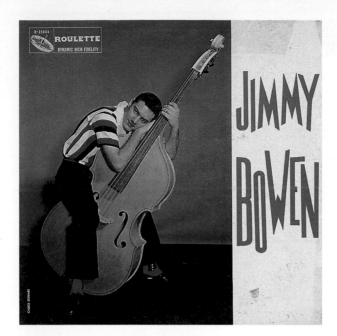

**Jimmy Bowen**
*Jimmy Bowen*
Roulette, 1957

Photo: Chuck Stewart

**Jack Scott**
*Jack Scott*
Carlton, 1959

Design: Unknown

**Buddy Knox & Jimmy Bowen**
*Buddy Knox & Jimmy Bowen*
Roulette, 1958

Photo: Alfred Gescheidt

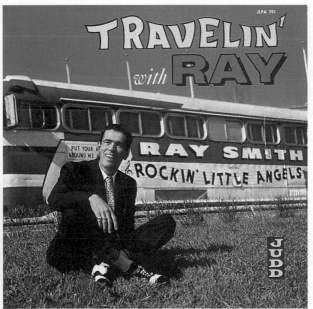

**Ray Smith**
*Travelin' With Ray*
Judd, 1960

Design: Unknown

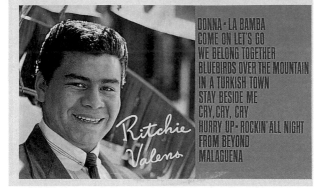

HIS INCOMPARABLE NEVER TO BE FORGOTTEN PERFORMANCES

RITCHIE VALENS HIS GREATEST HITS

DONNA – LA BAMBA
COME ON LET'S GO
WE BELONG TOGETHER
BLUEBIRDS OVER THE MOUNTAIN
IN A TURKISH TOWN
STAY BESIDE ME
CRY, CRY, CRY
HURRY UP – ROCKIN' ALL NIGHT
FROM BEYOND
MALAGUENA

Ritchie Valens
*His Greatest Hits*
Del Fi, 1963

Art Direction: Leon Beauchemin &
Donn Sanders

Ritchie Valens
*Ritchie Valens*
Del Fi, 1959

Design: Unknown

**Conway Twitty**
*Conway Twitty Sings*
MGM, 1959

Photo: Richard Meek

**Conway Twitty**
*Lonely Blue Boy*
MGM, 1960

Design: Unknown

# THE BEST OF THE

# Crests

## FEATURING JOHNNY MASTRO

**16 FABULOUS HITS**

including..."16 CANDLES" • "ANGELS LISTENED IN" • "STEP BY STEP" • "TROUBLE IN PARADISE"
• "ISN'T IT AMAZING" and others

LPC-904

**The Crests**
*The Best Of The Crests*
*Featuring Johnny Mastro*
Co-Ed, 1961

Design: Unknown

The only white member of the Crests was Johnny Mastro who is also the only one shown on the cover.

Der einzige weiße Musiker der Crests war Johnny Mastro, der auch als einziger auf dem Cover zu sehen ist.

Le seul membre blanc des Crests était Johnny Mastro, et c'est aussi le seul à figurer sur la pochette.

**Del Vikings**
*A Swinging, Singing Record Session*
Mercury, 1955

Photo: Williams/Nugent

**Jesse Belvin**
*Mr. Easy*
RCA Victor, 1960

Photo: Tommy Mitchell

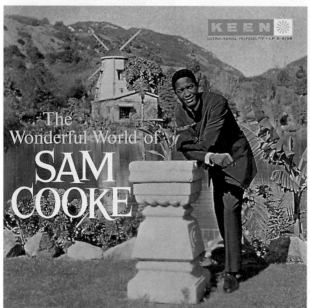

**Sam Cooke**
*The Wonderful World Of Sam Cooke*
Keen (ABKCO), 1960

Design: Unknown
© ABKCO Records

**Sam Cooke**
*I Thank God*
Keen (ABKCO), 1960

Design: Unknown
© ABKCO Records

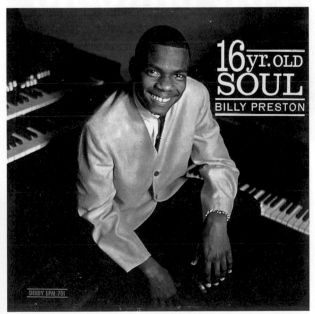

**Billy Preston**
*16 Yr. Old Soul*
SAR (ABKCO), 1963

Cover Photo: William Claxton
© ABKCO Records

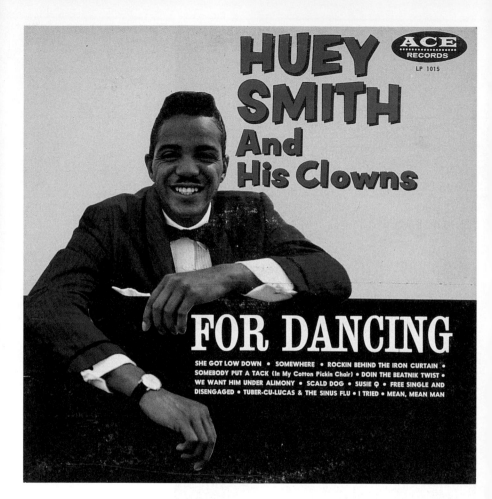

**Huey Smith And His Clowns**
*For Dancing*
Ace, 1961

Design: Unknown

**Johnny Otis**
*The Johnny Otis Show*
Capitol, 1958

Design: Unknown

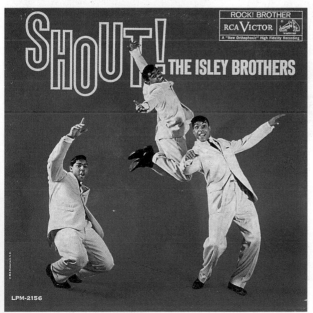

**The Isley Brothers**
*Shout!*
RCA Victor, 1959

Design: Unknown

**Bobby Day**
*Rockin' With Robin*
Chess, 1959

Design: Unknown

**Dee Clark**
*Dee Clark*
Abner, 1959

Photo: Don Bronstein

**Jackie Wilson**
*He's So Fine*
Brunswick, 1959

Design: Unknown

**The 5 Satins**
*The 5 Satins Sing*
Ember, 1957

Design: Unknown

**Jackie Wilson**
*Baby Workout*
Brunswick, 1963

Photo: Decca Photo Studio/
Hal Buksbaum

**Mickey And Sylvia**
*New Sounds*
Vik, 1957

Design: Unknown

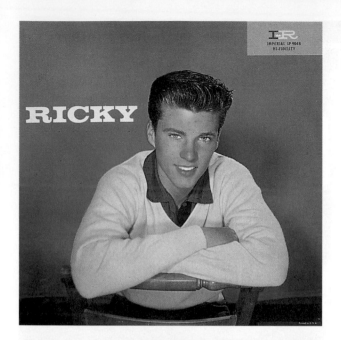

**Ricky Nelson**
*Ricky*
Imperial, 1957

Design: Unknown

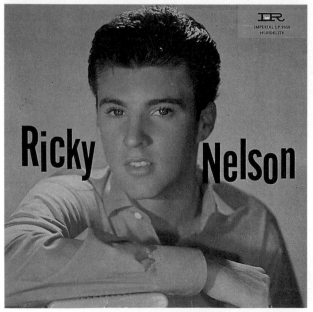

**Ricky Nelson**
*Ricky Nelson*
Imperial, 1957

Design: Unknown

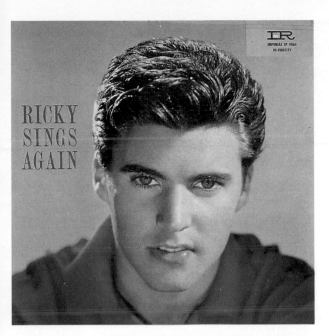

**Ricky Nelson**
*Ricky Sings Again*
Imperial, 1959

Design: Unknown

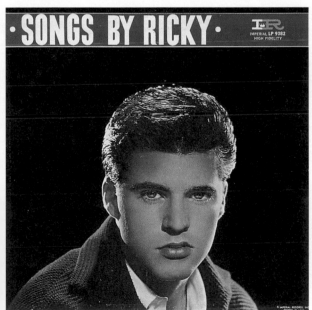

**Ricky Nelson**
*Songs By Ricky*
Imperial, 1959

Design: Unknown

**Connie Stevens**
*Conchetta*
Warner Bros., 1958

Design: Bert Six

**Brenda Lee**
*Emotions*
Decca, 1961

Design: Unknown

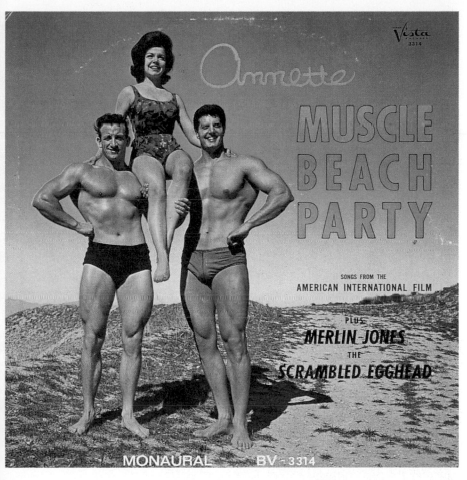

**Annette Funicello**
*Muscle Beach Party*
Buena Vista, 1964

Design: Unknown

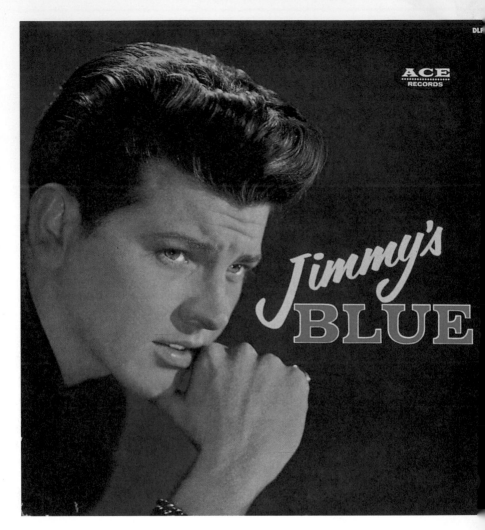

**Jimmy Clanton**
*Jimmy's Happy/Jimmy's Blue*
Ace, 1960

Design: Unknown

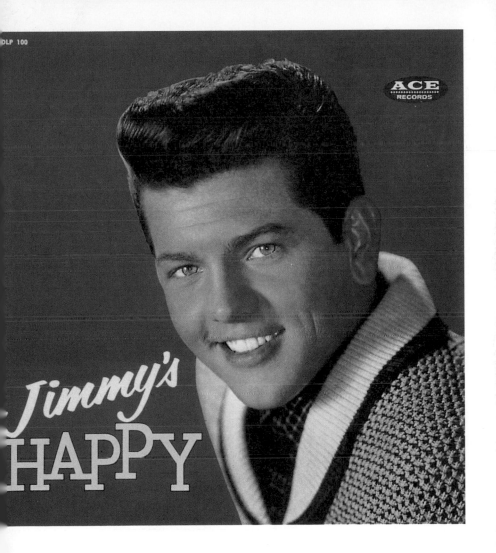

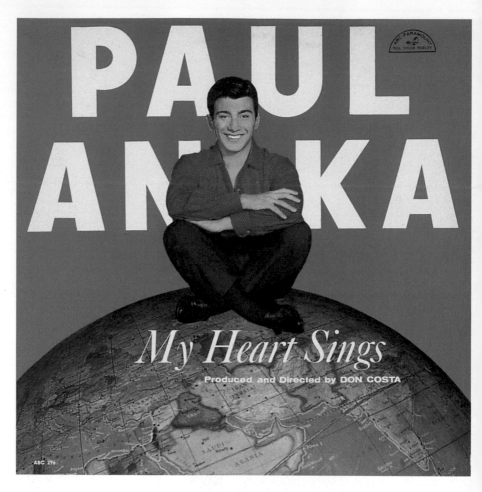

**Paul Anka**
*My Heart Sings*
ABC-Paramount, 1959

Design: Unknown

**Johnny Burnette**
*Johnny Burnette Sings*
Liberty, 1961

Design: Pate/Francis & Associates
Photo: Garrett-Howard

**The Marcels**
*Blue Moon*
Colpix, 1961

Design: Unknown

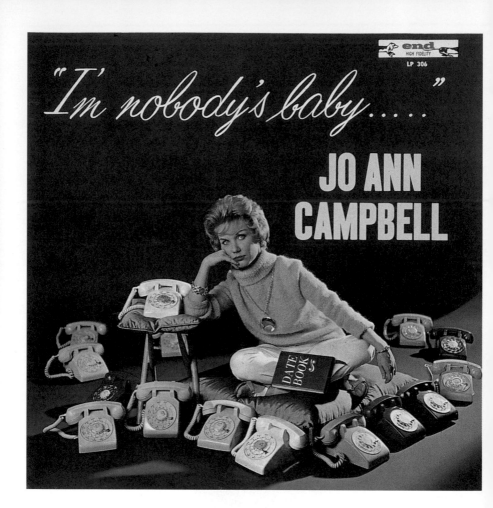

**Jo Ann Campbell**
*I'm Nobody's Baby …*
End, 1959

Design: Unknown

**Anita Bryant**
*In My Little Corner Of The World*
Carlton, 1961

Design: Unknown

**The Impalas**
*Sorry (I Ran All The Way Home)*
Cub, 1959

Photo: Bruno of Hollywood

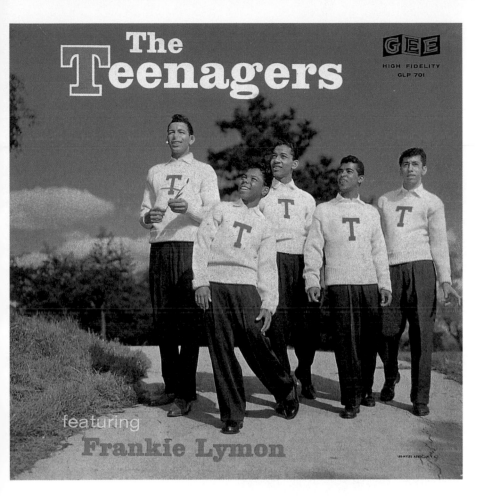

**Frankie Lymon And The Teenagers**
*The Teenagers Featuring Frankie Lymon*
Gee, 1957

Design: Lee-Miles Associates, New York City
Photo: Jack Zwillenger

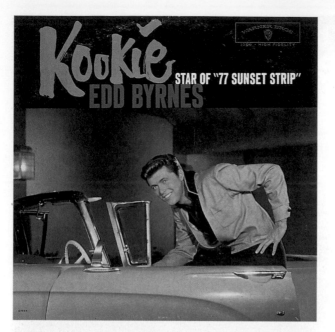

**Edd "Kookie" Byrnes**
*Kookie*
Warner Bros., 1959

Photo: Gene Kornmann

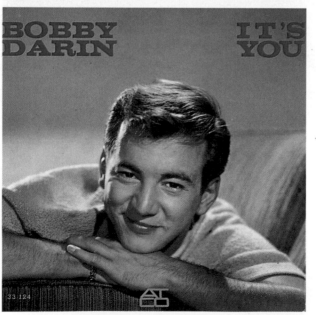

**Bobby Darin**
*It's You*
Atco, 1960

Design: Unknown
*Courtesy Atlantic Recording Corp.*

**Jimmy Clanton**
*My Best To You*
Ace, 1961

Design: Unknown

**Dion**
*Alone With Dion*
Laurie, 1960

Design: Connie DeNave
Art Direction: Walter Rich
Photo: Michael Levin

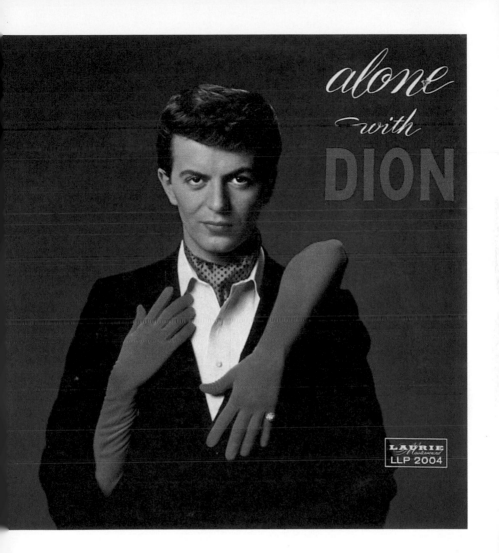

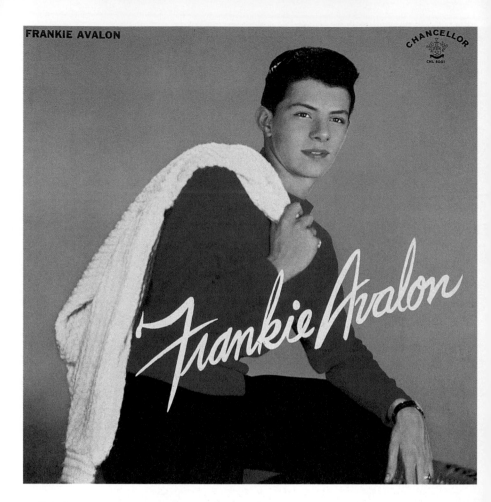

**Frankie Avalon**
*Frankie Avalon*
Chancellor, 1958

Photo: Bob Ghiraldini/Arsene Studios,
New York

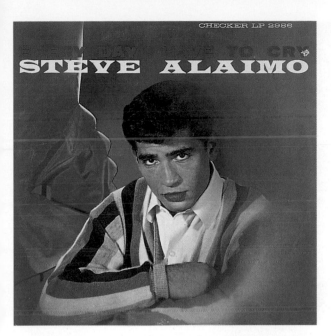

**Steve Alaimo**
*Every Day I Have To Cry*
Checker, 1963

Design: Howard Richmond

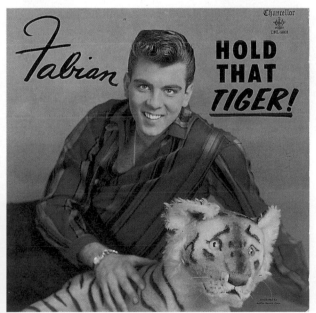

**Fabian**
*Hold That Tiger!*
Chancellor, 1959

Photo: Marvin Wellen / Iopix

**Damita Jo**
*I'll Save The Last Dance For You*
Mercury, 1961

Design: Unknown

**Frankie Ford**
*Let's Take A Sea Cruise*
Ace, 1959

Design: Unknown

**Connie Francis**
*The Exciting Connie Francis*
MGM, 1959

Photo: Curt Gunther

**Chantilly Lace Starring The Big Bopper**
*Helloo Baby!*
Mercury, 1959

Design: Unknown

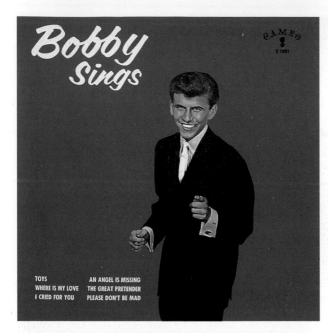

TOYS  AN ANGEL IS MISSING
WHERE IS MY LOVE  THE GREAT PRETENDER
I CRIED FOR YOU  PLEASE DON'T BE MAD

**Bobby Rydell**
*Bobby Sings, Bobby Swings*
Cameo (ABKCO), 1960

Design: Unknown
© ABKCO Records

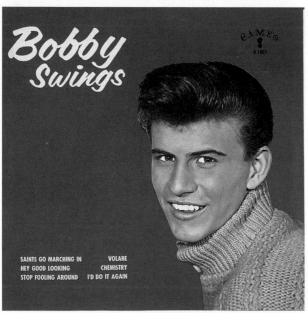

SAINTS GO MARCHING IN  VOLARE
HEY GOOD LOOKING  CHEMISTRY
STOP FOOLING AROUND  I'D DO IT AGAIN

(Back cover)
*Bobby Sings, Bobby Swings*

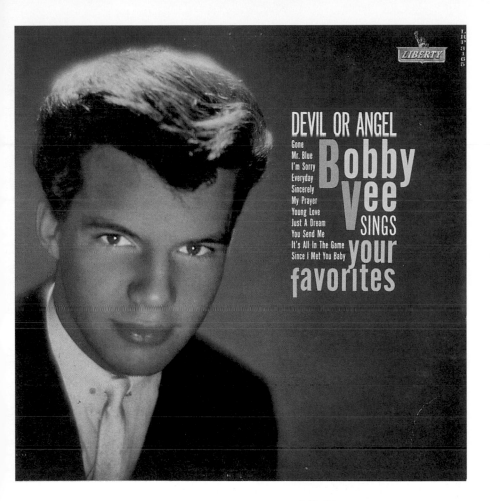

**Bobby Vee**
*Devil Or Angel*
Liberty, 1960s

Design: Pate/Francis Associates
Photos: Garrett-Howard, Inc.

**Freddie Bell And The Bell Boys**
*Rock & Roll... All Flavors*
Mercury, 1958

Design: Unknown

As inconsequential as this group may appear, this album does contain the version of *Hound Dog* that Elvis copped for his hit version.

So unbedeutend diese Gruppe auch erscheinen mag, ihr Album enthält die Version von *Hound Dog*, die Elvis für seinen Hit geklaut hat.

Aussi inintéressant que puisse apparaître ce groupe, cet album contient la version de *Hound Dog* dont Elvis s'empara pour en faire son hit.

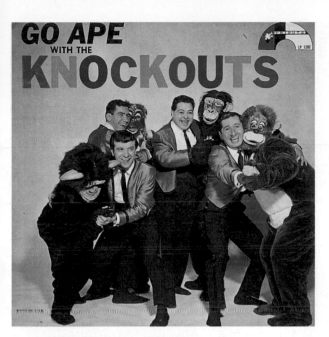

**The Knockouts**
*Go Ape With The Knockouts*
Tribute, 1964

Design: Lee-Myles Associates,
New York City

**The Playmates**
*At Play With The Playmates*
Roulette, 1958

Photo: Desmond Russell

**The Four Lovers**
*Joyride*
RCA Victor, 1956

Design: Unknown

This is the first album Frankie Valli (on the far left) recorded before forming the Four Seasons.

Dies ist das erste Album, das Frankie Valli (links außen) aufgenommen hat, bevor er die Four Seasons gründete.

Ceci est le premier album qu'enregistra Frankie Valli (à gauche) avant de former les Four Seasons.

**The Teddy Bears**
*The Teddy Bears Sing!*
Imperial, 1959

Photo: Garrett-Howard

**Duane Eddy**
*Have 'Twangy' Guitar Will Travel*
Jamie, 1958

Design: Unknown

Not only is the same shot used for two different covers (p. 183), but the same title is used for two different albums (see p. 183 top).

Hier wurde nicht nur dasselbe Foto für zwei verschiedene Cover verwendet (S. 183), sondern auch derselbe Titel für zwei unterschiedliche Alben (vgl. S. 183 oben).

Non seulement la même photo servit pour deux pochettes différentes (p. 183), mais le même titre fut utilisé pour deux albums distincts (cf. p. 183 en haut).

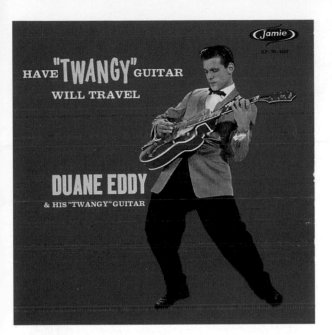

**Duane Eddy**
*Have 'Twangy' Guitar Will Travel*
(Different Cover)
Jamie, 1958

Design: Unknown

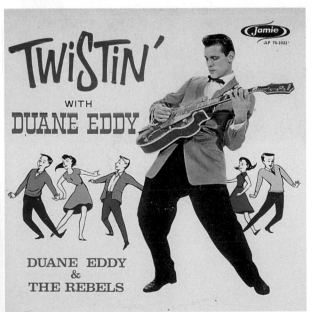

**Duane Eddy & The Rebels**
*Twistin' With Duane Eddy*
Jamie, 1962

Design: Unknown

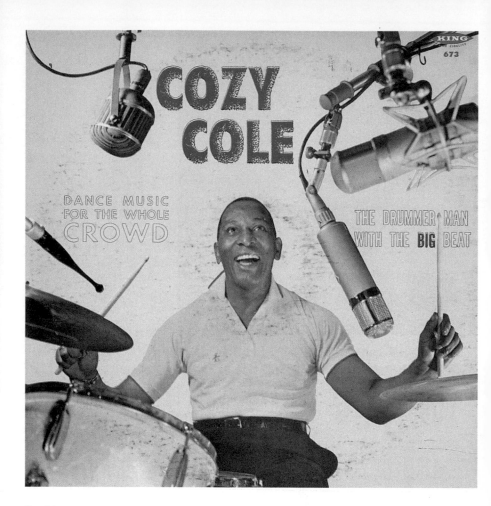

**Cozy Cole**
*Dance Music For The Whole Crowd*
King, 1960s

Design: Record Design Studio

**Preston Epps**
*Bongola*
Top Rank, 1961

Design: Unknown

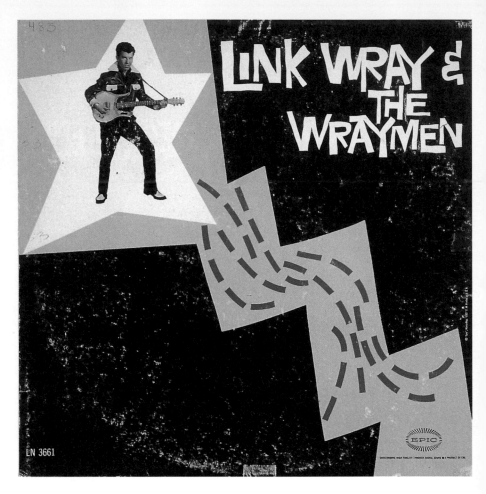

**Link Wray & The Wraymen**
*Link Wray & The Wraymen*
Epic, 1960

Design: Unknown

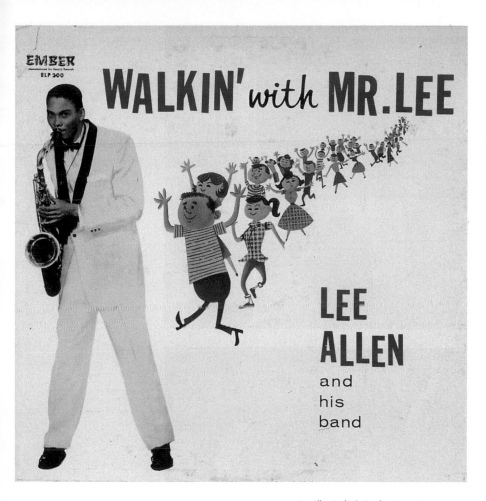

**Lee Allen And His Band**
*Walkin' With Mr. Lee*
Ember, 1958

Design: Unknown

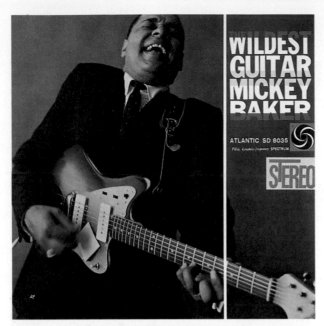

**Mickey Baker**
*Wildest Guitar*
Atlantic, 1959

Design: Marvin Israel
Photo: Elbert Budin
*Courtesy Atlantic Recording Corp.*

**Santo & Johnny**
*Santo & Johnny*
Canadian-American, 1959

Design: Unknown

**Santo & Johnny**
*Come On In …*
Canadian-American, 1962

Design: Unknown

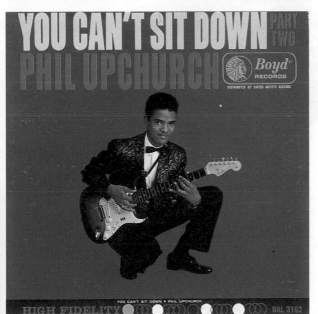

**Phil Upchurch**
*You Can't Sit Down, Part two*
Boyd, 1961

Design: Unknown

**Jorgen Ingmann**
*Apache*
Atco, 1961

Design: Loring Eutemey
*Courtesy Atlantic Recording Corp.*

FULL TONAL RANGE ‖‖‖‖ STEREO ‖‖‖‖ ATLANTIC SD 3001

# BAGPIPE BLUES

# RUFUS HARLEY

Looking for unusual, international instrumental acts, it's hard to top a Scandinavian guitarist dressed as an Indian or a black bag-pipe player.

Der als Indianer verkleidete skandinavische Gitarrist oder der schwarze Dudelsackspieler: Eine ungewöhnlichere Covergestaltung für eine Instrumentalnummer ist wohl kaum zu finden.

A propos d'interprétations instrumentales et internationales insolites, il est rare de tomber sur un guitariste scandinave costumé en indien ou en joueur de cornemuse.

**Rufus Harley**
*Bagpipe Blues*
Atlantic, 1966

Design: Fuentes/McCann
*Courtesy Atlantic Recording Corp.*

**Fendermen**
*Mule Skinner Blues*
Soma, 1960

Design: Unknown

**Duane Eddy**
*Girls! Girls! Girls!*
Jamie, 1961

Design: Garrett Howard

**Champs**
*Go Champs Go*
Challenge, 1958

Design: Unknown

**Johnny & The Hurricanes**
*Stormsville*
Warwick, 1960

Design: Unknown
*Courtesy Atlantic Recording Corp.*

**The Mellokings**
*Tonight – Tonight*
Herald, 1960

Design: Unknown

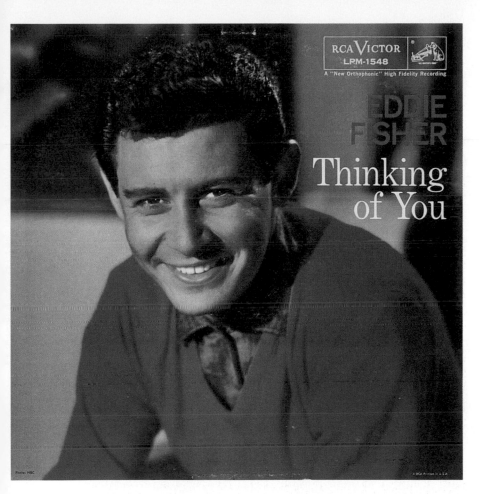

**Eddie Fisher**
*Thinking Of You*
RCA Victor, 1957

Photo: NBC

# 1960s

The sixties were the war years – and not just in Vietnam. In America, there was a full-tilt war between adolescence and age – it was US against THEM. US had long hair, free love, expanded consciousness, new highs, new lows, new clothes and new music. THEM was stunting, straight, selfish, archaic and imperialistic. All this was communicated through the expanding music scene.

As the teen idol and twist trends were strangling the life out of rock and roll, fresh sounds surfaced at home and abroad. In 1961, Bob Dylan played his first professional gig at Gerde's in New York and The Beatles opened at The Cavern in Liverpool. From the roots of American music a musical revolution sprang – a global battle of the bands in which growth and change won the day. Every branch of rock and roll grew to incredible new heights.

In 1962, The Beach Boys rode the first wave of the revolution with their hit *Surfin' Safari*, which started the fun-in-the-sun sound. Berry Gordy launched his Motown Records label with hits by The Miracles, Mary Wells and The Marvelettes. Black novelty records by groups like The Coasters and The Olympics were soon replaced by the more soulful sounds of the street – with artists such as Solomon Burke, Ben E. King,

Gladys Knight and Etta James. The following year, the soul ranks swelled with debut records by Otis Redding, Wilson Pickett and the blue-eyed soul of The Righteous Brothers.

In 1964, *Meet The Beatles* was released in America, and the whole country met The Beatles on the February 9th *Ed Sullivan* TV Show. Two months later, The Beatles occupied the top five positions on *Billboard Magazine's* "Top Hundred" chart, a feat never accomplished by any artist before or after. During that year, the British Invasion dominated the American hit parade with the debut records of The Animals, The Dave Clark Five, Gerry and The Pacemakers, The Hollies, The Kinks, Manfred Mann, The Rolling Stones, The Searchers and The Zombies.

At first the ranks of American rockers were decimated. Some groups like The Beau Brummels and The Sir Douglas Quintet tried to pass for British while others like Jimi Hendrix, P. J. Proby and The Walker Brothers just jumped ship, finding sanctuary and success in swinging London. By 1965, the American musicians regrouped and fought back. The Byrds covered Dylan's *Mr. Tambourine Man* electrically creating folk-rock, and Dylan himself went electric soon thereafter. The American troops finally turned the tide of battle by introducing drug warfare: the beginnings of psychedelic sound.

The psychedelic revolution started in San Francisco with The Grateful Dead, The Jefferson Airplane and Blue Cheer. Not to be outdone, Los Angeles added The Doors, Love and The Mothers of Invention. New York swelled the ranks with the Velvet Underground, The Fugs and Vanilla Fudge. The Brits countered with a leaner, meaner second wave of invasion bands such as The Who and The Yardbirds.

By 1967, both sides had realized that a continuous battle of the bands was too costly, so an international peace and love conference was convened in Monterey, CA. All the sounds of the sixties were represented, and the many diverse music cultures united into one international counterculture. The Monterey International Pop Festival was so successful that it was repeated in Woodstock, Altamont and the Isle of Wight – with varying degrees of success.

As the seventies began, the war years were finally coming to an end. However, the casualty rate was staggering, with Jimi Hendrix, Janis Joplin and Jim Morrison all dying at the age of 27.

Die sechziger Jahre standen im Zeichen des Krieges, und das nicht nur in Vietnam. In den USA kam es zu einem regelrechten Krieg zwischen den Generationen – auf der einen Seite standen die SPIESSER, auf der anderen Seite WIR. WIR, das bedeutete lange Haare, freie Liebe, Bewußtseinserweiterung, Hochs und Tiefs, neue Kleidung und neue Musik. Die SPIESSER waren verknöchert, kleinkariert, egozentrisch, altmodisch und imperialistisch. Das alles schlug sich in der immer vielseitigeren Musikszene nieder.

Während die Teenageridole und der Twist dem Rock 'n' Roll den Lebensnerv abschnürten, zeichneten sich in den USA und anderswo ganz neue Musikrichtungen ab. 1961 hatte Bob Dylan seinen ersten professionellen Gig im New Yorker Gerde's, und die Beatles gaben im Cavern Club in Liverpool ihr Debüt. Die Musik, die in den USA wurzelte, gelangte nach Europa und führte nun zu einer echten musikalischen Revolution, einem weltweiten „Sängerstreit" der Rockgruppen, bei dem die musikalische Weiterentwicklung den eigentlichen Sieg davontrug. Jede Spielart des Rock 'n' Roll erreichte im Verlauf dieser Revolution bis dato ungeahnte Höhen.

1962 ritten die Beach Boys auf der ersten Welle der Revolution mit ihrem Hit *Surfin' Safari* und begründeten den „Fun in the Sun"-Sound. Berry Gordy hob seine Plattenfirma Motown Records aus der Taufe und verzeichnete mit Hits von den Miracles, Mary Wells und den Marvelettes einen kometenhaften Aufstieg. An die Stelle neuer Platten von schwarzen Gruppen wie The Coasters und The Olympics trat schon bald der stark am Soul orientierte Sound der Straße von Sängern wie Solomon Burke, Ben E. King, Gladys Knight und Etta James. 1963 boomte der Soul, als Otis Redding, Wilson Pickett und die weiße Soul-Gruppe The Righteous Brothers ihre ersten Platten auf den Markt brachten.

1964 kam in den USA das Album *Meet The Beatles* heraus, und am 9. Februar des Jahres konnten alle US-Bürger die Beatles in der Ed-Sullivan-Show im Fernsehen kennenlernen. Zwei Monate später belegten die Beatles die ersten fünf Plätze der „Top Hundred"-Hitparade des *Billboard Magazine*, ein bislang einmaliges Bravourstück. Im Laufe desselben Jahres kam es in der amerikanischen Hitparade zu einer regelrechten britischen Invasion, denn Gruppen wie The Animals, The Dave Clark Five, Gerry and The Pacemakers, The Hollies, The Kinks, Manfred Mann, The Rolling Stones, The Searchers und The Zombies landeten mit ihren Debütplatten auf den ersten Plätzen.

Zunächst dezimierte sich das amerikanische Heer der Rockmusiker. Einige Gruppen wie The Beau Brummels und das Sir Douglas Quintet gaben sich britisch, während andere wie Jimi Hendrix, P.J. Proby und The Walker Brothers einfach das nächste Schiff nahmen und im Swinging London nicht nur Zuflucht fanden, sondern auch Erfolg hatten. 1965 formierten sich die amerikanischen Musiker neu und schlugen zurück. The Byrds brachten eine Rock-Version von Dylans *Mr. Tambourine Man* heraus und begründeten damit den Folk Rock, und auch Dylan selbst schloß bald darauf seine Gitarre an einen Elektroverstärker an. Schließlich wendeten die amerikanischen „Truppen" das Blatt in der Schlacht, indem sie bei ihrer Kriegsführung Drogen einsetzten und den „Psychedelic Rock" ins Leben riefen.

Die psychedelische Revolution begann in San Francisco mit The Grateful Dead, The Jefferson Airplane und Blue Cheer. Los Angeles ließ sich nicht lumpen und mobilisierte The Doors, Love und The Mothers of Invention. New York ließ The Velvet Unterground, The Fugs und Vanilla Fudge aufmarschieren. Die Briten reagierten mit einer schwächeren, bissigen Gegenoffensive und schickten Gruppen wie The Who und The Yardbirds ins Feld.

Im Jahre 1967 erkannten beide Seiten, daß eine Fortsetzung des „Banden"-Krieges zu teuer war, und so kam es im kalifornischen Monterey zu einer internationalen Friedens-und-Liebes-Konferenz. Es waren sämtliche Sounds vertreten, und die vielen unterschiedlichen Musikkulturen vereinigten sich zu einer einzigen internationalen Gegenkultur. Das Monterey International Pop Festival war so erfolgreich, daß es in Woodstock, Altamont und auf der Isle of Wight wiederholt wurde, wenn auch mit unterschiedlichem Erfolg.

Anfang der siebziger Jahre wurde der Krieg endgültig beigelegt, doch mit erschütternden Verlusten: Jimi Hendrix, Janis Joplin und Jim Morrison waren alle drei im Alter von 27 Jahren gestorben.

Les années soixante furent les années de guerre, et pas seulement au Vietnam. En Amérique, la guerre régnait entre la jeunesse et les adultes – c'était NOUS contre EUX. NOUS avait des cheveux longs, pratiquait l'amour libre, la conscience élargie, avait de nouveaux hauts, de nouveaux bas, de nouveaux vêtements et une nouvelle musique. EUX était ratatiné, strict, égoïste, archaïque et impérialiste. Tout cela se communiquait à travers l'élargissement considérable de la scène musicale.

Alors que les idoles des adolescents et les adeptes du twist étaient en train d'étouffer le rock 'n' roll, des sonorités nouvelles firent leur apparition chez nous et de l'autre côté de l'Atlantique. En 1961, Bob Dylan donna son premier récital chez Gerde's à New York, et les Beatles firent l'ouverture de la Cavern à Liverpool. Les racines musicales américaines qui avaient été transplantées produisirent une révolution musicale, une guerre mondiale des groupes dont le vainqueur fut une nouvelle croissance musicale. A travers cette révolution, chaque branche du rock 'n' roll évolua vers de nouveaux sommets.

En 1962, les Beach Boys conduisirent la première vague de la révolution avec leur tube *Surfin' Safari*, lançant le son fun-in-the-sun. Berry Gordy lança sa marque, Motown Records avec des tubes par les Miracles, Mary Wells et les Marvelettes. Les disques de nouveautés noires de groupes comme les Coasters et les Olympics furent bientôt remplacés par les sons de la rue beaucoup plus accrocheurs d'artistes tels que Solomon Burke, Ben E. King, Gladys Knight et Etta James. L'année suivante, les premiers disques d'Otis Redding, Wilson Pickett et la «soul aux yeux-bleus» des Righteous Brothers vinrent grossir les rangs de la soul music.

En 1964, *Meet The Beatles* sortit en Amérique, et tout le pays rencontra effectivement les Beatles dans le *Ed Sullivan* TV Show du 9 février. Deux mois plus tard, le groupe occupait les cinq premières places au hit-parade du *Billboard Magazine's* Top, un exploit resté unique en son genre. Cette année-là, l'Invasion Britannique domina le hit-parade américain avec les premiers disques des Animals, du Dave Clark Five, de Gerry and The Pacemakers, des Hollies, des Kinks, de Manfred Mann, des Rolling Stones, des Searchers et des Zombies.

Les rangs des rockers américains furent décimés. Des groupes comme Beau Brummels et le Sir Douglas Quintet tentèrent de se faire passer pour anglais, tandis que d'autres comme Jimi Hendrix, P.J.Proby et les Walker Brothers sautèrent dans le bateau, pour trouver un refuge

et le succès dans le Swinging London. En 1965, les musiciens américains resserrèrent les rangs et organisèrent la riposte. Les Byrds élec-
trifièrent le *Mr Tambourine Man* de Dylan et créèrent le folk-rock, et
Dylan lui-même s'électrifia très tôt après. Les troupes américaines inver-
sèrent le cours de la bataille en introduisant la guerre des stupéfiants,
début du son psychédélique.

La révolution psychédélique commença à San Francisco avec le
Grateful Dead, Jefferson Airplane et Blue Cheer. Pour ne pas rester à
l'écart, Los Angeles ajouta les Doors, Love et les Mothers Of Invention.
New York grossit les rangs avec le Velvet Underground, les Fugs et
Vanilla Fudge. Les Anglais réagirent par une seconde vague moins
importante de groupes envahisseurs comme les Who et les Yardbirds.

En 1967, on prit conscience des deux côtés que la bataille des
groupes était trop dispendieuse, et une conférence de paix et d'amour
internationale fut organisée à Monterey, Californie. Tous les sons des
années soixante étaient représentés, et les nombreuses cultures musicales unies en une seule contre-culture internationale. Le Festival Pop
International de Monterey eut un tel succès que l'expérience fut renou
velée, avec des fortunes diverses, à Woodstock, Altamont et à l'Ile de
Wight.

Quand les années soixante-dix commencèrent, les années de guerre
touchaient à leur fin. Pourtant, le taux d'accidents augmenta de façon
vertigineuse avec les disparitions, à vingt-sept ans tous les trois, de Jimi
Hendrix, Janis Joplin et Jim Morrison.

**Chubby Checker**
*For Twisters Only*
Parkway (ABKCO), 1961

Design: Al Cahn
© ABKCO Records

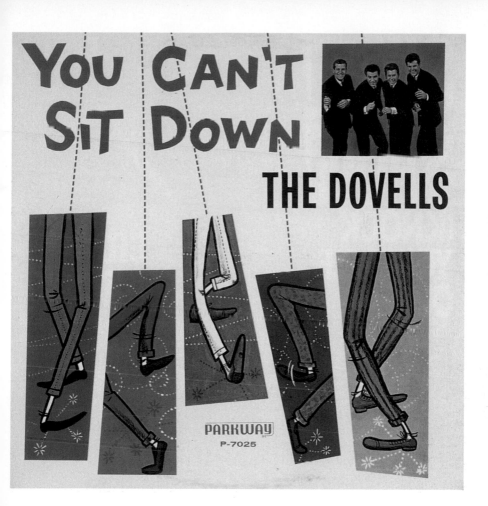

**The Dovells**
*You Can't Sit Down*
Parkway (ABKCO), 1963

Design: Unknown
© ABKCO Records

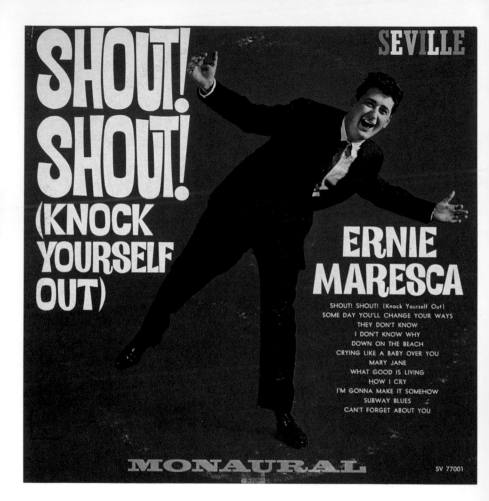

**Ernie Maresca**
*Shout! Shout! (Knock Yourself Out)*
Seville, 1962

Design: Barry Blum/Harry Farmlett

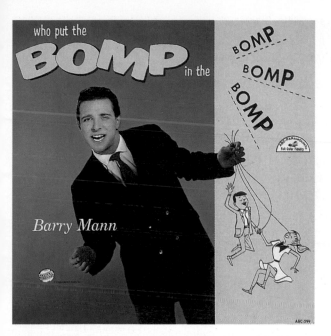

**Barry Mann**
*Who Put The Bomp*
*In The Bomp, Bomp, Bomp*
ABC-Paramount, 1963

Design: ARW

**The Exciters**
*Tell Him*
United Artists, 1963

Photo: Maurice Seymour, New York

**The Olympics**
*Doin' The Hully Gully*
Arvee, 1960

Design: Unknown

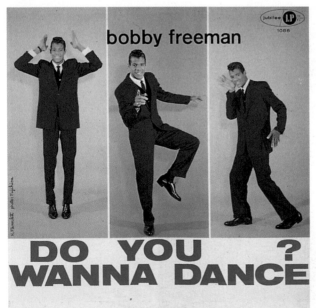

**Bobby Freeman**
*Do You Wanna Dance?*
Jubilee, 1959

Design: Harry Farmlett
Photo: Fujihira

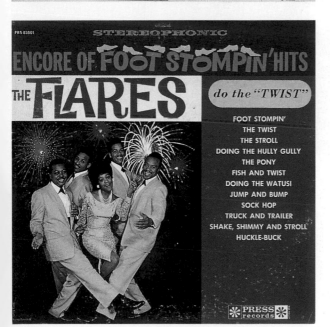

**Johnny Thunder**
*Loop De Loop*
Diamond, 1963

Art Direction: Arnold Meyers

**The Flares**
*Encore Of Foot Stompin' Hits*
Press, 1961

Design: Unknown

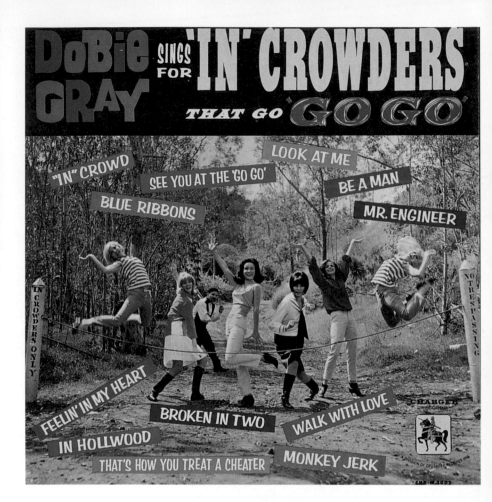

**Dobie Gray**
*Dobie Gray Sings For 'In' Crowders*
Charger, 1965

Photo: Vince Conti

Even as late as the mid-sixties, these two black artists had whites pictured on their covers.

Noch Mitte der sechziger Jahre wurden Weiße auf den Covern der Alben dieser beiden schwarzen Künstler abgebildet.

Jusqu'au milieu des années 60, ces deux musiciens noirs étaient représentés par des blancs sur leurs couvertures.

**Titus Turner**
*Sound Off*
Jamie, 1961

Design: Unknown

**Joey Dee**
*Dance, Dance, Dance*
Roulette, 1961

Design: Moskof/Morrison, Inc.
Photo: Bob Ritta

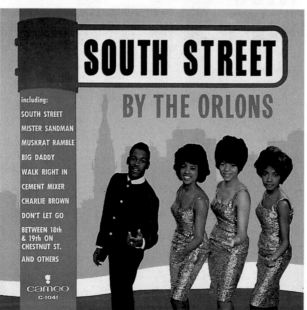

**The Orlons**
*South Street*
Cameo (ABKCO), 1963

Design: Unknown
© ABKCO Records

**The Olympics**
*Dance By The Light Of The Moon*
Arvee, 1961

Design: Unknown

**Dick Dale And His Del-Tones**
*Mr. Eliminator*
Capitol, 1964

Design: Capitol Photo Studio/
Ken Veeder

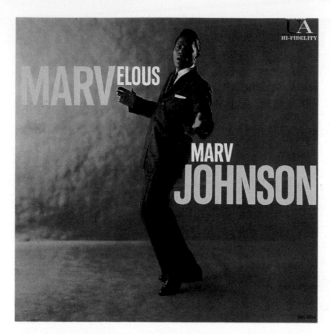

**Marv Johnson**
*Marvelous Marv Johnson*
United Artists, 1960

Design: Bacon/Braren/Lewine

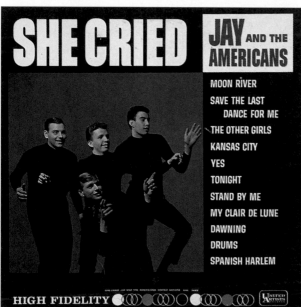

**Jay And The Americans**
*She Cried*
United Artists, 1962

Photo: Maurice Seymour

**Gary "U.S." Bonds**
*Dance 'Til Quarter To Three With 'U.S.' Bonds*
LEGRAND, 1961

Design: Walter Rich

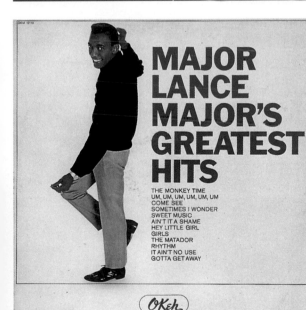

**Major Lance**
*Major's Greatest Hits*
Okeh, 1965

Photo: Sandy Speiser

**The Beach Boys**
*Surfer Girl*
Capitol, 1963

Design: Capitol Photo Studio/
Ken Veeder

**The Beach Boys**
*Surfin' Safari*
Capitol, 1962

Photo: Capitol Photo Studio/
Ken Veeder

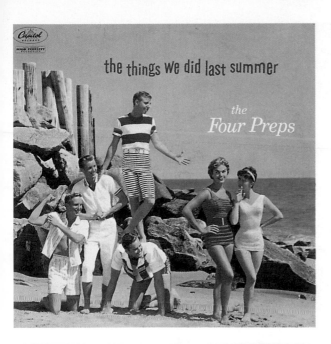

**The Four Preps**
*The Things We Did Last Summer*
Capitol, 1958

Design: Unknown

**Jan & Dean**
*Jan & Dean Take Linda Surfin'*
Liberty, 1963

Design: Studio Five

**The Tornadoes**
*Bustin' Surfboards*
Josie, 1963

Design: Unknown
*Josie Courtesy of Gerald H. Sanders*

**The Trashmen**
*Surfin' Bird*
Garrett, 1964

Photo: Ted Volante

During the surf craze, any instrumental could be released as a surf album although it had nothing to do with surf music. This Freddy King album is a fine example.

Während der Surf-Welle konnte jedes alte Instrumentalalbum als Surf-Album wiederaufgelegt werden. Ein Beispiel dafür ist diese Platte von Freddy King.

A l'époque de la surf music, n'importe quel vieil album instrumental sans aucun rapport avec cette musique pouvait être réédité comme un album de surf. Celui de Freddy King en est un bon exemple.

**Freddy King**.
*Freddy King Goes Surfin'*
King, 1963

Design: Unknown

Recorded Live at The Tulagi in Boulder, Colorado.

Diddy-Wah-Diddy
Good Golly Miss Molly
Johnny B. Goode
Roll Over Beethoven
Linda Lou
Be-Bop-A-Lula
Let the Good Times Roll
Sticks and Stones
Greenback Dollar
Summertime
Bony Moronie
Baja Blast

**A**STRONAUTS
**O**RBIT
**K**AMPUS

RCA VICTOR

LPM-2903

**The Astronauts**
*Astronauts Orbit Kampus*
RCA Victor, 1964

Design: Unknown

One of the biggest surf bands, the Astronauts were actually from Boulder, Colorado, not exactly known for its great waves.

Die Astronauts, eine der erfolgreichsten Surf-Bands, stammten in Wahrheit aus Boulder in Colorado, das eigentlich nicht gerade für seine großen Wellen bekannt ist.

L'un des plus grands groupes de surf, Les Astronauts, venait en fait de Boulder, Colorado, un endroit qui n'est pas réputé pour ses grosses vagues.

**Bruce Johnston**
*Surfin' 'Round The World*
Columbia, 1963

Photo: Leigh Weiner

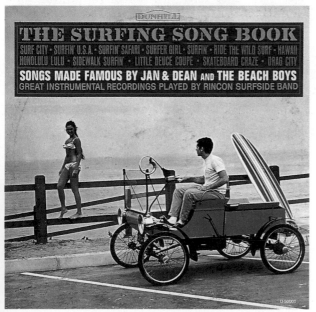

**Rincon Surfside Band**
*The Surfing Song Book*
Dunhill, 1965

Design: Unknown

**The Ventures**
*Walk Don't Run*
Dolton, 1960

Design: Pate/Francis Associates
Photo: Garrett-Howard

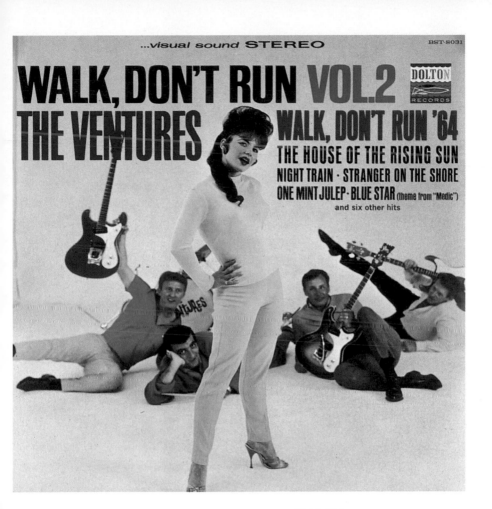

The Ventures
*Walk Don't Run – Vol. 2*
Dolton, 1964

Design: Studio Five

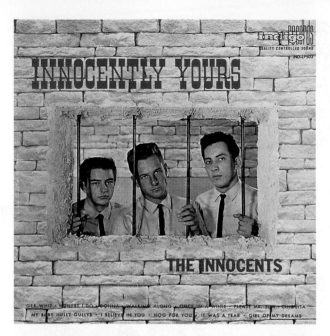

**The Innocents**
*Innocently Yours*
Indigo, 1961

Photo: Newcomb Studios, Pasadena

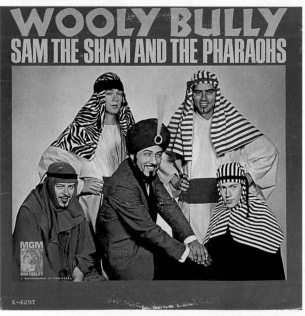

**Sam The Sham And The Pharaohs**
*Wooly Bully*
MGM, 1965

Photo: Bill Webb/Joy Webb

**The Rivieras**
*Let's Have A Party*
USA, 1964

Design: Don Bronstein

**The Hollywood Argyles**
*The Hollywood Argyles*
*Featuring Gary Paxton*
Lute, 1960

Design: Unknown

**FIRST ALBUM**

# THE "YOU KNOW WHO" GROUP

**THE BOYS WITH THAT GREAT NEW ENGLISH SOUND**

**THIS ALBUM INCLUDES:**

☐ ROSES ARE RED MY LOVE

☐ HEY YOU AND THE WIND AND THE RAIN

☐ IT'S A FUNNY THING (THAT MONEY CAN DO)

☐ AUTUMN LEAVES

☐ IT WAS ONLY YESTERDAY

☐ HOW CAN SHE LIVE (WITHOUT ME)

☐ BLUE IS THE NIGHT

☐ REELIN AND ROCKIN

☐ RED RIVER VALLEY

☐ THIS DAY LOVE

☐ TELL ME (HOW DO I SAY GOODBY?)

☐ ALBERTA

INTERNATIONAL
ALLIED RECORDS LTD.

MONO 14420

**The "You Know Who" Group**
*The "You Know Who" Group*
International, 1965

Design: Unknown

They sounded exactly like New Jersey's The Four Seasons; yet, the cover boasts that these boys have that great new English sound. Perhaps they were trying to pass themselves off as the Beatles.

Diese Band hörte sich genauso an wie The Four Seasons aus New Jersey, doch das Cover pries sie als die Jungs mit dem tollen neuen Sound aus England an. Möglicherweise wollten sie als die Beatles durchgehen.

Ce groupe sonnait exactement comme les Four Seasons du New Jersey. Pourtant, la pochette nous les présente comme des types qui ont le grand nouveau son anglais.

**Casinos**
*Then You Can Tell Me Goodbye*
Fraternity, 1967

Design: Robert Carter
Photo: Barry Weinstein

**The Fleetwoods**
*Mr. Blue*
Dolton, 1959

Design: Pate/Francis & Associates
Photo: Chao Chen Yang,
Seattle (Wash.)

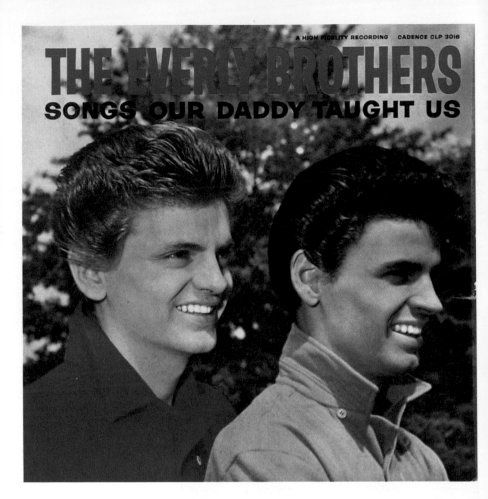

**The Everly Brothers**
*Songs Our Daddy Taught Us*
Cadence, 1958

Photo: Bob Kornheiser
*Courtesy Atlantic Recording Corp.*

**FOLK SONGS** *by* _____
*the everly brothers*

I'M HERE TO GET MY BABY OUT OF JAIL • LIGHTNING EXPRESS • BARBARA ALLEN • KENTUCKY
ROVING GAMBLER • LONG TIME GONE • ROCKIN'ALONE IN AN OLD ROCKIN' CHAIR
OH SO MANY YEARS • THAT SILVER HAIRED DADDY OF MINE • PUT MY LITTLE SHOES AWAY
WHO'S GONNA SHOE YOUR PRETTY LITTLE FEET • DOWN IN THE WILLOW GARDEN

**Cadence**

CLP 3059

During the Folk craze, just like surf music, old albums were re-released. These two Everly albums are the same, only the album title has been changed to make it more current.

Wie bei der Surf-Musik wurden während der Folk-Welle alte Alben wiederaufgelegt. Diese beiden Alben der Everly Brothers sind identisch, nur der Titel wurde geändert, damit er aktueller klang.

Durant la folkmania, comme au temps de la surf music, d'anciens albums furent réédités. Ces deux albums des Everly n'en sont qu'un, seul le titre a été changé pour être au goût du jour.

**The Everly Brothers**
*Folk Songs By The Everly Brothers*
Cadence, 1958/1963

Design: Unknown

**Peter, Paul And Mary**
*Peter, Paul And Mary*
Warner Bros., 1962

Design: Milton Glaser
Photo: Bernard Cole

**The Kingston Trio**
*Sold Out*
Capitol, 1960

Design: Unknown

the SPRINGFIELDS

FOLK SONGS FROM THE HILLS

SETTLE DOWN
GREENBACK DOLLAR
WABASH CANNONBALL
MIDNIGHT SPECIAL
ALONE WITH YOU
THERE'S A BIG WHEEL
COTTONFIELDS
FOGGY MOUNTAIN TOP
MAGGIE
DARLING ALLALEE
LITTLE BY LITTLE
MOUNTAIN BOY

**PHILIPS** *hi-fi* PHM 200-078 *Monaural*

Dusty Springfield and her brother Tom started recording as members of a folk trio during the folk revival, before Dusty established herself as a solo star.

Dusty Springfield und ihr Bruder Tom nahmen ihre ersten Platten während des Folk-Revivals als Mitglieder eines Folk-Trios auf, bevor Dusty ihre Solokarriere begann.

Avant de devenir une star en solo, Dusty Springfield avait commencé par enregistrer avec son frère Tom dans un trio folk à l'époque du grand retour en vogue de cette musique.

**The Springfields**
*Folk Songs From The Hills*
Philips, 1963

Design: Unknown

**Bob Dylan**
*Bringing It All Back Home*
Columbia, 1965

Photo: Daniel Kramer

**Bob Dylan**
*Bob Dylan*
Columbia, 1962

Photo: Don Hunstein

**Bob Dylan**
*The Freewheelin' Bob Dylan*
Columbia, 1963

Photo: Don Hunstein

BOOKENDS / SIMON & GARFUNKEL

**Simon & Garfunkel**
*Bookends*
Columbia, 1968

Photo: Richard Avedon

# Joan Baez/5

**Joan Baez**
*Joan Baez/5*
Vanguard, 1964

Design: Unknown

**The Simon Sisters**
*Cuddlebug*
Kapp, 1964

Photo: Alex Greco

Carly and her sister Lucy had a few hits as a duo before Carly's solo career took off.

Carly und ihre Schwester Lucy landeten als Duo ein paar Hits, bevor Carlys Solokarriere begann.

Carly et sa sœur Lucy eurent quelques hits en duo avant que la première ne démarre une carrière solo.

**Judy Collins**
*Judy Collins #3*
Elektra, 1964

Design: William S. Harvey
Photo: Jim Marshall
*Courtesy Elektra Entertainment Group*

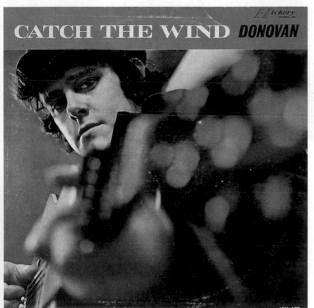

**Donovan**
*Catch The Wind*
Hickory, 1965

Design: Unknown

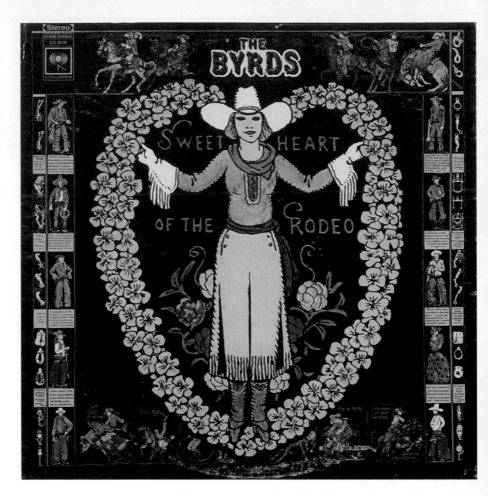

**The Byrds**
*Sweetheart Of The Rodeo*
Columbia, 1968

Design: Geller & Butler Advertising
Illustration: © 1933 Jo Mora

**Buffalo Zone**
*Sweethearts Of The Rodeo*
CBS, 1990

Art Direction: Bill Johnson
Illustration: Dennas Davis

**Lloyd Price**
*Lloyd Price Sings The Million Sellers*
ABC-Paramount, 1961

Design: Harry Farmlett
Photo: Montague Everett

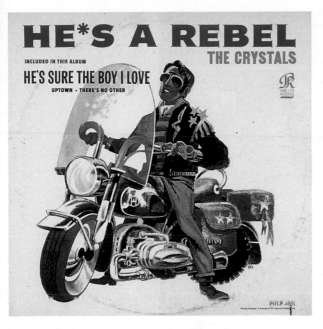

**The Crystals**
*He's A Rebel*
Philles Records (Phil Spector
Records, Inc.), 1963

Design: Unknown
© Phil Spector Records, Inc.

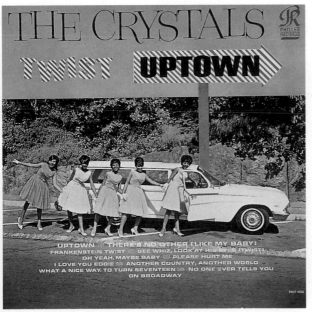

**The Crystals**
*Twist Uptown*
Philles Records (Phil Spector
Records, Inc.), 1962

Design: Studio Five
© Phil Spector Records, Inc.

**The Dixie Cups**
*Chapel Of Love*
Red Bird, 1964

Design: Loring Eutemey
Photo: Hugh Bell

**The Shirelles**
*Tonight's The Night*
Scepter, 1961

Design: Lee-Miles Associates,
New York City

**Bob B. Soxx And The Blue Jeans**
*Zip-A-Dee Doo Dah*
Philles Records (Phil Spector Records, Inc.),
1963

Design: Bob Abrams
© Phil Spector Records, Inc.

**The Shirelles**
*Foolish Little Girl*
Scepter, 1963

Design: Unknown

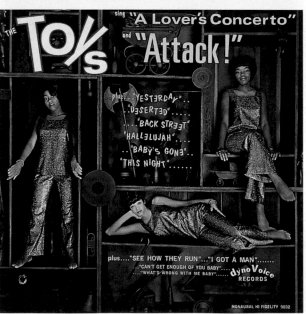

**The Toys**
*The Toys Sing "Lover's Concerto" And "Attack!"*
Dynovoice, 1966

Design: Bob Crewe
Photo: Ron Harris

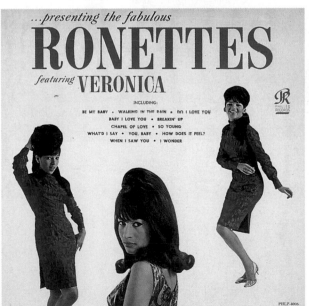

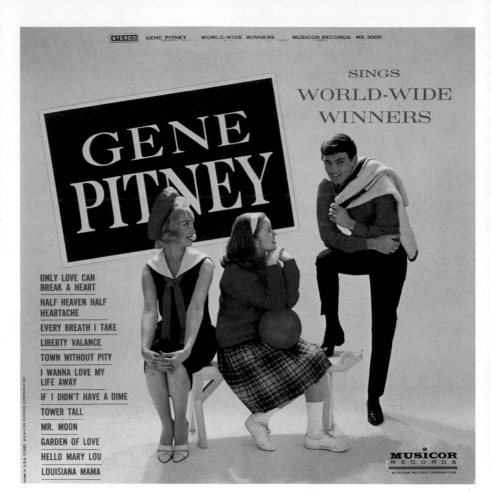

**Gene Pitney**
*Gene Pitney Sings World-Wide Winners*
Musicor, 1963

Design: Unknown

**Gene Pitney**
*Dedicated To My Teen Queens*
Musicor, 1964

Design: Norman Art Studio, Chicago

Two album covers, two models, one set of sweaters and one photo session shows once again how small thinking some of the small record companies were.

Zwei Album-Cover, zwei Fotomodelle, eine Garnitur Pullover und eine Fotosession machen wieder einmal deutlich, wie phantasielos einige der kleineren Plattenfirmen dachten.

Deux pochettes d'albums, deux mannequins, une paire de sweaters et une seule séance de photos qui montrent une fois encore le manque d'imagination de certaines petites compagnies de disques.

**The Shangri-Las**
*Leader Of The Pack*
Red Bird, 1965

Design: Loring Eutemey
Photo: Hugh Bell

**The Angels**
*My Boyfriend's Back*
Smash, 1963

Design: Unknown

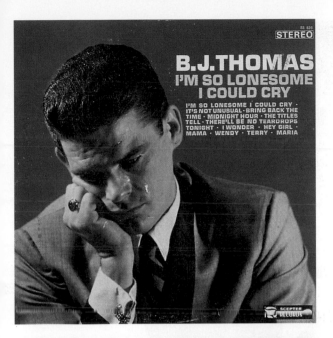

**B.J. Thomas**
*I'm So Lonesome I Could Cry*
Scepter, 1966

Design: Burt Goldblatt

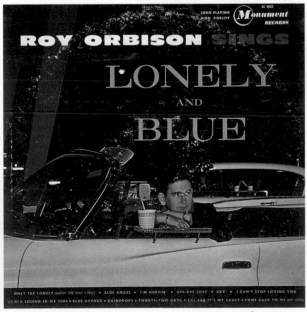

**Roy Orbison**
*Lonely And Blue*
Monument, 1961

Design: Unknown

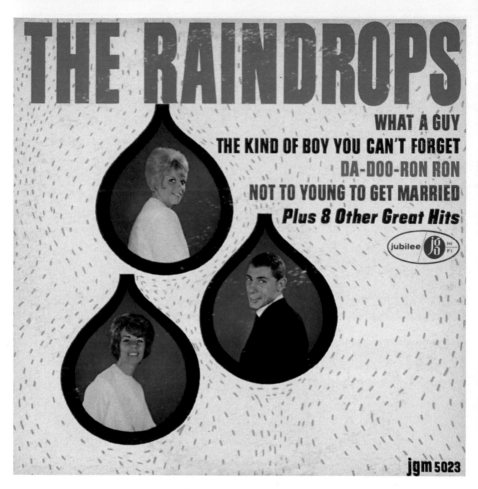

**The Raindrops**
*The Raindrops*
Jubilee, 1963

Design: Stephen P. Haas Studios

Besides being a great practitioner of the "girl group" sound, the Raindrops were basically just Jeff Barry and Ellie Greenwich, two of the most important songwriters of the sixties.

Die Raindrops, herausragende Vertreter des „Girl Group"-Sounds, bestanden im Grunde nur aus Jeff Barry und Ellie Greenwich, zwei der bedeutendsten Songschreiber der sechziger Jahre.

Grands spécialistes du «girl group sound», les Raindrops étaient composés de Jeff Barry et d'Ellie Greenwich, deux des plus importants auteurs-compositeurs des années soixante.

This album featured Wilson's teen-tragedy hit *Last Kiss*. Rumor has it that first printings of this cover actually had blood dripping from the girl's face but it was air-brushed out.

Wichtigstes Stück auf diesem Album war Wilsons Teenager-Tragödien-Hit *Last Kiss*. Auf den ersten Ausgaben dieses Covers tropfte dem Mädchen angeblich sogar Blut vom Gesicht, das später retuschiert wurde.

Cet album contenait le hit de Wilson: *Last Kiss*. On dit que les premières copies de cet album montré aient du sang dégoulinant sur le visage de la fille.

**J. Frank Wilson And The Cavaliers**
*Last Kiss*
Josie, 1964

Design: Unknown

FULL *dynamics frequency* SPECTRUM

ATLANTIC 1259

# THE GREAT RAY CHARLES

STEREO

**Ray Charles**
*The Great Ray Charles*
Atlantic, 1959

Design: Marvin Israel
Photo: Lee Friedlander
*Courtesy Atlantic Recording Corp.*

This original cover was later changed to *Twist With Ray Charles* to capitalize on the Twist craze as was done with the surf and folk fads.

Das Originalcover bekam später den Titel *Twist With Ray Charles*, um von der Twist-Welle zu profitieren, wie man es zuvor schon bei der Surf- und Folk-Welle praktiziert hatte.

Cette pochette originale fut plus tard transformée en *Twist With Ray Charles* afin de tirer profit de la folie du twist, de la même façon qu'on l'avait fait avec les modes surf et folk.

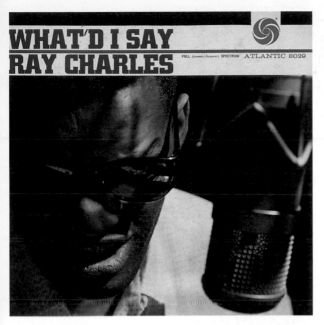

**Ray Charles**
*What'd I Say*
Atlantic, 1959

Design: Marvin Israel
Photo: Lee Friedlander
*Courtesy Atlantic Recording Corp.*

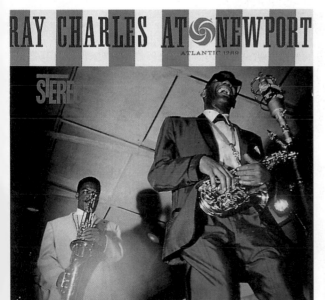

**Ray Charles**
*Ray Charles At Newport*
Atlantic, 1958

Design: Marvin Israel
Photo: Lee Friedlander
*Courtesy Atlantic Recording Corp.*

**Gene Chandler**
*The Duke Of Earl*
Vee-Jay, 1962

Design: Unknown

**James Brown**
*A Soulful Christmas*
King, 1969

Design: Unknown

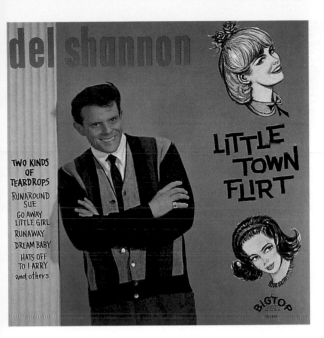

**Del Shannon**
*Little Town Flirt*
Big Top, 1963

Design: Unknown

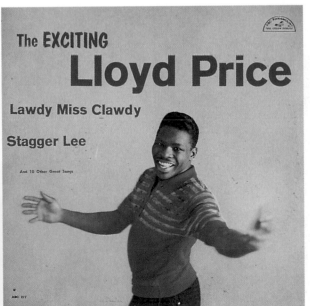

**Lloyd Price**
*The Exciting Lloyd Price*
ABC-Paramount, 1959

Design: Matthew Schultz

**James Brown**
*James Brown Presents
His Show Of Tomorrow*
King, 1968

Design: Unknown

**James Brown**
*I Can't Stand Myself
When You Touch Me*
King, 1968

Design: Roger McElya

**James Brown**
*It's A Man's Man's Man's World*
King, 1966

Design: Unknown

**James Brown**
*Showtime*
Smash, 1964

Design: Unknown

HOLD ON
CUPID
PORTRAIT OF MY LOVE
CINDY
ALWAYS TOGETHER
WHAT KIND OF FOOL
RAINDROPS
YOUR FRIENDS
I WANT TO LOVE YOU
NATURE BOY

**Dee Clark**
*Hold On... It's Dee Clark*
Vee-Jay, 1961

Design: Unknown

**Jerry Butler**
*Aware Of Love*
Vee-Jay, 1961

Design: Unknown

clarence henry
you always hurt the one you love
ARGO LP 4009

All three of these black artists (Clark, Butler, Henry) had generic white people on their album covers.

Alle drei schwarzen Künstler (Clark, Butler, Henry) hatten Weiße auf den Covern ihrer Alben.

Ces trois artistes noirs (Clark, Butler, Henry) eurent des individus blancs sur leur pochette d'album.

**Clarence Henry**
*You Always Hurt The One You Love*
Argo, 1961

Design: Unknown

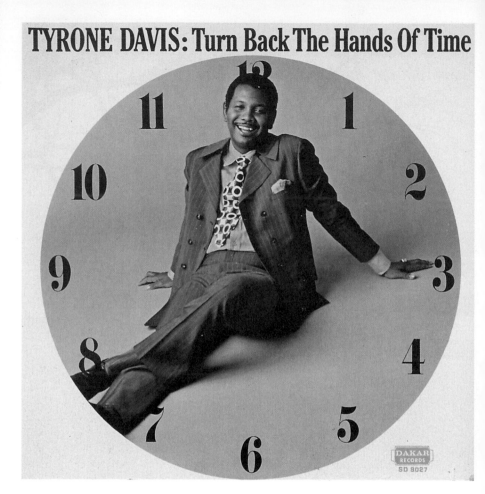

**Tyrone Davis**
*Turn Back The Hands Of Time*
Dakar, 1970

Design: Loring Eutemey
Photo: Joel Brodsky

**The Tymes**
*So Much In Love*
Parkway (ABKCO), 1963

Design: Unknown
© ABKCO Records

**The Marathons**
*Peanut Butter*
Arvee, 1961

Design: Unknown

**The Impressions**
*Keep On Pushing*
ABC-Paramount, 1964

Photo: Don Bronstein

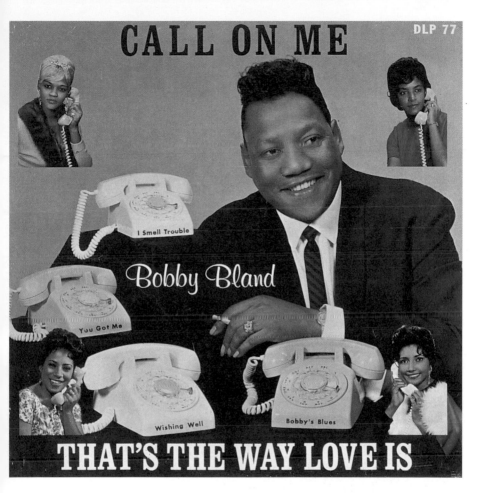

**Bobby Bland**
*Call On Me/That's The Way Love Is*
Duke, 1963

Design: Mitchell & Garner

**Mary Wells**
*The One Who Really Loves You*
Motown, 1962

Design: Barni Wright

Berry Gordy's Motown Records put generic cartoons on these early record covers to appeal to a teenage America.

Berry Gordys Motown Records gestaltete diese frühen Platten-cover mit Cartoons, um bei den amerikanischen Teenagern anzukommen.

La Motown Records de Berry Gordy mit des personnages de dessins animés sur les pochettes de ses premiers albums afin de séduire une Amérique adolescente.

**The Marvelettes**
*Please Mr. Postman*
Tamla, 1961

Design: Barni

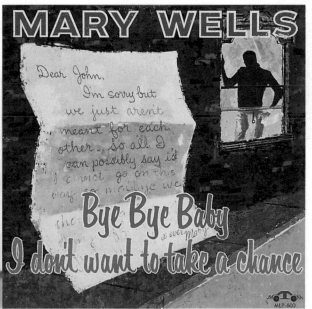

**Mary Wells**
*Bye Bye Baby/*
*I Don't Want To Take A Chance*
Motown, 1961

Design: Barni

**Martha And The Vandellas**
*Heat Wave*
Gordy, 1963

Design: Bernie Yeszin

**The Miracles**
*Hi... We're The Miracles*
Tamla, 1961

Design: Wakefield & Mitchell
Photo: Pictorial Studios, Inc.

**The Miracles**
*Cookin' With The Miracles*
Tamla, 1962

Design: Bill Mitchell

**Mary Wells**
*Two Lovers And Other Great Hits*
Motown, 1963

Design: Barni Wright

**Mary Wells**
*My Guy*
Tamla/Motown, 1964

Photo: David Redfern

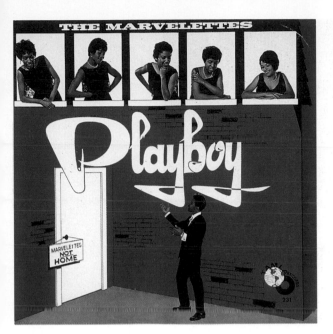

**The Marvelettes**
*Playboy*
Tamla, 1962

Design: Louyce Wakefield &
Barni Wright

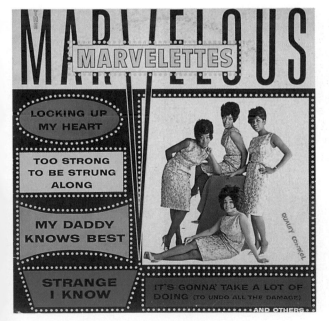

**The Marvelettes**
*The Marvelous Marvelettes*
Tamla, 1963

Design: Barni Wright

**Ike & Tina Turner**
*Ike & Tina Turner's Kings Of Rhythm Dance*
Sue, 1962

Design: Unknown

**Ike & Tina Turner**
*Dynamite!*
Sue, 1963

Design: Unknown

**Inez & Charlie Foxx**
*Inez & Charlie Foxx*
Sue, 1966

Design: Frank Lerner
Photo: Richard Litwin

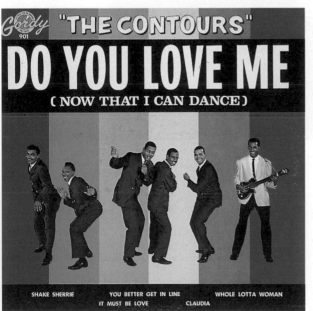

**The Contours**
*Do You Love Me (Now That I Can Dance)*
Gordy, 1962

Design: Barni Wright

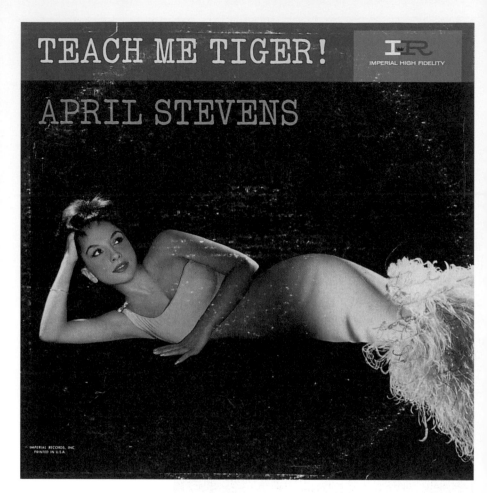

**April Stevens**
*Teach Me Tiger!*
Imperial, 1960

Design: Unknown

Brother and sister, Nino & April had been trying as solo artists for years before they hit big as a duo.

Die Geschwister Nino & April hatten sich erst jahrelang als Solokünstler versucht, bevor sie als Duo den großen Durchbruch schafften.

Frère et sœur dans la vie, Nino & April avaient essayé pendant des années de s'imposer en solo avant d'obtenir ensemble leur premier grand hit.

**Nino Tempo & April Stevens**
*Deep Purple*
Atco, 1963

Design: Loring Eutemey
Photo: John Engstead
*Courtesy Atlantic Recording Corp.*

**Nino Tempo**
*Nino Tempo's Rock 'N Roll Beach Party*
Liberty, 1958

Photo: Gene Lester

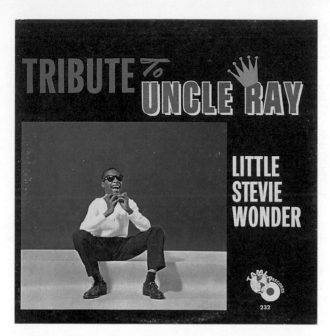

**Little Stevie Wonder**
*Tribute To Uncle Ray*
Tamla, 1963

Design: Barni Wright

**Marvin Gaye**
*I Heard It Through The Grapevine*
Tamla, 1968

Design: Unknown

STEREO

The TEMPTATIONS
WISH
IT WOULD
RAIN

**The Temptations**
*Wish It Would Rain*
Gordy, 1968

Photo: Motown GA-DF

stereo

**Jr. Walker And The All Stars**
*Soul Session*
Soul, 1966

Design: Horace Junior

SOUL
SESSION
JR.WALKER
AND THE ALL STARS

STEREO

DS-50006

DUNHILL

# THE MAMA'S AND THE PAPA'S

## IF YOU CAN BELIEVE YOUR EYES AND EARS

**The Mama's And The Papa's**
*If You Can Believe Your Eyes And Ears*
Dunhill, 1966

Photo: Guy Webster

This is one of the only rock albums that had three covers. The original and the second cover were considered too dirty. So the third cover was created blocking out the whole bathroom motif.

Eines der wenigen Rockalben, das drei Cover hatte. Das Original und das zweite Cover wurden als zu unanständig empfunden. So schuf man das dritte Cover, auf dem das Badezimmermotiv verschwand.

Ceci est l'un des seuls albums de rock à avoir eu trois pochettes. La pochette originale et la seconde furent jugées trop dégoûtantes. Sur la troisième pochette, le motif de la salle de bains avait disparu.

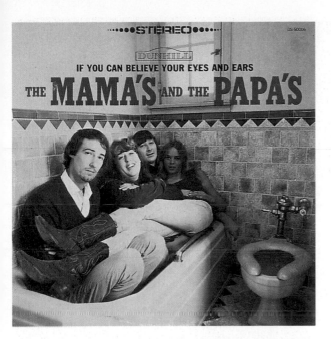

**The Mama's And The Papa's**
*If You Can Believe Your Eyes And Ears*
Dunhill, 1966

Photo: Guy Webster

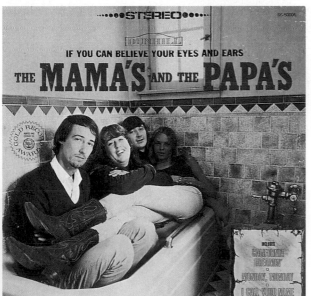

**The Mama's And The Papa's**
*If You Can Believe Your Eyes And Ears*
Dunhill, 1966

Photo: Guy Webster

**Nancy Sinatra**
*Sugar*
Reprise, 1967

Design: Ron Joy

**Paul & Paula**
*We Go Together*
Philips, 1963

Design: Wm. A. Smith

**Crosby, Stills & Nash**
*Crosby, Stills & Nash*
Atlantic, 1969

Design: Unknown
*Courtesy Atlantic Recording Corp.*

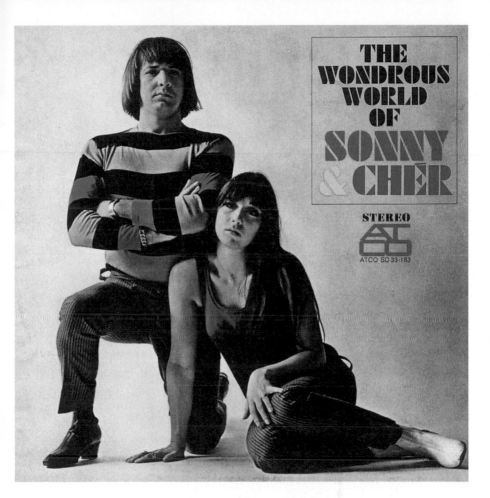

**Sonny & Cher**
*The Wondrous World Of Sonny & Cher*
Atco, 1966

Design: Haig Adishian
Photo: Jerry Schatzberg
*Courtesy Atlantic Recording Corp.*

**The Turtles**
*It Ain't Me Babe*
White Whale, 1965

Design: Peter Whorf Graphics

**The Byrds**
*Turn! Turn! Turn!*
Columbia, 1966

Photo: Guy Webster

**Tiny Tim**
*God Bless Tiny Tim*
Reprise, 1968

Art Direction: Ed Thrasher

**Question Mark And The Mysterians**
*96 Tears*
Cameo (ABKCO), 1966

Art Direction: Douglas Fiske
© ABKCO Records

**Count Five**
*Psychotic Reaction*
Double Shot, 1966

Design: Bernard Yeszin Graphics

**The Barbarians**
*The Barbarians*
Laurie, 1960s

Design: Miller, Bodden & Rich,
Philadelphia

**The Standells**
*Why Pick On Me/Sometimes Good
Guys Don't Wear White*
Tower, 1966

Photo: Howard Risk

**Wayne Cochran And His C.C. Riders**
*High And Ridin'*
Bethlehem, 1970s

Design: Dan Ruest Studio
Photo: John Paradisi

**Crow Music**
*Crow Music*
Amaret, 1960s

Design: Unknown

**Steppenwolf**
*Monster*
Dunhill, 1969

Design: Unknown

STEPPENWOLF MONSTER

**The Youngbloods**
*Elephant Mountain*
RCA Victor, 1969

Photo: Charles L. Heald

**Shiva's Headband**
*Take Me To The Mountains*
Capitol, 1970

Cover Art: Jim Franklin

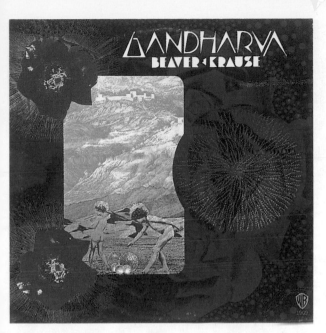

**Beaver & Krause**
*Gandharva*
Warner Bros., 1971

Design: Satty/D. Singer

**Quicksilver Messenger Service**
*Happy Trails*
Capitol, 1969

Design: George Hunter For
Globe Paintings
Lettering: Ken Hollister

**Dr. Timothy Leary PH.D.**
*L.S.D.*
Pixie, 1966

Design: Unknown

As part of the acid rock movement, even Timothy Leary cranked out a couple of albums. This is the better cover of the two.

Als Teil der Acid-Rock-Bewegung brachte sogar Timothy Leary zwei Alben heraus. Hier das bessere Cover.

Figure clé du mouvement acid rock, Timothy Leary sortit lui-même deux albums. Ceci est la meilleure pochette des deux.

**The Thirteenth Floor Elevators**
*The Psychedelic Sounds Of 13th Floor Elevators*
International Artists, 1967

Design: John Cleveland, Austin (Texas)
*International Artists Courtesy Of Charly Records*

**It's A Beautiful Day**
*It's A Beautiful Day*
Columbia, 1969

Photo: Globe Propaganda

**Buffalo Springfield**
*Buffalo Springfield Again*
Atco, 1967

Design: Loring Eutemey
Illustration: Eve Babitz
*Courtesy Atlantic Recording Corp.*

**Grateful Dead**
*Grateful Dead*
Warner Bros., 1967

Collage: Kelly
Photo: Herb Greene

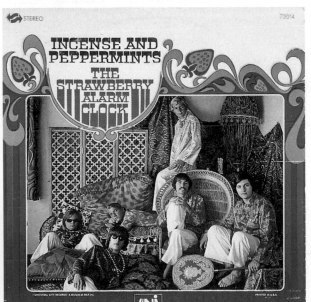

**The Strawberry Alarm Clock**
*Incense And Peppermints*
Uni, 1967

Photo: Ed Caraeff

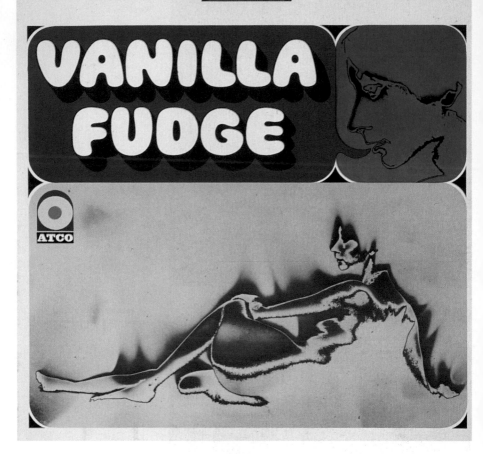

**Vanilla Fudge**
*Vanilla Fudge*
Atco, 1967

Design: Haig Adishian
Photo: Bruce Laurance
*Courtesy Atlantic Recording Corp.*

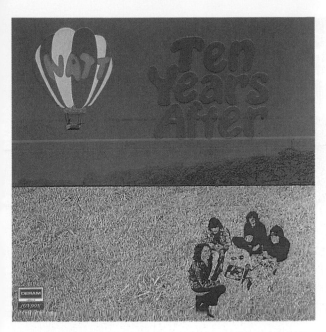

**Ten Years After**
*Watt*
Deram, 1960s/70s

Design: John Fowlie
Color Processing: Graham Nash

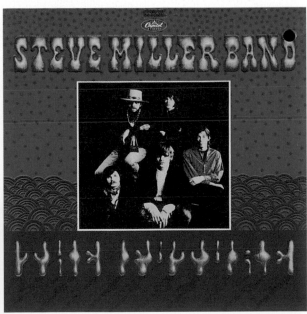

**The Steve Miller Band**
*Children Of The Future*
Capitol, 1968

Design: Victor Moscoso
Photo: Elaine Mayes

**Mad River**
*Mad River*
Capitol, 1968

Photo: George Jerman

**The Steve Miller Band**
*Sailor*
Capitol, 1968

Photo: Thomas Weir

**Ten Years After**
*Sssh.*
Deram, 1969

Photo: John Fowlie/Graham Nash

ENTROPY / BLACK SHEEP OF THE FAMILY / POST WAR SATURDAY ECHO / GOOD LORD KNOWS
UP ON THE GROUND / GEMINI / MAKE UP YOUR MIND / LAUGHIN' TACKLE

**Quatermass**
*Quatermass*
Harvest, 1960s

Design: Hipgnosis

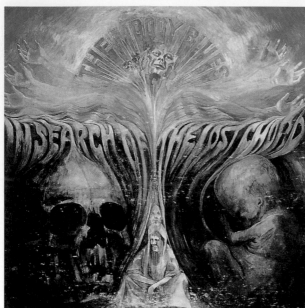

**The Moody Blues**
*In Search Of The Lost Chord*
Deram, 1968

Design: Philip Travers

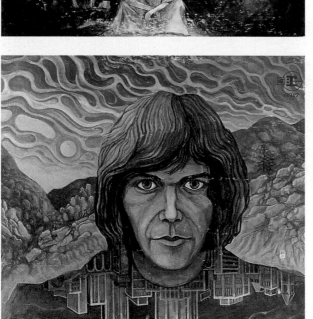

**Neil Young**
*Neil Young*
Reprise, 1968

Art Direction: Neil Young
Portrait: Roland Diehl

**Moby Grape**
*Wow*
Columbia, 1968

Design: Bob Cato

**The Byrds**
*Mr. Tambourine Man*
Columbia, 1965

Photo: Barry Feinstein

**The Jimi Hendrix Experience**
*Are You Experienced*
Track, 1967

Design: Unknown

**The Jimi Hendrix Experience**
*Are You Experienced*
Reprise, 1967

Art Direction: Ed Thrasher
Photo. Karl Ferris

**Cream**
*Disraeli Gears*
Atco, 1967

Artwork: Martin Sharp
Photos: Bob Whitaker
*Courtesy Atlantic Recording Corp.*

**The West Coast Pop Art Experimental Band**
*The West Coast Pop Art Experimental Band Part One*
Reprise, 1967

Design: Charles E. White, III
Photo: Carl Frith

**The Incredible String Band**
*The 5000 Spirits*
Elektra, 1967

Design: Simon & Marijke
*Courtesy Elektra Entertainment Group*

**Derek & The Dominos**
*Layla*
Atco, 1970

Painting: Frandsen De Schonberg
*Courtesy Atlantic Recording Corp.*

**Bee Gees**
*Bee Gees' 1st*
Atco, 1967

Design: Klaus Voorman
*Courtesy Atlantic Recording Corp.*

**Iron Butterfly**
*In-A-Gadda-Da-Vida*
Atco, 1968

Design: Loring Eutemey
Photo: Stephen Paley
*Courtesy Atlantic Recording Corp.*

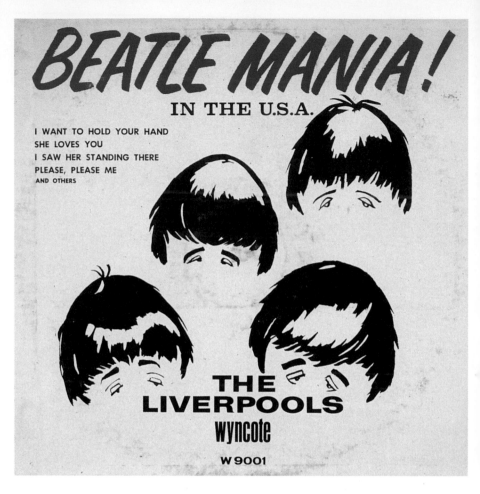

**The Liverpools**
*Beatle Mania! In The U.S.A.*
Wyncote, 1960s

Design: Unknown

The Beatles bonanza was so big that these budget labels thought they could confuse the public into buying these rip-off albums. Note how they each implied that they might be the Fab Four.

Das Geschäft mit den Beatles war derart lukrativ, daß Low-Budget-Label glaubten, sie könnten die Öffentlichkeit zum Kauf dieser Nepp-Alben verleiten. Jedes dieser drei Cover suggeriert, es könne sich um die „Fabulous Four" handeln.

Le filon Beatles était si riche que même ces petites compagnies crurent qu'elles pourraient tromper le public et leur faire acheter ces albums fauchés. Notez comment chacune des pochettes suggère qu'il pourrait s'agir des «Fab Four».

The Manchesters
*Beatlerama*
Diplomat, 1960s

Design: Unknown

B. Brock And The Sultans
*Do The Beetle*
Crown, 1964

Design: F.B. Smith/W. Paul Bailey
Advertising, Culver City (California)

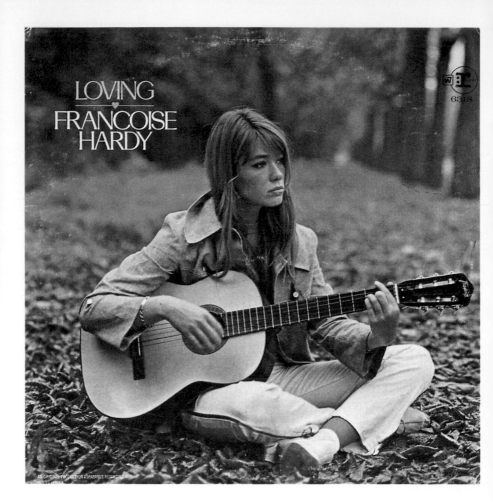

**Françoise Hardy**
*Loving*
Reprise, 1960s

Art Direction: Ed Thrasher

# OLYMPIA 64

**PHILIPS**

The British Invasion was so gigantic that other European countries tried to get in on the action. France seemed to have a little luck with these two artists, but Britannia ruled the airwaves.

Die britische Invasion war so erfolgreich, daß andere europäische Länder versuchten, auf den fahrenden Zug aufzuspringen. Frankreich hatte mit diesen beiden Künstlern anscheinend sogar ein wenig Glück, aber die Briten beherrschten den Äther.

L'invasion britannique fut si colossale que d'autres pays européens tentèrent de prendre part à l'action. La France parut avoir une petite chance avec ces deux artistes, mais l'Angleterre régnait sur les ondes.

**Johnny Hallyday**
*Olympia 64*
Philips, 1960s

Photo: Wiezniak/J.P. Le Loir Fornier et Studio Boissiere

**Tom Jones**
*It's Not Unusual* (live cover)
Parrot, 1965

Design: Unknown

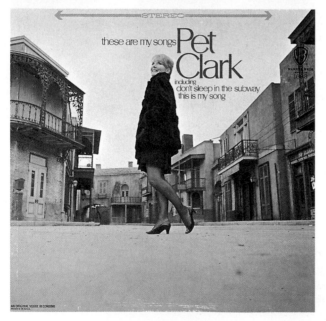

**Petula Clark**
*These Are My Songs*
Vogue, 1967

Art Direction: Ed Thrasher

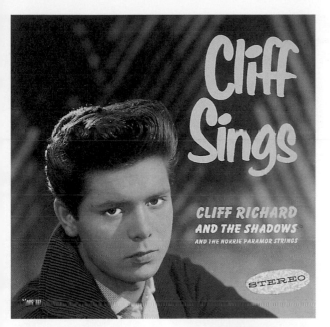

**Cliff Richard And The Shadows**
*Cliff Sings*
ABC-Paramount, 1960

Design: Unknown

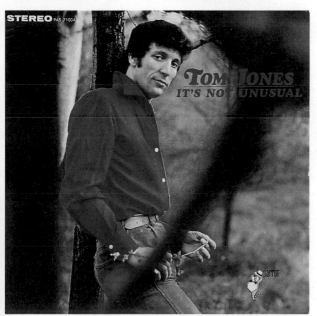

**Tom Jones**
*It's Not Unusual* (red shirt cover)
Parrot, 1965

Design: Unknown

**James Taylor**
*James Taylor*
Apple, 1969

Photo: Richard Imrie/J.B.A.
© Apple Corps Ltd.

James Taylor

**Sir Douglas Quintet**
*The Best Of Sir Douglas Quintet*
Tribe, 1966

Design: Harry Farmlett
Photo: Moshe Brakha

This Texas band actually shot their cover portrait in silhouette and gave themselves a British sounding name just to compete with the foreign influx that was dominating the airwaves.

Diese texanische Band ließ sich für das Coverporträt als Silhouette ablichten und gab sich einen britisch klingenden Namen, um mit der Konkurrenz ausländischer Gruppen mithalten zu können.

Ce groupe du Texas réalisa son image de pochette en silhouettes et se donna un nom aux consonances anglaises afin de rivaliser avec la vague d'étrangers portée par le vent soufflant d'Angleterre.

**The Spencer Davis Group**
*Gimme Some Lovin'*
United Artists, 1967

Design: Unknown

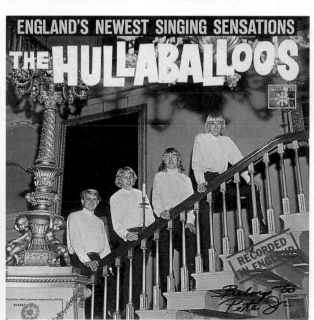

**The Hullaballoos**
*The Hullaballoos On Hullaballoo*
Roulette, 1965

Design: Unknown

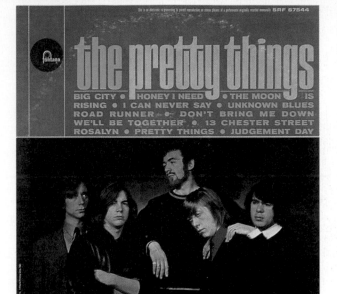

The Pretty Things
*The Pretty Things*
Fontana, 1965

Design: Unknown

The Troggs
*Wild Thing*
Fontana, 1966

Design: Unknown

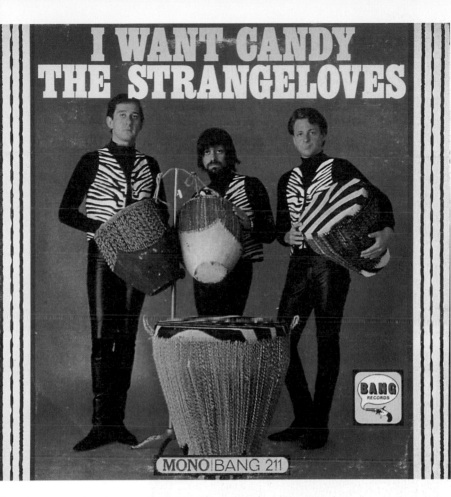

I WANT CANDY
THE STRANGELOVES

BANG
RECORDS

MONO | BANG 211

These three New York producers and writers tried to pass themselves off as Australians to cash in on the foreign invasion.

Diese drei New Yorker Produzenten und Autoren gaben sich als
Australier aus, um aus der ausländischen Invasion Profit zu
schlagen.

Ces trois auteurs et producteurs new-yorkais tentèrent de se
faire passer pour australiens afin de profiter de l'invasion étran-
gère.

**The Strangeloves**
*I Want Candy*
Bang, 1965

Design: Haig Adishian
Photo: Nick Samardge

**The Yardbirds**
*Five Live*
Columbia/EMI, 1964

Photo: Richard Rosser

**The Animals**
*The Animals*
EMI/Regal, 1960s

Photo: Fleetway Publications

**The Kinks**
*You Really Got Me*
Reprise, 1965

Design: Unknown

**The Animals**
*The Animals*
MGM, 1964

Design: Unknown

**Them**
*Angry Young Them*
Decca, 1965

Design: Unknown

**Them**
*Them Featuring Here Comes The Night*
Parrot, 1965

Design: Unknown

**Them**
*Them Again*
Decca, 1966

Design: Unknown

**The Dave Clark Five**
*The Dave Clark Five Return!*
Epic, 1965

Design: Unknown

**Manfred Mann**
*The Manfred Mann Album Featuring Do Wah Diddy Diddy*
Ascot, 1964

Design: Unknown

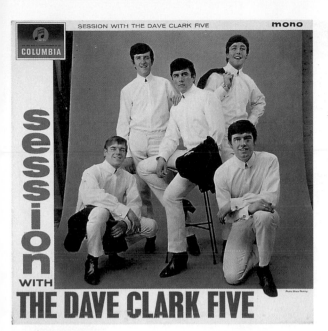

**The Dave Clark Five**
*Sessions With The Dave Clark Five*
Columbia, 1960s

Photo: Bruce Fleming

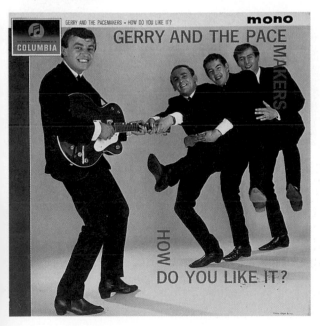

**Gerry And The Pacemakers**
*How Do You Like It?*
Columbia, 1963

Photo: Edgar Brind

**The Who**
*My Generation*
Virgin, 1965

Design: Unknown

**The Who**
*The Who Sell Out*
Decca, 1967

Design: David King/Roger Law
Photos: David Montgomery

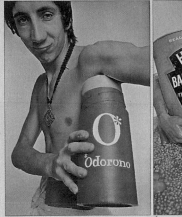 

THE WHO SELL OUT   DECCA   THE WHO SELL OUT

Replacing the stale smell of excess with the sweet smell of success, Peter Townshend, who, like nine out of ten stars, needs it. Face the music with Odorono. Use all day, deodorant that turns perspiration into inspiration.

This way to a cowboy's breakfast. Daltry rides again. Thinks: "Thanks to Heinz Baked Beans everyday is a super day." Those who know how many beans make five eat Heinz beans inside and outside at every opportunity. Get saucy.

(Back cover)
*The Who Sell Out*

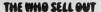

THE WHO SELL OUT   THE WHO SELL OUT

There used to be a dark side to Keith Moon. Not now. Not any more. If acne is preventing you from reaching your acme, use Medac, the spot remover that makes your pits flit. Put Medac on the spot now.

John Entwistle was a nine and a half stone weakling until Charles Atlas made a man of him at nine and three-quarter stone. Now those huggy bear biceps bring those beach beauties running. Put muscles among the mussels. Tense yourself skinny.

"Decca", "Gold Label Series", "New World of Sound" and "Harlequin Design" are registered trademarks.
**DECCA RECORDS, A Division of MCA INC.,** New York, N. Y., USA

**Jethro Tull**
*This Was*
Reprise, 1969

Design: Unknown

**The Rolling Stones**
*The Rolling Stones – England's Newest HitMakers*
ABKCO Records, 1964

Photo: Nicholas Wright
© ABKCO Records

**The Rolling Stones**
*Their Satanic Majesties Request*
ABKCO Records (London), 1967

Design: Michael Cooper
© ABKCO Records

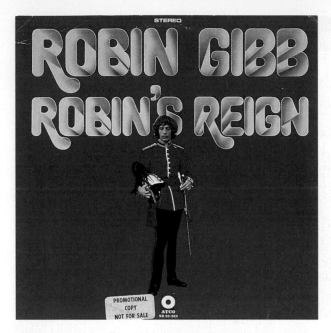

**Robin Gibb**
*Robin's Reign*
Atco, 1970

Design: Hamish Grimes
Photo: Ray Washbourne
*Courtesy Atlantic Recording Corp.*

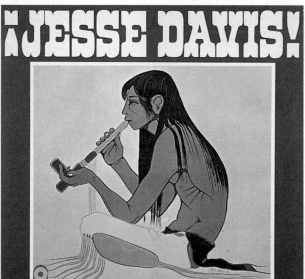

**Jesse Davis**
*Jesse Davis*
Atlantic, 1970

Design: Jesse Edwin Davis,
For Washita Prods.
Painting: Jesse Edwin Davis
*Courtesy Atlantic Recording Corp.*

BEE GEES
ODESSA

Although probably not captured by this photo, the cover and back of this album are red felt. Later editions were just red paper.

Obwohl auf dem Foto wahrscheinlich nicht zu erkennen, sind das Cover und die Rückseite dieses Albums aus rotem Filz. Spätere Ausgaben waren lediglich aus rotem Papier.

Bien qu'on ne s'en rende probablement pas compte sur cette photo, le recto et le verso de cette pochette sont en velours rouge. Les éditions suivantes furent réalisées en papier rouge.

**Bee Gees**
*Odessa*
Atco, 1969

Design: Unknown
*Courtesy Atlantic Recording Corp.*

**Bob Dylan**
*Planet Waves*
Columbia, 1974

Painting: Bob Dylan

**Captain Beefheart And His Magic Band**
*Shiny Beast (Bat Chain Puller)*
Warner Bros., 1978

Design: Brad Kanawar
Art Direction: John Cabalka

**Joni Mitchell**
*Mingus*
Asylum, 1979

Art Direction: Glen Christensen
Painting: Joni Mitchell
*Courtesy Elektra Entertainment Group*

**The Who**
*The Who By Numbers*
MCA, 1975

Drawing: John Entwhistle

**Mike Bloomfield & Al Kooper**
*The Live Adventures Of Mike
Bloomfield & Al Kooper*
Columbia, 1969

Design: Virginia Team
Painting: Norman Rockwell

**Joni Mitchell**
*Clouds*
Reprise, 1969

Art Direction: Ed Thrasher
Painting: Joni Mitchell

**Bob Dylan**
*Self Portrait*
Columbia, 1970

Design: Ron Coro
Painting: Bob Dylan

**John Lennon**
*Walls And Bridges*
Apple, 1974

Design: Roy Kohara
Drawings: John Lennon
Photo: Bob Gruen

**The Band**
*Music From Big Pink*
Capitol, 1968

Design: Milton Glaser
Painting: Bob Dylan

**Crosby, Stills, Nash And Young**
*So Far*
Atlantic, 1974

Art Direction: Gary Burden
For R. Twerk
Cover Art: Joni Mitchell
*Courtesy Atlantic Recording Corp.*

**Joni Mitchell**
*Ladies Of The Canyon*
Reprise, 1970

Design: Joni Mitchell

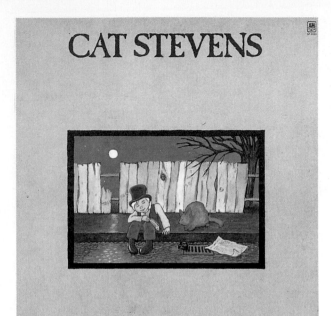

**Cat Stevens**
*Teaser And The Firecat*
A&M, 1971

Illustration: Cat Stevens

**Cat Stevens**
*Tea For The Tillerman*
A&M, 1971

Illustration: Cat Stevens

**Cat Stevens**
*Mona Bone Jakon*
A&M, 1971

Illustration: Cat Stevens

**The Velvet Underground**
*The Velvet Underground And Nico*
Verve, 1967

Painting: "Banana" by Andy Warhol

**The Jeff Beck Group**
*Beck-Ola*
Epic, 1967

Painting: "La Chambre D'Écoute"
by René Magritte

**Ray Charles**
*The Genius Hits The Road*
ABC-Paramount, 1960

Design: Viceroy/Everett

**Ray Charles**
*Country And Western Meets Rhythm And Blues*
ABC-Paramount, 1965

Design: Robert Flynn/Viceroy
Photo: Howard Morehead

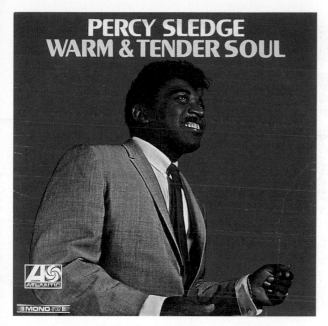

**Percy Sledge**
*Warm & Tender Soul*
Atlantic, 1966

Design: Haig Adishian
Photo: Hermann Bachmann
*Courtesy Atlantic Recording Corp.*

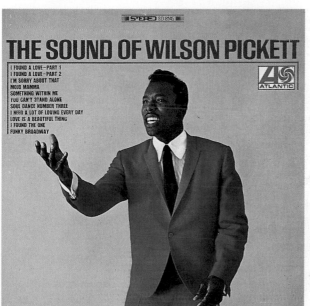

**Wilson Pickett**
*The Sound Of Wilson Pickett*
Atlantic, 1967

Design: Haig Adishian
Photo: Nick Samardge
*Courtesy Atlantic Recording Corp.*

**Big Brother & The Holding Company**
*Cheap Thrills*
Columbia, 1968

Design: Unknown

**The Flamin Groovies**
*Supersnazz*
Epic, 1969

Artwork: Bob Zoell

**Archie Bell & The Drells**
*Tighten Up*
Atlantic, 1968

Design: Loring Eutemey
*Courtesy Atlantic Recording Corp.*

**Freddie Hughes**
*Send My Baby Back*
Scepter, 1968

Design: Burt Goldblatt

**Eddie Floyd**
*Knock On Wood*
Stax, 1967

Design: Ronnie Stoots

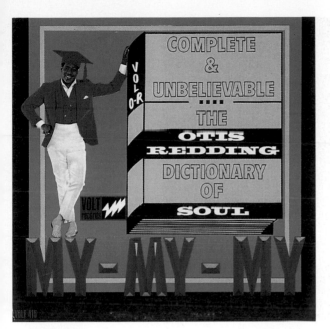

**Otis Redding**
*The Otis Redding Dictionary Of Soul*
Volt, 1966

Design: Ronnie Stoots

**Sam & Dave**
*Hold On, I'm Comin'*
Stax, 1966

Design: Ronnie Stoots

**Barbara Lynn**
*You'll Lose A Good Thing*
Jamie, 1962

Design: Unknown

**Claudine Clark**
*Party Lights*
Chancellor, 1962

Design: Chic Laganella
Photo: Michael Denning,
Philadelphia

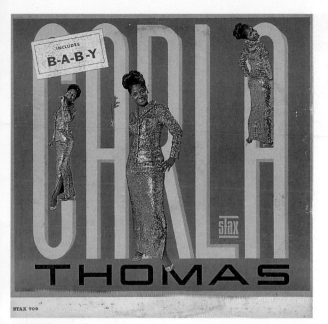

**Carla Thomas**
*Carla*
Stax, 1966

Design: Ronnie Stoots
Photos: Bill Kingsley

**Etta James**
*Etta James Rocks The House*
Argo, 1964

Design: Don Bronstein
Photo: J. B. Lecroy

**Aretha Franklin**
*Aretha Franklin: Soul '69*
Atlantic, 1969

Design: Loring Eutemey
Photo: Jean-Pierre Leloir
*Courtesy Atlantic Recording Corp.*

**Brenda Holloway**
*Every Little Bit Hurts*
Tamla, 1964

Design: Yeszin/Mead

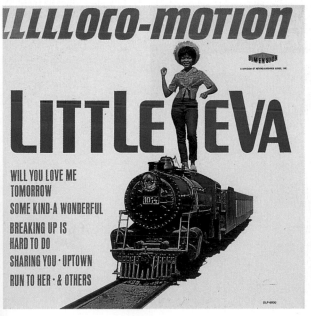

**Little Eva**
*Lllloco-Motion*
Dimension, 1962

Design: Unknown

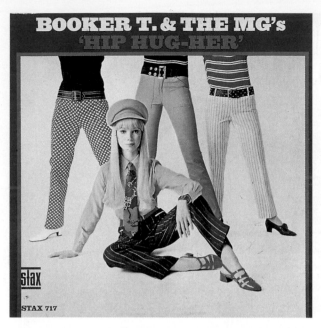

**Booker T. & The MG's**
*'Hip Hug-Her'*
Stax, 1967

Design: Loring Eutemey
Photo: George Rosenblatt
*Courtesy Atlantic Recording Corp.*

**Arthur Conley**
*Sweet Soul Music*
Atco, 1967

Design: Loring Eutemey
Photo: George Rosenblatt

**Johnnie Taylor**
*Wanted One Soul Singer*
Atlantic, 1967

Design: Ronnie Stoots
*Courtesy Atlantic Recording Corp.*

**Fontella Bass**
*The 'New' Look*
Checker, 1966

Design: Don Bronstein

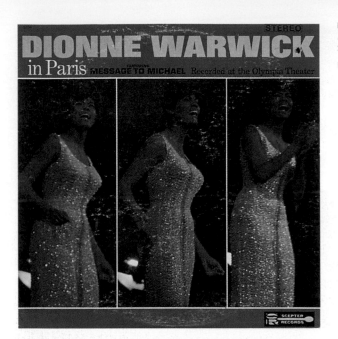

**Dionne Warwick**
*Dionne Warwick In Paris*
Scepter, 1966

Design: Burt Goldblatt

**Dionne Warwick**
*Make Way For Dionne Warwick*
Scepter, 1964

Design: Unknown

**Dionne Warwick**
*Very Dionne*
Scepter, 1970

Art Direction: Dick Smith
Photo: Harry Langdon

**Margie Joseph**
*Margie Joseph Makes A New Impression*
Volt, 1971

Art Direction: The Graffiteria/David Krieger
Photo: Joel Brodsky

**Roberta Flack**
*Chapter Two*
Atlantic, 1970

Design: Ira Friedlander
Photo: Jack Robinson
*Courtesy Atlantic Recording Corp.*

**Dave Mason**
*Alone Together*
Blue Thumb, 1970

Design: Tom Wilkes/
Barry Feinstein/Camouflage

As packaging got more fancy in the sixties, this album with its five-fold cover is probably the most elaborate of the decade.

In den sechziger Jahren wurde die Verpackung immer ausgefallener. Dieses Album, dessen Cover sich viermal ausklappen läßt, ist wohl das ausgefeilteste des Jahrzehnts.

Alors que l'emballage devenait plus original dans les années soixante, cet album avec sa pochette en cinq volets fut probablement la plus élaborée de la décennie.

**Small Faces**
*Ogdens' Nut Gone Flake*
Immediate, 1968

Design: Unknown

STEREO

**Beatles**
*Sgt. Pepper's Lonely Hearts Club Band*
Capitol, 1967

Design: MC Productions & The Apple
Photo: Michael Cooper
© Apple Corps Ltd.

**Beatles**
*Meet The Beatles*
Capitol, 1964

Photo: Robert Freeman
© Apple Corps Ltd.

**Beatles**
*Hey Jude*
Apple, 1970

Design: Unknown
© Apple Corps Ltd.

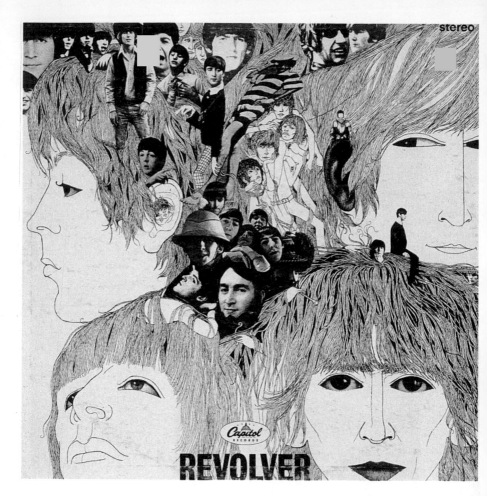

**Beatles**
*Revolver*
Capitol, 1966

Design: Klaus Voorman
© Apple Corps Ltd.

This is the cover-up outer sleeve of the totally nude John & Yoko album cover. Out of respect for Yoko's wishes, we cannot show the nude covers. Needless to say, the album was banned.

Dies ist die mit braunem Papier umhüllte Ausgabe des Albums. Auf dem Originalcover, das wir auf Yokos Wunsch hin nicht zeigen, sind John & Yoko splitternackt zu sehen. Selbstredend wurde das Originalcover verboten.

Ceci est l'habillade de la pochette de l'album de John & Yoko sur laquelle ils figurent totalement nus. Selon la volonté de Yoko, nous ne pouvons montrer cette pochette. Inutile de dire que l'album fut interdit.

**John Lennon & Yoko Ono**
*Two Virgins: Unfinished Music – Vol. 1*
Apple, 1968

Design: Unknown

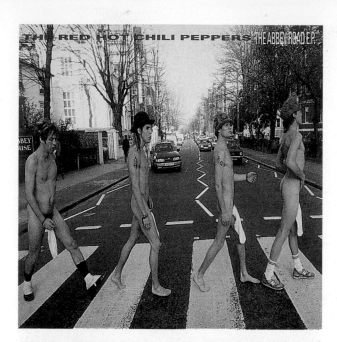

**Red Hot Chili Peppers**
*The Abbey Road EP*
EMI-Manhattan, 1988

Design: Abrahams Pants
Photo: Chris Clunn

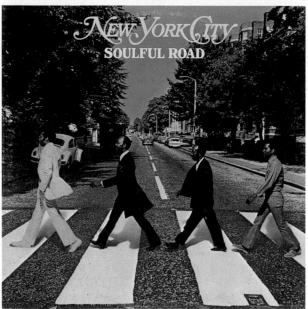

**New York City**
*Soulful Road*
Chelsea, 1973

Design: Big Cigar
Photo: Ian MacMillian

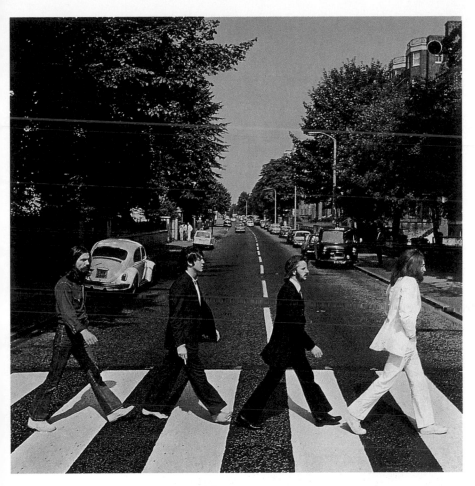

**Beatles**
*Abbey Road*
Capitol/EMI, 1969

Photo: Iain MacMillan
© Apple Corps Ltd.

**Blind Faith**
*Blind Faith*
Atco, 1969

Design: Bob Seidemann
*Courtesy Atlantic Recording Corp.*

Although this cover was banned and replaced by another cover, this is still the most common copy of the album.

Obwohl das Plattencover verboten und durch ein anderes ersetzt wurde, ist es immer noch die am meisten verbreitete Version des Albums.

Bien que cette pochette eût été interdite et remplacée par une autre, il s'agit pourtant de la version la plus répandue de cet album.

The Grape was one of the most highly touted San Francisco bands that failed to sell. This album was banned before the offending finger over the washboard was air-brushed out.

The Grape war eine der Bands aus San Francisco, für die sehr viel Werbung gemacht wurde, ohne daß es sich finanziell auszahlte. Dieses Album war verboten, bis der anstößige Finger über dem Waschbrett wegretuschiert wurde.

The Grape, l'un des groupes les plus branchés de San Francisco, ne connut jamais de succès commercial. Cet album fut interdit jusqu'à ce que le doigt offensant sur la planche à laver eût été supprimé.

**Moby Grape**
*Moby Grape*
Columbia, 1967
Photo: Jim Marshall

**The Jimi Hendrix Experience**
*Electric Ladyland*
Track, 1968

Design: David King
Photo: David Montgomery

THE JIMI HENDRIX EXPERIENCE  ELECTRIC LADYLAND

This cover with the nude women was banned in the USA and only released in Europe.

Dieses Cover mit den nackten Frauen war in den USA verboten und erschien nur in Europa.

La pochette avec les femmes nues fut interdite aux Etats-Unis et ne sortit qu'en Europe.

# 1970s

After the unconditional surrender of the "we" generation of the sixties, the "me" generation of the seventies came to power. As the war babies entered their thirties, "we" started to become "them". The sound of a generation was splintered into various musical genres that reflected narcissism rather than idealism.

The first trend of the seventies seemed to be the dismantling of successful sixties bands. In 1971, The Beatles broke up officially to pursue separate careers. That same year, Michael Jackson and Rod Stewart scored their first hits without their groups, and they joined the swelling ranks of solo singing stars such as Elton John, Billy Joel, Cat Stevens, James Taylor and Jim Croce. In addition, many female singers such as Linda Ronstadt, Carly Simon, Carole King and Olivia Newton-John became stars on their own. Not surprisingly, the subject matter for all these new superstars was simply themselves. For those wanting more diverse forms of music, Led Zepplin and Kiss kept the hysterical heavy-metal sound alive. For pure posturing, Alice Cooper introduced shock-rock, while Marc Bolan, David Bowie and The New York Dolls invented glitter rock. In The Grateful Dead tradition, The Allman Brothers and The Marshall Tucker Band expanded the boogie-band concept with their southern rock sound. Thanks to Miles Davis and Weather Report, there was yet another hybrid form of music called jazz-rock. The progressive rock bandwagon was represented by Yes, Roxy Music and Pink Floyd, whose album *Dark Side of the Moon* set the all-time record for sales longevity – over fifteen years on the pop charts. For pure pop, there was no group bigger or better than Sweden's Abba.

With all the excesses of success in popular music, many fans searched elsewhere for a rougher, rootsier form of music. Not knowing where to look at first, the rocking fifties was revived with the release of such films as *Grease* and *American Graffiti*. The emergence of Bob Seger and Bruce Springsteen was yet another sign of good-old rock and roll regaining popularity. Then the release of the first all-Jamaican film *The Harder They Come* introduced reggae music and made Jimmy Cliff and Bob Marley international stars.

The splintering rock scene of the seventies was united commercially with the release of the disco-dance film *Saturday Night Fever*. The accompanying album could not be manufactured fast enough to meet the demand and, with 25 million copies sold, soon became the biggest selling soundtrack album of all time. Gloria Gaynor, The Village People and Donna Summer helped disco attain a popularity with all ages not seen since "The Twist", and once again rock became predictable and acceptable.

As if in protest – the disenfranchised and disenchanted started the punk-rock movement – refusing to dance their troubles away. From England came The Sex Pistols, The Clash and Elvis Costello, while America contributed The Ramones, Blondie and Patti Smith. Though the movement itself was short lived, punk rock did bring outrage and rebellion back into rock and roll. By the end of the seventies, this harder rock sound was being spread by such new bands as The Cars, Talking Heads and The Police.

The diversity of the seventies music scene proved that rock and roll would never be one unifying movement. Trends came and went more rapidly as the public's need for new sounds seemed continually insatiable.

Nachdem die „Wir"-Generation der sechziger Jahre bedingungslos kapituliert hatte, gelangte die „Ich"-Generation an die Macht. Die Kriegskinder waren jetzt Anfang Dreißig, und aus „wir" wurde allmählich „sie". Die Musik einer Generation splitterte sich in unterschiedliche Genres auf, die eher Narzismus als Idealismus widerspiegelten.

Der erste Trend in den siebziger Jahren war die Auflösung erfolgreicher Gruppen der sechziger Jahre. 1971 trennten sich die Beatles offiziell, um ihre Solokarrieren zu verfolgen. Im selben Jahr landeten Michael Jackson und Rod Stewart die ersten Hits ohne ihre Gruppen und reihten sich in die wachsende Zahl der Solistenstars wie Elton John, Billy Joel, Cat Stevens, James Taylor und Jim Croce ein. Sängerinnen wie Linda Ronstadt, Carly Simon, Carole King und Olivia Newton-John wurden Stars. Das zentrale Thema dieser neuen Superstars waren – wie nicht anders zu erwarten – ausschließlich sie selbst.

Für alle, die ein abwechslungsreicheres Musikspektrum interessierte, hielten Led Zeppelin und Kiss den wilden Heavy-Metal-Sound am Leben. Aus reiner Lust an der bühnenwirksamen Provokation führte Alice Cooper den Shock-Rock ein, während Marc Bolan, David Bowie und The New York Dolls den Glitter-Rock erfanden. In der Tradition von The Grateful Dead entwickelten die Allman Brothers und die Marshall Tucker Band das Konzept der Boogie-Band mit ihrem Rock-Sound der Südstaaten weiter. Dank Miles Davis und Weather Report gab es noch eine weitere Mischung namens Jazz Rock. Die progressive Rockwelle repräsentierten Yes, Roxy Music und Pink Floyd, die mit ihrem Album *Dark Side Of The Moon* sämtliche Dauerverkaufsrekorde brachen – über 15 Jahre in den Pop-Charts. Auf dem Gebiet der reinen Popmusik war die schwedische Gruppe Abba ohne jede ernstzunehmende Konkurrenz.

Angesichts des übermäßigen Erfolgs der Popmusik hielten viele Fans anderswo nach einer rauheren, ursprünglicheren Musikform Ausschau. Während sie noch überlegten, wohin sie sich da wenden sollten, erlebten die „Rocking Fifties" eine Renaissance, als die Filme *Grease* und *American Graffiti* in die Kinos kamen. Ein weiteres Zeichen für die neue Popularität des guten alten Rock 'n' Roll war das Auftauchen von Bob Seger und Bruce Springsteen in der Musikszene. Der erste jamaikanische Film *The Harder They Come* machte den Reggae bekannt und Jimmy Cliff und Bob Marley zu internationalen Stars.

Der aufgesplitterten Rockszene der siebziger Jahre entsprach in kommerzieller Hinsicht der Disco-Tanzfilm *Saturday Night Fever*. Das

Soundtrack-Album konnte gar nicht schnell genug produziert werden, so groß war die Nachfrage, und mit 25 Millionen verkauften Exemplaren verzeichnete es bald einen beispiellosen Rekordumsatz. Gloria Gaynor, The Village People und Donna Summer machten den Rock erneut berechenbar und akzeptabel und trugen dazu bei, daß die Disco-Musik bei allen Generationen einen Beliebtheitsgrad erreichte, wie es ihn seit dem Twist nicht mehr gegeben hatte.

Aus Protest riefen die gesellschaftlichen Außenseiter und Desillusionierten, die sich weigerten, ihre Probleme „wegzutanzen", die Punk-Rock-Bewegung ins Leben. Aus England kamen The Sex Pistols, The Clash und Elvis Costello, während Amerika The Ramones, Blondie und Patti Smith beisteuerten. Der Bewegung selbst war zwar kein langes Leben beschieden, doch der Punk Rock brachte schockierende und rebellische Elemente zurück in den Rock 'n' Roll. Gegen Ende der siebziger Jahre wurde dieser härtere Rock-Sound von neuen Bands wie The Cars, Talking Heads und The Police verbreitet.

Die Vielfalt der Musikszene der siebziger Jahre machte deutlich, daß der Rock 'n' Roll nie wieder eine einheitliche Bewegung sein würde. Die Trends wechselten genauso schnell, wie das scheinbar unersättliche Publikum nach immer neuen Sounds verlangte.

Après la reddition inconditionnelle de la génération «nous» des années soixante, la génération «moi» des années soixante-dix prit le pouvoir. A mesure que les enfants de la guerre abordaient la trentaine, «nous» devenait «eux». Le son d'une génération éclata en divers genres musicaux qui reflétaient le narcissisme plutôt que l'idéalisme.

La première caractéristique des années soixante-dix parut être la désintégration des grands groupes des années soixante. En 1971, les Beatles se séparèrent officiellement pour entamer des carrières séparées. La même année, Michael Jackson et Rod Stewart eurent leurs premiers tubes sans leurs groupes et rejoignirent les rangs de stars de comme Elton John, Billy Joel, Cat Stevens, James Taylor et Jim Croce. En outre, de nombreuses chanteuses comme Linda Ronstadt, Carly Simon, Carole King et Olivia Newton-John devinrent des stars. Les sujets des chansons de ces nouvelles superstars était, comme on s'en doute, elles-mêmes tout simplement.

Pour ceux qui recherchaient des formes musicales plus variées, Led Zeppelin et Kiss maintenaient vivant le son hystérique du heavy metal. Pour le simple geste, Alice Cooper introduisit le shock rock, alors que Marc Bolan, David Bowie et les New York Dolls inventaient le glitter rock. Dans la lignée du Grateful Dead, les Allman Brothers et le Marshall Tucker Band développèrent l'idée du groupe de boogie avec leur son de rock sudiste. Grâce à Miles Davis et à Weather Report, il y avait maintenant une autre forme hybride de musique appelée jazz rock. Le convoi des musiciens de rock progressif était entraîné par Yes, Roxy Music, et Pink Floyd dont l'album *Dark Side of the Moon* a établi le record de longévité des ventes – plus de quinze ans dans la liste des meilleures ventes aux Etats-Unis. Pour la pop à l'état pur, il n'y avait pas de meilleur groupe que le suédois Abba.

Avec l'éclatant succès de l'excès dans la musique populaire, de nombreux fans cherchèrent ailleurs une forme de musique plus brutale et authentique. Comme ils ne savaient pas où tourner leur regard, les années cinquante réapparurent grâce au succès de films comme *Grease* et *American Graffiti*. L'apparition de Bob Seger et de Bruce Springsteen fut un autre signe du regain de popularité du bon vieux rock 'n' roll. La sortie du premier film entièrement jamaïcain *The Harder They Come* («Tout Tout de Suite») fit découvrir le reggae et transforma Jimmy Cliff et Bob Marley en stars internationales.

La scène rock éclatée des années soixante-dix fut commercialement unie par la sortie du film disco *Saturday Night Fever*. L'album de la musique du film ne put être pressé en assez grandes quantités pour satisfaire immédiatement la demande et devint, avec 25 millions d'exemplaires vendus, la plus grosse vente de musique de film de tous les temps. Gloria Gaynor, Village People et Donna Summer permirent au disco d'atteindre une popularité, sans exemple depuis le twist, auprès de toutes les générations et, rendirent à nouveau le rock prévisible et acceptable.

Comme en signe de protestation, les affranchis et les désenchantés démarrèrent le mouvement punk, refusant d'oublier leurs problèmes dans la danse. D'Angleterre arrivèrent les Sex Pistols, les Clash et Elvis Costello, alors que l'Amérique apportait sa contribution avec les Ramones, Blondie et Patti Smith. Quoique le mouvement lui-même n'eût qu'une brève existence, le punk ramena l'outrance et la révolte dans le rock 'n' roll. A la fin des années soixante-dix, ce son plus dur fut répandu par de nouveaux groupes comme les Cars, Talking Heads et Police.

La diversité de la scène musicale des années soixante-dix prouva que le rock 'n' roll ne serait jamais plus un mouvement unitaire. Les tendances apparaissaient et disparaissaient de plus en plus rapidement, alors que les besoins du public en sons nouveaux paraissaient impossibles à satisfaire.

**Elton John**
*Tumbleweed Connection*
Uni, 1970

Design: Unknown

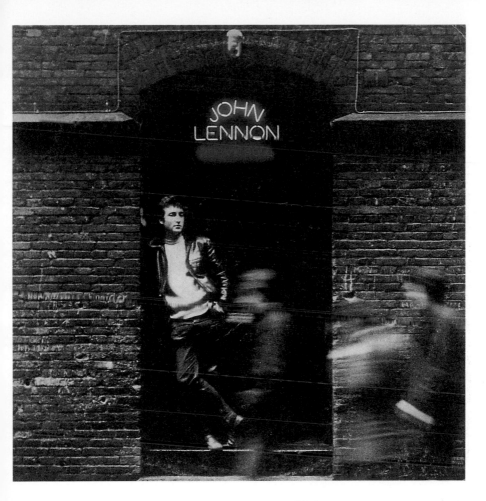

**John Lennon**
*Rock 'N' Roll*
Apple, 1975

Design: Roy Kohara
Photo: Jürgen Vollmer

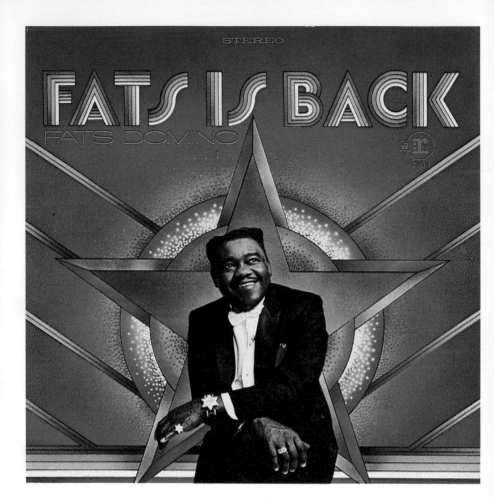

**Fats Domino**
*Fats Is Back*
Reprise, 1968

Art Direction: Ed Thrasher
Photo: Dave Willardson

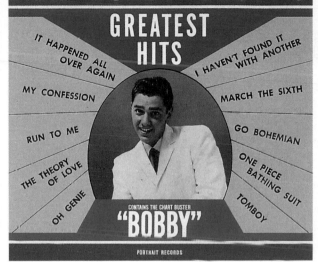

**Neil "Bobby" Scott**
*Neil 'Bobby' Scott's Greatest Hits*
Portrait, 1960s

Design: Unknown

**The Maytals**
*The Sensational Maytals*
BMN, 1964/65

Design: Ronnie Nasralla
Photo: Wally & Brian Motta

**Burning Spear**
*Man In The Hills*
Island, 1976

Photo: Kim Gottlieb

**Marcia Griffiths**
*Sweet Bitter Love*
Trojan, 1970s

Design: Unknown

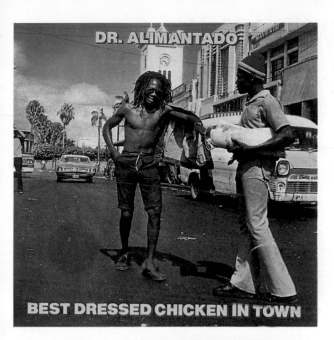

**Dr. Alimantado**
*Best Dressed Chicken In Town*
Greensleeves, 1978

Photo: D. K. James

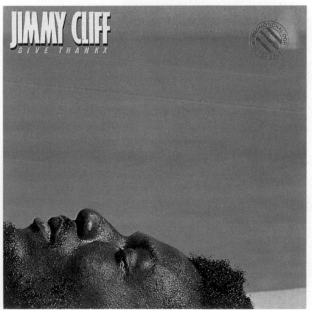

**Jimmy Cliff**
*Give Thankx*
Warner Bros., 1976

Design: Bob Himmel/
AGI, New York
Photo: Ruiko Yoshida, Tokyo

**Pure Prairie League**
*If The Shoe Fits*
RCA, 1976

Art Direction: Acey Lehman
Artwork: John Thompson

**The Siegel – Schwall Band**
*R.I.P. Siegel/Schwall*
Wooden Nickel, 1974

Art Direction: Acy Lehman
Cover Illustration:
Harvey Dinnerstein

**The Doobie Brothers**
*Stampede*
Warner Bros., 1975

Design: John & Barbara Casado
Art Direction: Ed Thrasher
Photo: Michael & Jill Maggid

**Mary Kay Place**
*Aimin' To Please*
Columbia, 1977

Design: Tom Steele/
Roger Carpenter
Illustration: Joe Heiner
Photo: Gene Gurly

**Wilderness Road**
*Wilderness Road*
Columbia, 1970s

Design: John Craig
Photo: Bob Prokop

**Wet Willie**
*Keep On Smilin'*
Capricorn, 1974

Design: Richard Mantel
Photo: Al Clayton

**Marshall Tucker Band**
*A New Life*
Capricorn, 1974

Design: Wondergraphics/
J. Flourney Holmes/D. Powell

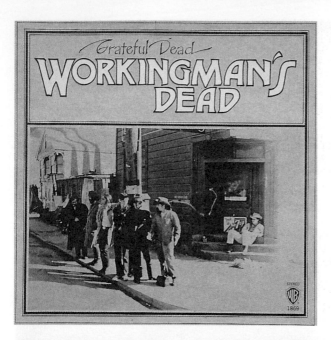

**Grateful Dead**
*Workingman's Dead*
Warner Bros., 1970

Design: Mouse Studios/
Toon N' Tree

**Crosby, Stills, Nash & Young**
*Déjà vu*
Atlantic, 1970

Design: Gary Burden
Photo: Tom Gundelfinger
*Courtesy Atlantic Recording Corp.*

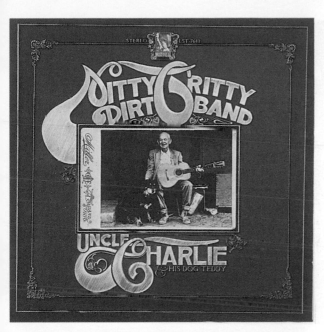

**Nitty Gritty Dirt Band**
*Uncle Charlie & His Dog Teddy*
Liberty, 1970

Design: Dean O. Torrance/
Kittyhawk Graphics Executive Art

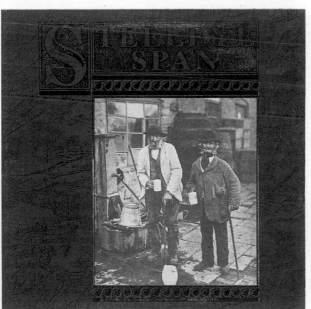

**Steeleye Span**
*Then Man Mop Or Mr. Reservoir
Butler Rides Again*
Pegasus, 1971

Design: Unknown

**Juice Newton**
*Can't Wait All Night*
RCA, 1984

Design: Kosh/Ron Larsen
Photo: Robert Blakeman

**Stephen Stills**
*Thoroughfare Gap*
Columbia, 1978

Design: Stephen Stills/John Berg
Photo: Jim McCrary

**Carole King**
*Thoroughbred*
Ode, 1976

Design: Chuck Beeson

**Procol Harum**
*A Salty Dog*
A&M, 1969

Design: Dickinson

**Joe Walsh**
*The Smoker You Drink The Player You Get*
Dunhill, 1973

Design: Jimmy Wachtel

**The Sutherland Bros. & Quiver**
*Lifeboat*
Island, 1973

Design: Barney Bubbles/C.C.S.

**The Pretty Things**
*Silk Torpedo*
Swan Song, 1974

Design: Hipgnosis
*Courtesy Atlantic Recording Corp.*

**Jethro Tull**
*Aqualung*
Reprise, 1971

Painting: Burton Silverman

**Led Zeppelin**
*Led Zeppelin*
Atlantic, 1969

Design: Graphreaks
Illustration: "The Hermit" by
Barrington Colby, MOM
*Courtesy Atlantic Recording Corp.*

**Genesis**
*Nursery Cryme*
Buddah, 1971

Design: Unknown

**Aynsley Dunbar**
*"To Mum, From Aynsley And The Boys"*
Blue Thumb, 1968

Design: Bryan Morrison
Photo: Hipgnosis

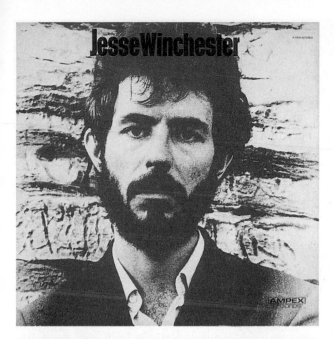

**Jesse Winchester**
*Jesse Winchester*
Ampex, 1971

Design: Bob Cato
Photo: Jeremy Taylor

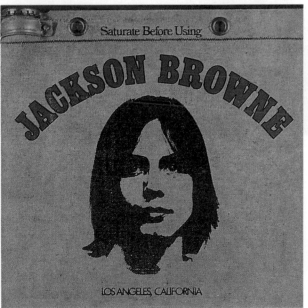

**Jackson Browne**
*Jackson Browne*
Asylum, 1972

Art Direction: Gary Burden
for R. Twerk
Photo: Henry Diltz
*Courtesy Elektra Entertainment Group*

**J. J. Cale**
*Okie*
Shelter, 1974

Design: Big Cigar
Illustration: Richard Germinaro

**J. J. Cale**
*Naturally*
Shelter, 1971

Cover painting: Rabon

**Hall & Oates**
*Abandoned Luncheonette*
Atlantic, 1973

Design: Unknown
*Courtesy Atlantic Recording Corp.*

**City Boy**
*Young Men Gone West*
Mercury, 1977

Art Direction: Sue DuBois
Liner Illustration: Geoff Halpin
Photo: Bob Carlos Clarke

**Captain & Tennille**
*Dream*
A&M, 1978

Design: Junie Okaki
Art Direction: Roland Young
Photo: Norman Seef

**Stackridge**
*Pinafore Days*
Sire, 1974

Design: John Kosh
Photo: John Swannell

**Dr. John**
*Dr. John's Gumbo*
Atco, 1972

Design: Barry Feinstein/Tom Wilkes
for Camouflage Prods.
*Courtesy Atlantic Recording Corp.*

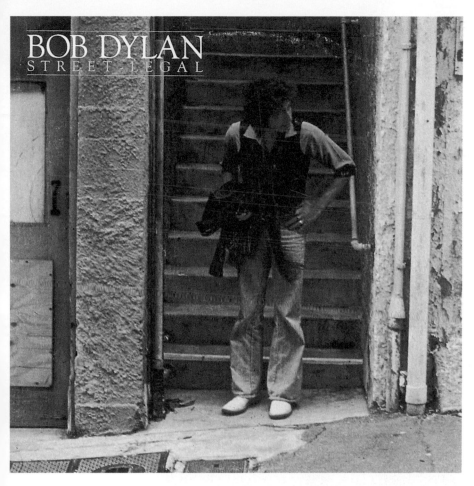

**Bob Dylan**
*Street Legal*
Columbia, 1978

Design: George Corsillo/Gribbitt
Art Direction: Tim Bryant/Gribbitt
Photo: Howark Alk

**Supercharge**
*Supercharge*
Virgin, 1976

Design: Ed Lee
Photo: Eric Meola

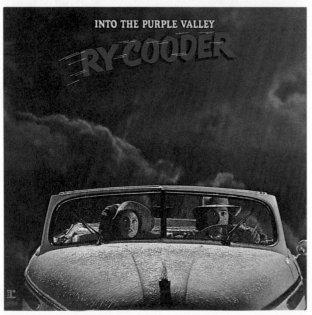

**Ry Cooder**
*Into The Purple Valley*
Reprise, 1972

Art Direction: Ed Thrasher
Photo: Marty Evans

**Chris Spedding**
*Chris Spedding*
Rak/EMI, 1976

Design: Gered Mankowitz
(Tinting by Arthur Allen)

**Neil Young**
*On The Beach*
Reprise, 1974

Design: Gary Burden
for R. Twerk & Co.
Photo: Bob Seidemann

**Pavlov's Dog**
*Pampered Menial*
ABC, 1975

Design: Unknown

**Bob Seger System**
*Mongrel*
Capitol, 1970

Design: Tom Weschler

**The Laughing Dogs**
*The Laughing Dogs*
Columbia, 1979

Design: Andrea Klein/John Berg
Photo: Jerry Abramowitz

**Daddy Cool**
*Teenage Heaven*
Reprise, 1972

Design: Ed Thrasher

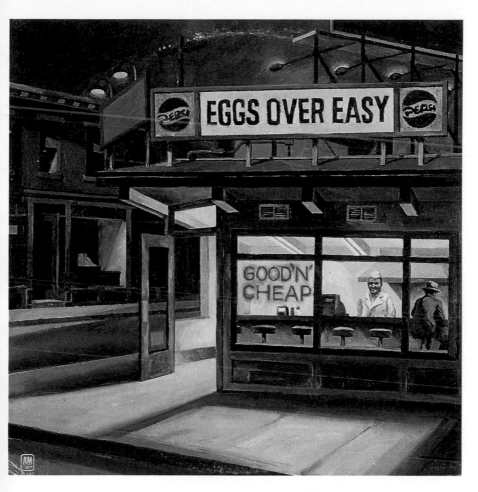

**Eggs Over Easy**
*Good 'N' Cheap*
A&M, 1974

Art Direction: Roland Young
Illustration: Joe Garnett

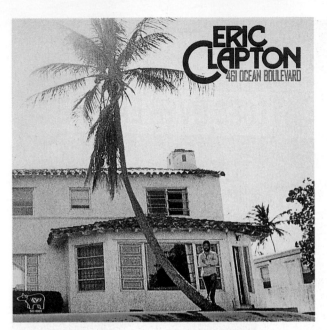

**Eric Clapton**
*461 Ocean Boulevard*
RSO, 1974

Art Direction: Bob Defrin
Photo: David Gahr

**John Lennon**
*John Lennon/Plastic Ono Band*
Apple, 1970

Design: John & Yoko
Photo: Dan Richter

**Audience**
*The House On The Hill*
Elektra, 1971

Design: Hipgnosis/Howard Werth
US Art Direction: Robert L. Heimall
*Courtesy Elektra Entertainment Group*

**Peter Gabriel**
*Peter Gabriel*
Atco, 1977

Design: Hipgnosis
*Courtesy Atlantic Recording Corp.*

**John Lennon &**
**The Plastic Ono Band**
*Live Peace In Toronto 1969*
Apple, 1970

Design: Unknown

**Genevieve Waite**
*Romance Is On The Rise*
Paramour, 1974

Design: Ruth Ansel
Photo: Richard Avedon
(Tinting by Bob Bishop)

**Bob Seger**
*Smokin' O.P.'s*
Palladium, 1972

Design: Thomas Weschler

**Bette Midler**
*Bette Midler*
Atlantic, 1973

Design: Loring Eutemey
*Courtesy Atlantic Recording Corp.*

**The Manhattan Transfer**
*The Manhattan Transfer*
Atlantic, 1975

Art Direction: Bob Defrin
Drawing: Fred Eric Spione
*Courtesy Atlantic Recording Corp.*

**The Pointer Sisters**
*That's A Plenty*
Blue Thumb, 1974

Art Direction: Herb Greene
Cover Art: Randy Tutem

**The Manhattan Transfer**
*Extensions*
Atlantic, 1979

Design: Taki Ono
Illustration: Pater Sato
*Courtesy Atlantic Recording Corp.*

**Brinsley / Schwarz**
*Despite It All*
Capitol, 1970

Design: Unknown

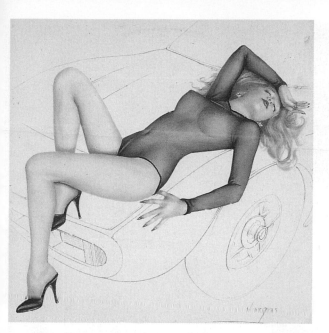

**The Cars**
*Candy-o*
Elektra, 1979

Design & Art Direction: Ron Coro/
Johnny Lee
Concept: David Robinson
Painting: Albert Vargas
*Courtesy Elektra Entertainment Group*

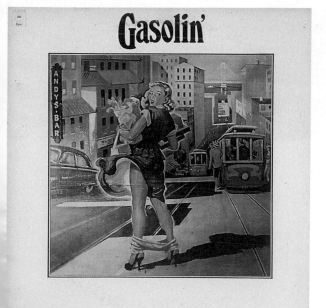

**Gasolin'**
*Gasolin'*
Epic, 1974

Painting: Tage Hansen

**Shoot**
*On The Frontier*
EMI, 1973

Art Direction: Fabio Nicoli/
Gered Mankowitz

**Gambler**
*Teenage Magic*
EMI, 1979

Design: Rod Dyer, Inc.

**Little Feat**
*The Last Record Album*
Warner Bros., 1975

Design: Unknown

**Little Feat**
*Waiting For Columbus*
Warner Bros., 1978

Design: Unknown

**Little Feat**
*Down On The Farm*
Warner Bros., 1975

Design: Eddy Herch
Art Direction & Painting: Neon Park

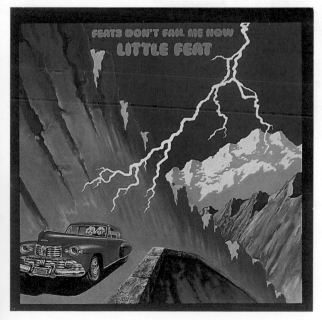

**Little Feat**
*Feats Don't Fail Me Now*
Warner Bros., 1974

Design: Neon Park

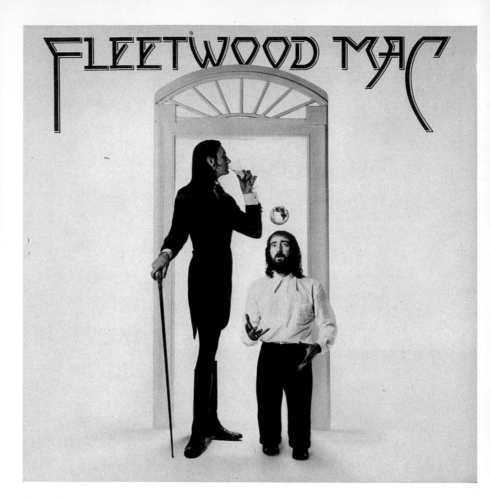

**Fleetwood Mac**
*Fleetwood Mac*
Reprise, 1975

Design: Des Strobel/AGI
Photo: Herbert Worthington

**Fleetwood Mac**
*Rumours*
Warner Bros., 1977

Design: Unknown

**Badfinger**
*Badfinger*
Warner Bros., 1974

Design: John Kosh
Photo: Peter Howe

**Badger**
*White Lady*
Epic, 1974

Design: John Berg
Cover Art: David Croland

**Blue Oyster Cult**
*Agents Of Fortune*
Columbia, 1976

Design: John Berg/Andy Engel

**Wishbone Ash**
*Live Dates*
MCA, 1973

Design: Hipgnosis
Drawing: Colin Elgie

**Grateful Dead**
*Europe '72*
Warner Bros., 1972

Design: Kelley/Mouse Studios

**Mott The Hoople**
*Mott The Hoople*
Atlantic, 1970

Drawing: M.C. Escher
*Courtesy Atlantic Recording Corp.*

**Beaver & Krause**
*In A Wild Sanctuary*
Warner Bros., 1970

Art Direction: Ed Thrasher
Etching: "Three Worlds" by M.C. Escher

**Jefferson Airplane**
*After Bathing At Baxter's*
RCA, 1967

Design: Jefferson Airplane/
Ron Cobb

**Aerosmith**
*Draw The Line*
Columbia, 1977

Design: John Berg
Art: Al Hirschfeld

**Leon Redbone**
*On The Track*
Warner Bros., 1975

Design: Chuck Jones

**The Kinks**
*Schoolboys In Disgrace*
RCA, 1975

Art Direction: Chris Hopper
Illustration: Mickey Finn

**Move**
*Shazam*
A&M, 1969

Design: Nickleby

**Jefferson Airplane**
*Thirty Seconds Over Winterland*
Grunt, 1973

Design: Bruce Steinberg

**Phil Ochs**
*Gunfight At Carnegie Hall*
A&M, 1975

Art Direction: Mike Yazzolino
Cover Art: Larry Hall

**The Manhattan Transfer**
*Jukin'*
Capitol, 1971

Design: Curtis Gathje

**Montrose**
*Warner Bros. Presents 'Montrose'!*
Warner Bros., 1975

Illustration: Harry Rossit

**Judi Pulver**
*Pulver Rising*
MGM, 1973

Design: Jimmy Watchell/S. Botticelli
Photo: Lorrie Sullivan/Jimmy Watchtell

**Melissa Manchester**
*For The Working Girl*
Arista, 1980

Design: Ria Lewerke-Shapiro
Photo: George Hurrell

**Golden Earring**
*Moontan*
MCA, 1974

Photo: Ronnie Hertz

**Sweet**
*Off The Record*
Capitol, 1977

Design: Norman Goodman
Artwork: Terry Pastor

**Spinners**
*The Best Of Spinners*
Atlantic, 1978

Art Direction: Bob Defrin
Illustration: David Williardson
*Courtesy Atlantic Recording Corp.*

**Harry Nilsson**
*A Little Touch Of Schmilsson In The Night*
RCA, 1973

Photo: Tom Hanley Of Bloomsbury

**T. Rex**
*The Slider*
Warner Bros., 1972

Photo: Ringo Starr

**Rickie Lee Jones**
*Rickie Lee Jones*
Warner Bros., 1979

Design: Mike Salisbury
Photo: Norman Seef

**Van Morrison**
*Wavelength*
Warner Bros., 1978

Design: Brad Kanawyer
Art Direction: John Cabalka
Photo: Norman Seef

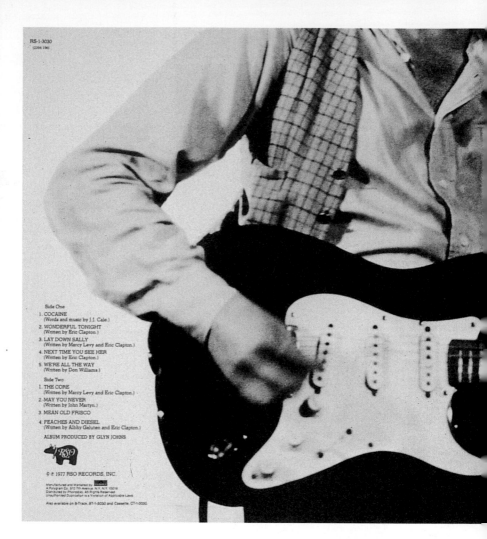

Side One

1. COCAINE
(Words and music by J.J. Cale.)
2. WONDERFUL TONIGHT
(Written by Eric Clapton.)
3. LAY DOWN SALLY
(Written by Marcy Levy and Eric Clapton.)
4. NEXT TIME YOU SEE HER
(Written by Eric Clapton.)
5. WE'RE ALL THE WAY
(Written by Don Williams.)

Side Two

1. THE CORE
(Written by Marcy Levy and Eric Clapton.)
2. MAY YOU NEVER
(Written by John Martyn.)
3. MEAN OLD FRISCO
4. PEACHES AND DIESEL
(Written by Albhy Galuten and Eric Clapton.)

ALBUM PRODUCED BY GLYN JOHNS

℗ © 1977 RSO RECORDS, INC.

Manufactured and Marketed by [RSO]
A Polygram Co. 810 7th Avenue. N.Y. N.Y. 10019
Distributed by Phonodisc. All Rights Reserved.
Unauthorized Duplication is a Violation of Applicable Laws.

Also available on 8-Track, 8T-1-3030 and Cassette. CT-1-3030.

**Eric Clapton**
*Slowhand*
RSO, 1977

Design & Art Direction:
David Stewart for El & Nell, Inc.
Photo: Watal Asanuma

ERIC CLAPTON
SLOWHAND

**Bruce Springsteen**
*Born To Run*
Columbia, 1975

Design: John Berg/Andy Engel
Photo: Eric Meola

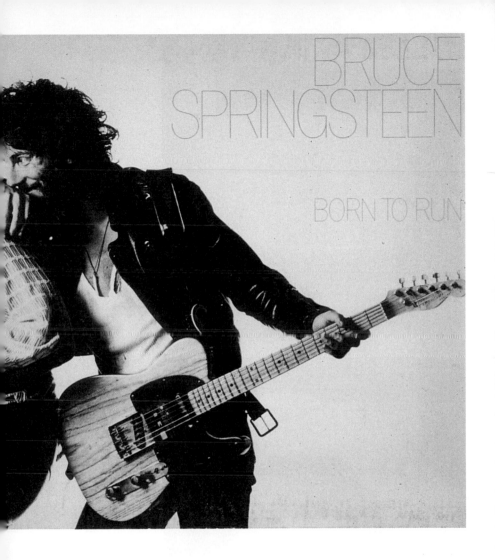

**Richard & Linda Thompson**
*Pour Down Like Silver*
Island, 1975

Design: ABD Al-Lateef
Photo: ABD Al-Adheim

**Marianne Faithfull**
*Broken English*
Island, 1979

Photo: Dennis Morris

**Nico**
*The Marble Index*
Elektra, 1968

Design: Robert L. Heimell
Art Direction: William S. Harvey
Photo: Guy Webster
*Courtesy Elektra Entertainment Group*

**Paul Simon**
*Paul Simon*
Columbia, 1971

Design: Ron Coro/John Berg
Photos: P. A. Harper

**Jeff Beck**
*Blow By Blow*
Epic, 1975

Design: John Berg
Art: John Collier

**Creedence Clearwater Revival**
*Green River*
Fantasy, 1969

Photos: Basul Parik

**Leo Kottke**
*My Feet Are Smiling*
Capitol, 1973

Design: John Van Hamersveld
Photo: Norman Seef

**Billy Joel**
*The Stranger*
Columbia, 1977

Photo: Jim Houghton

**Lou Reed**
*Coney Island Baby*
RCA, 1976

Design: Mick Rock

**Joe Jackson**
*Look Sharp!*
A&M, 1979

Art Direction: Michael Ross
Photo: Brian Griffin

**Graham Nash**
*Wild Tales*
Atlantic, 1973

Art Direction: Gary Burden for R. Twerk
Photo: Joel Bernstein
*Courtesy Atlantic Recording Corp.*

**Bob Dylan**
*Desire*
Columbia, 1975

Photo: Ken Regan

**John Phillips**
*Warlok*
Dunhill, 1970

Design: Tom Gundelfinger

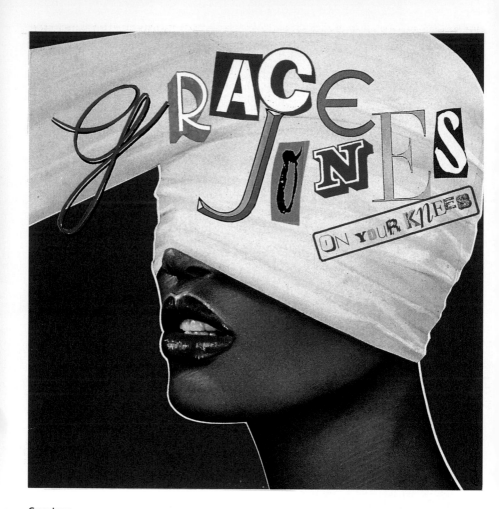

**Grace Jones**
*On Your Knees*
Island, 1979

Design: Richard Bevistein

PROMOTIONAL
COPY
NOT FOR SALE

**King Crimson**
*In The Court Of The Crimson King*
Atlantic, 1969

Design: Barry Godber
*Courtesy Atlantic Recording Corp.*

**Joni Mitchell**
*Don Juan's Reckless Daughter*
Asylum, 1977

Design: Joni Mitchell
Art Direction: Glen Christensen
Photo: Norman Seef
*Courtesy Elektra Entertainment Group*

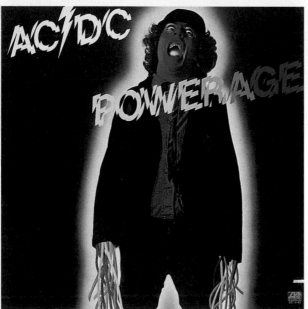

**AC/DC**
*Powerage*
Atlantic, 1978

Art Direction: Bob Defrin
Photo: Jim Houghton
*Courtesy Atlantic Recording Corp.*

**Captain Beefheart & His Magic Band**
*Trout Mask Replica*
Warner Bros., 1977

Design: Carl Schenkel
Photo: Ed Caraeff/Carl Schenkel

**Lucifer's Friend**
*Lucifer's Friend*
Billingsgate, 1973

Design: Juligan Studio

**Neil Young**
*After The Gold Rush*
Reprise, 1970

Art Direction: Gary Burden
Photo: Joel Bernstein

**Graham Parker And The Rumour**
*The Parkerilla*
Mercury, 1978

Photo: Frances Newman

**Al Kooper**
*Act Like Nothing's Wrong*
United Artists, 1976

Design & Photo: Norman Seef
Concept: Al Kooper

**Robert Palmer**
*Pressure Drop*
Island, 1975

Design: Graham Hughes

**The Creation**
*The Creation '66–'67*
Charisma Perspective, 1973

Design: Hipgnosis

**Wishbone Ash**
*New England*
Atlantic, 1976

Design: Hipgnosis
*Courtesy Atlantic Recording Corp.*

**Keith Moon**
*Two Sides Of The Moon*
MCA, 1975

Art Direction: George Okaki
Concept: Gary Stromberg/
Bruce Reiley Skip/John & Keith
Photo: Jim McCrary/
Robert Failla Rainbow Photography

**Wishbone Ash**
*There's The Rub*
MCA, 1974

Design: Hipgnosis

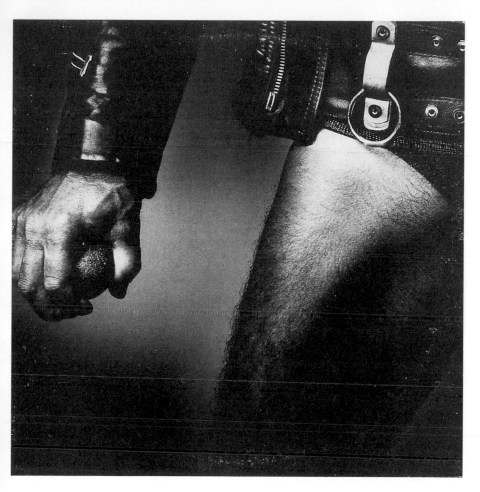

**Accept**
*Balls To The Walls*
Portrait, 1984

Design: Jean Lessenich
Idea: Deaffy & A. Janowiak
Photo: Dieter Eikelpoth

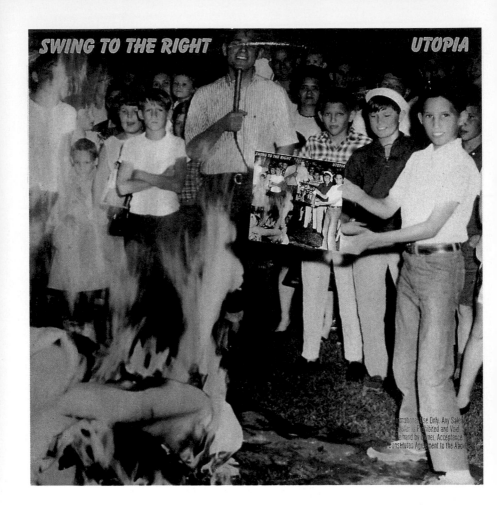

**Utopia**
*Swing To The Right*
Bearsville, 1982

Design: Lisa Amowitz/The Creative Directors,
Inc., New York City
Art Direction: John Wagman
*Courtesy Atlantic Recording Corp.*

**Jefferson Airplane**
*Crown Of Creation*
RCA Victor, 1968

Design: J. Van Hammersveld
Photo: Hiro

**Nazareth**
*Malice In Wonderland*
A&M, 1980

Design: Amy Nagasawa
Photo: Bernard Faucon

**Lynyrd Skynyrd**
*Street Survivors*
MCA, 1977

Art Direction: George Osaki
Concept & Photo: David Alexander

**Lynyrd Skynyrd**
*Street Survivors*
MCA, 1977

Art Direction: George Osaki
Concept & Photo: David Alexander

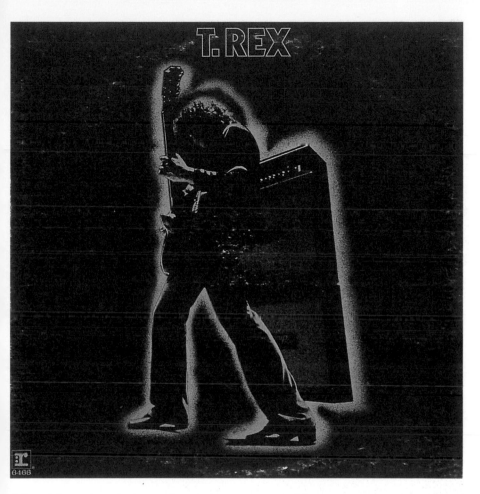

(left page) Due to the tragic plane crash, in which two group members died, the fire cover was changed.

(links) Nach dem tragischen Flugzeugabsturz, bei dem zwei Gruppenmitglieder ums Leben kamen, wurde das Cover mit dem Feuer abgeändert.

(A gauche) En raison du tragique accident d'avion au cours duquel deux membres du groupe trouvèrent la mort, la pochette sur loquelle du feu est représenté, fut changée.

**T. Rex**
*Electric Warrior*
Warner Bros., 1971

Design: Hipgnosis
Photo: Spud Murphy

**Pink Floyd**
*Wish You Were Here*
Columbia, 1975

Design: Hipgnosis

**Santana**
*Abraxas*
Columbia, 1970

Design: Mati
Photo: Marian Schmidt

**Yes**
*Relayer*
Atlantic, 1974

Design: Roger Dean
© Roger Dean
*Courtesy Atlantic Recording Corp.*

**Glider**
*Glider*
United Artists, 1977

Art Direction:
Herbert Worthington, III
Painting: Annie Neilson

**Osibisa**
*Osibisa*
Decca, 1971

Design: Roger Dean
© Roger Dean

**Rush**
*Hemispheres*
Mercury, 1978

Art Direction:
Hugh Syme & Bob King
Graphics: Hugh Syme
Photo: Fin Costello

**Average White Band**
*The Best Of Average White Band*
RCA, 1979

Design: Laurence Hoadley
Photos: Duffy

**Yes**
*Going For The One*
Atlantic, 1977

Design: Hipgnosis
*Courtesy Atlantic Recording Corp.*

**Deep Purple**
*Stormbringer*
Warner Bros., 1974

Design: John Cabalka
Art Direction: Ed Thrasher
Illustration: Joe Garnett

**Meat Loaf**
*Bat Out Of Hell*
Epic, 1977

Design: Ed Lee
Concept: Jim Steinmen
Illustration: Richard Corben

**The Graeme Edge Band Featuring Adrian Gurvitz**
*Kick Off Your Muddy Boots*
Threshold, 1975

Design: Petagno III

**Firefall**
*Firefall*
Atlantic, 1976

Concept: Jock Bartley
Artwork: Ralph Wernli
Art Direction: Bob Defrin
*Courtesy Atlantic Recording Corp.*

**Led Zeppelin**
*Houses Of The Holy*
Atlantic, 1973

Design: Hipgnosis
*Courtesy Atlantic Recording Corp.*

**Robert Palmer**
*Sneakin' Sally Through The Alley*
Island, 1974

Design: Graham Hughes

**Rocky Burnette**
*The Son Of Rock And Roll*
EMI, 1979

Design: Cream
Photo: H. W. Worthington, III

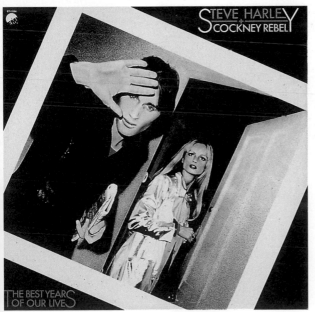

**Steve Harley / Cockney Rebel**
*The Best Years Of Our Lives*
EMI, 1975

Design: Mick Rock

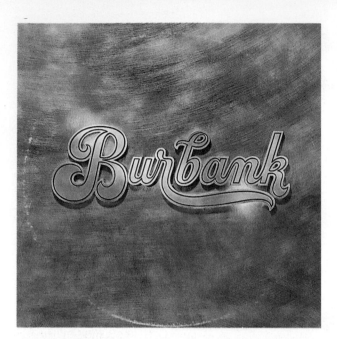

**Various Artists**
*Burbank*
Warner Bros., 1972

Art Direction: Ed Thrasher

**Commodores**
*Commodores*
Motown, 1977

Design: Stan Martin/OV.
Illustration: Tom Nikosey

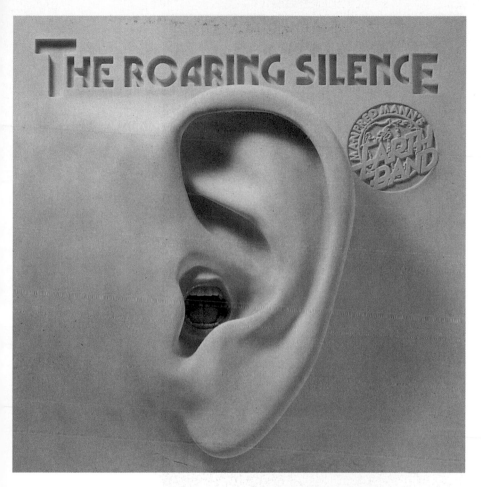

**Manfred Mann's Earth Band**
*The Roaring Silence*
Warner Bros., 1976

Design: Shirtsleeve Studios

**Chicago**
*Chicago X*
Columbia, 1976

Design: John Berg
Photo: Columbia Records
Photo Studio

**Chicago**
*Chicago 13*
Columbia, 1979

Design: Tony Lane
Painting: Gary Meyer

**Chicago**
*Chicago XIV*
Columbia, 1980

Design: John Berg/Tony Lane

**Chicago**
*Chicago*
Columbia, 1970

Design: John Berg
Artwork: Nick Fasciano

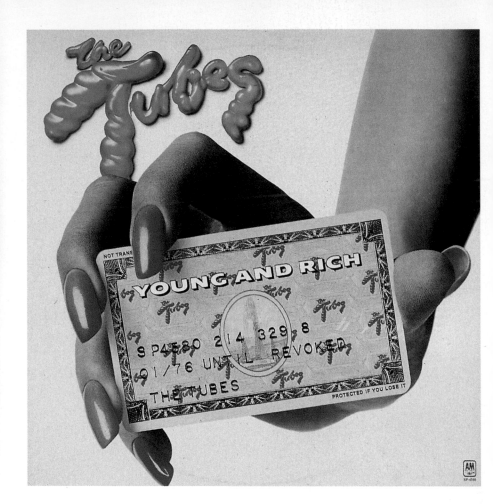

**The Tubes**
*Young And Rich*
A&M, 1976

Design: Michael Cotton/
Prairie Prince
Photo: Harry Mittman

**The Tubes**
*The Tubes*
A&M, 1975

Design: M. Cotton & P. Prince
Art Direction: Roland Young
Photo: Ian Patrick

**Heat Wave**
*Too Hot To Handle*
Epic, 1977

Design: Paula Scherr
Illustration: Robert Grossman

**The James Montgomery Band**
*The James Montgomery Band*
Island, 1976

Design: Mike Fink/Rod Dyer, Inc.
Illustration: Mick Haggerty

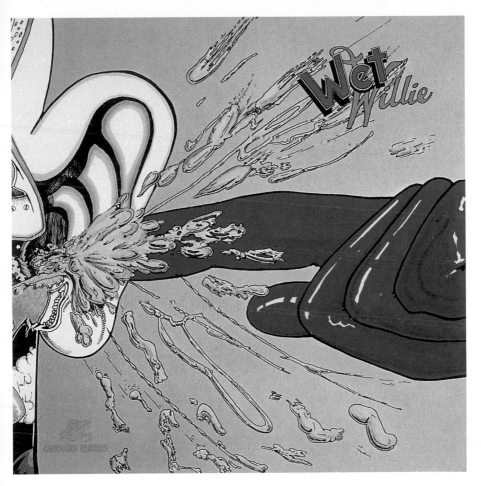

**Wet Willie**
*Wet Willlie*
Capricorn, 1970s

Design: Athens Art Co-op/Wonder Graphics,
Athens (Georgia)

Lent for Promotional Use Only. Any Sale or
Unauthorized Transfer is Prohibited and Void. Subject
to Return Upon Demand by Owner. Acceptance of This
Record Constitutes Agreement to the Above.

**Chicago**
*Chicago 16*
Full Moon/Warner Bros., 1982

Design: Kosh/Ron Larsen

**Zephyr**
*Going Back To Colorado*
Warner Bros., 1971

Art Direction: Ed Thrasher

**Gloria Gaynor**
*Gloria Gaynor's Park Avenue South*
Polydor, 1978

Design: Basil Pao/AGI
Cover Art: Christian Piper

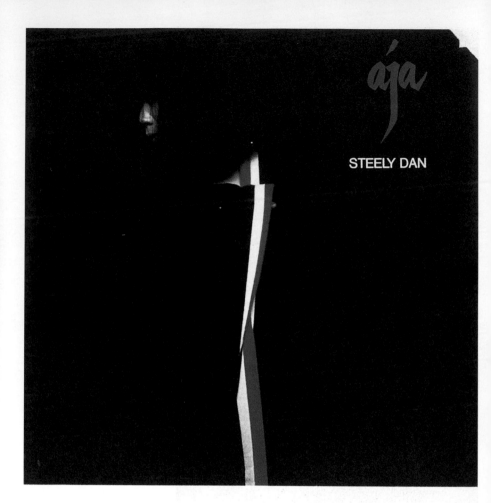

**Steely Dan**
*Aja*
ABC, 1977

Design: Patricia Matsui & Geoff Western
Art Direction: Oz Studio
Photo: Hideki Fujii

**The Who**
*Tommy*
Decca, 1969

Design: Mike McInnerney

**The London Symphony Orchestra**
*Tommy*
Ode, 1972

Design: Wilkes & Braun, Inc.

**Grand Funk Railroad**
*E Pluribus Funk*
EMI, 1972

Design: Craig Braun, Inc.
Concept: Terry Knight

**The Police**
*Roxanne* (Picture Disc)
A&M, 1978

Design: Unknown

**The Police**
*Don't Stand So Close To Me / De Do Do Do, De Da Da Da* (Picture Disc)
A&M, 1981

Design: Unknown

**Various Artists**
*No Wave... To Go* (Picture Disc)
A&M, 1978

Design: Unknown

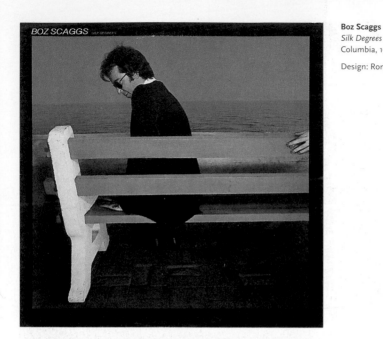

**Boz Scaggs**
*Silk Degrees*
Columbia, 1976

Design: Ron Coro/Nancy Donald

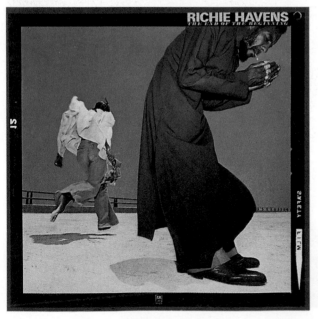

**Richie Havens**
*The End Of The Beginning*
A&M, 1976

Design: Junie Osaki
Art Direction: Roland Young
Photo: Moshe Brakhe

**Fabulous Poodles**
*Mirror Stars*
Epic, 1978

Design: Hipgnosis

**Joan Edwards And The Vogue Recording
Orchestra**
*Go West, Young Man, Go West!* (Picture Disc)
Vogue, 1940s

Design: Unknown

The picture disc was actually introduced in the forties as these two examples show. The seventies and eighties found many records released on colored vinyl or with full picture discs.

Die Picturedisk wurde, wie diese beiden Beispiele belegen, bereits in den vierziger Jahren eingeführt. In den siebziger und achtziger Jahren erschienen viele Platten aus farbigem Vinyl oder als regelrechte Bildscheiben.

Comme en témoignent ces deux exemples, c'est dans les années quarante qu'apparut le picture-disc. Dans les années soixante-dix et quatre-vingts, on pressa beaucoup de disques dans des vinyles de couleur ou avec des images.

**Art Kassel And His Orchestra**
*Sweetheart* (Picture Disc)
Vogue, 1940s

Design: Unknown

**Various Artists**
*Burbank's Finest 100% All Meat*
Warner Bros., 1975

Design: Ed Thrasher/John & Barbara
Casado/Jack Sckar

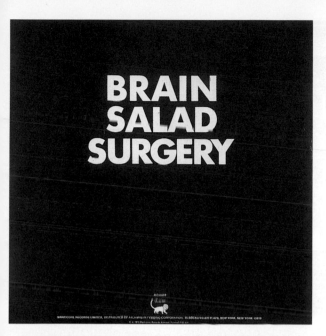

**Emerson, Lake & Palmer**
*Brain Salad Surgery*
Manticore, 1973

Design: Fabio Nicoli Associates

**Bad Company**
*Run With The Pack*
Swan Song, 1976

Design: Kosh/AGI
*Courtesy Atlantic Recording Corp.*

**Family**
*Bandstand*
United Artists, 1972

Design: Unknown

**Traffic**
*The Low Spark Of High Heeled Boys*
Island, 1971

Design: Tony Wright

**Traffic**
*Shoot Out At The Fantasy Factory*
Island, 1973

Illustration: Tony Wright

**Squeeze**
*Squeeze*
A&M, 1979

Design: Chuck Beeson
Concept: Jeff Ayeroff
Illustration: Cindy Marsh
Photo: Mark Hanauer

**Raspberries**
*Side 3*
Capitol/EMI, 1973

Design: Rod Dyer
Art Direction: John Hoernle
Photo: Bob Gruen/Leandro Correa

**Gentle Giant**
*Octopus*
Columbia, 1973

Design: John Berg/Kenny Kneitel
Concept: John Berg
Artwork: Fluid Drive
Illustration: Charles White III
Lettering: Michael Doret

**Alice Cooper**
*School's Out*
Warner Bros., 1972

Design: Wilkes & Braun, Inc.
Concept: Sound Packing Corp.

**Led Zeppelin**
*Physical Graffiti*
Swan Song, 1978

Design & Concept: AGI Mike Doud,
London/Peter Corriston, New York
*Courtesy Atlantic Recording Corp.*

**John Cale**
*The Academy In Peril*
Warner Bros., 1972

Design: Andy Warhol
Photos: Ed Thrasher

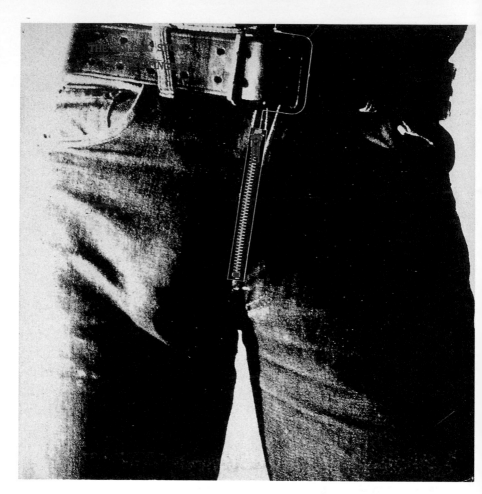

**The Rolling Stones**
*Sticky Fingers*
Rolling Stones, 1971

Design: Craig Braun, Inc.
Concept & Photo: Andy Warhol

**The Rolling Stones**
*Some Girls*
Rolling Stones, 1978

Design: Peter Corriston

chic cheer    i want your love
le freak      at last i am free
savoir faire  sometimes you win
happy man   (funny) bone

**Chic**
*C'est Chic*
Atlantic, 1978

Art Direction: Bob Defrin
Photo: Joel Brodsky
*Courtesy Atlantic Recording Corp.*

**Detroit Emeralds**
*I'm In Love With You*
Westbound, 1973

Art Direction: David Krieger
Photo: Joel Brodsky
*Courtesy Atlantic Recording Corp.*

**Harold Melvin & The Blue Notes**
*Harold Melvin & The Blue Notes*
Philadelphia International, 1972

Photo: Don Hunstein

**Harold Melvin & The Blue Notes**
*I Miss You*
Philadelphia International, 1972

Photos: Steinbicker/Houghton, Inc.

**The Doors**
*Strange Days*
Elektra, 1967

Concept & Art Direction: William S. Harvey
Photo: Joel Brodsky
*Courtesy Elektra Entertainment Group*

**Grand Funk Railroad**
*Shinin' On*
Capitol, 1974

Design: Andrew Cavaliere/Lynn
Goldsmith
Art Direction: Lynn Goldsmith
Cover Art: Neil Adams/Walt
Simonson for Shorewood Graphics

**The Soft Machine**
*The Soft Machine*
Probe, 1968

Design: Brian Goto/Eli Aliman/
Henry Epstein

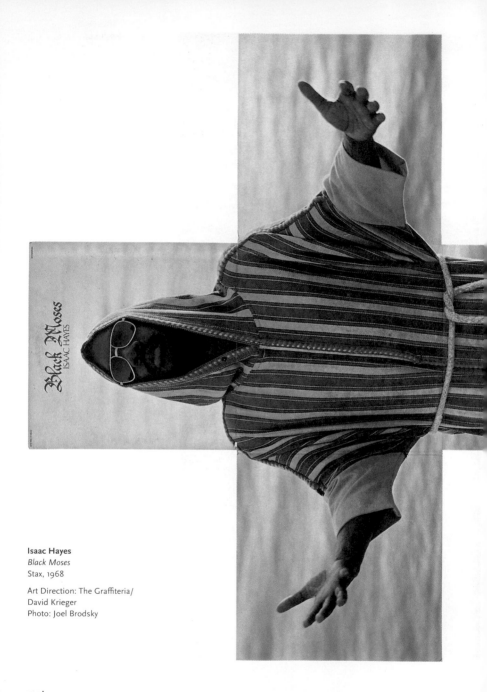

**Isaac Hayes**
*Black Moses*
Stax, 1968

Art Direction: The Graffiteria/
David Krieger
Photo: Joel Brodsky

**Peter Brown**
*Do You Wanna Get Funky With Me?*
Drive, 1977

Design: Peter Brown/Henry Stone/
Cory Wade
Photo: Peter Brown

**Freda Payne**
*Out Of Payne Comes Love*
ABC, 1975

Design: Earl R. Klasky
Photo: Antonin Kratochvil

**Joan Armatrading**
*Back To The Night*
A&M, 1975

Art Direction: Favio Nicoli
Photo: Clive Arrowsmith

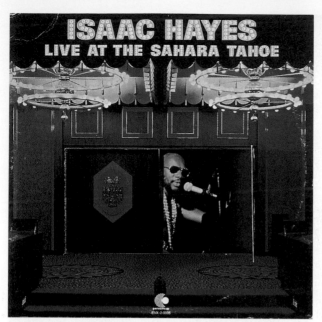

**Isaac Hayes**
*Isaac Hayes Live At The Sahara Tahoe*
Stax, 1973

Design: Ron Gordon/David Hogan

**Marvin Gaye**
*What's Going On*
Tamla, 1971

Art Direction: Curtis McNair
Photo: Hendin

**Al Green**
*I'm Still In Love With You*
Hi, 1972

Design: Unknown

**Maxine Nightingale**
*Right Back Where We Started From*
United Artists, 1976

Concept: Pierre Tubbs/Derek Richards
Art Direction: Dave Murphy
Photo: Derek

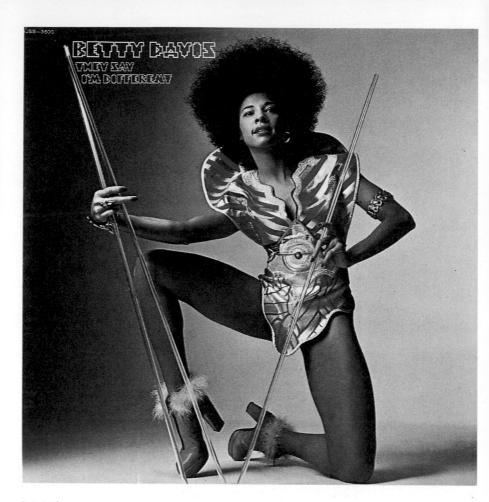

**Betty Davis**
*They Say I'm Different*
Just Sunshine, 1973

Design: Ron Levine
Art Direction: Bill Levy
Photo: Mel Dixon

**Betty Wright**
*Hard To Stop*
Atlantic, 1973

Design: Loring Eutemey
Photo: Joel Brodsky
*Courtesy Atlantic Recording Corp.*

**P. P. Arnold**
*Kafunta*
Immediate, 1970s

Design: Loog At The House
Of Immediate
Photo: Gered Mankowitz

**Ike & Tina Turner**
*Outta Season*
Blue Thumb, 1969

Design & Photo: Amos & Andy

**The Doors**
*Morrison Hotel*
Elektra, 1970

Design: Gary Burden
Photo: Henry Diltz
*Courtesy Elektra Entertainment Group*

**The Eagles**
*Hotel California*
Asylum, 1976

Photo: David Alexander
*Courtesy Elektra Entertainment Group*

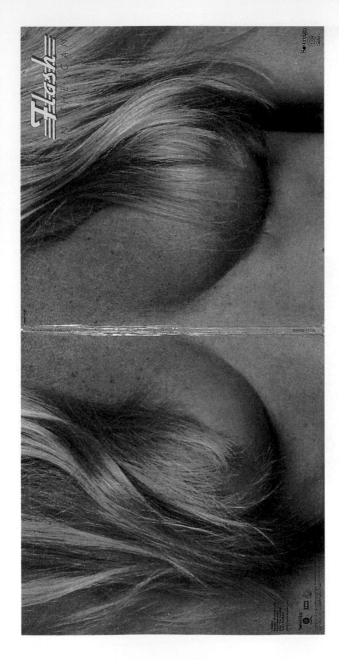

**Flash**
*In The Can*
Capitol, 1972

Design: John Hoernle
Photo: Rick Rankin

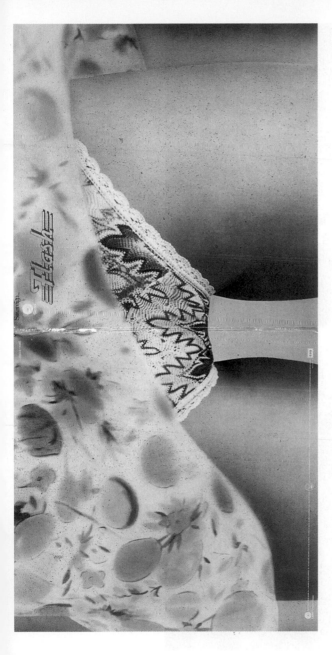

**Flash**
*Flash*
Capitol, 1972

Design: Unknown

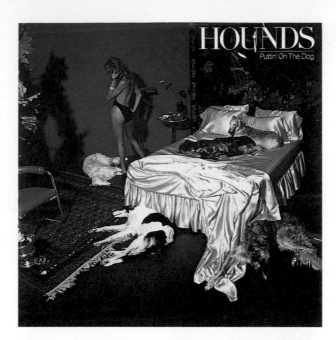

**The Hounds**
*Puttin' On The Dog*
Columbia, 1975

Photo: McGowan/Coder

**Silverhead**
*16 And Savaged*
MCA, 1973

Design: Chelita Secunda
Photo: Keith Morris

**Sad Cafe**
*Fanx Ta–Ra*
RCA, 1977

Design: Graves Aslett Associates,
Ltd., London
Concept: Carole Lisberg
Photo: Gered Mankowitz

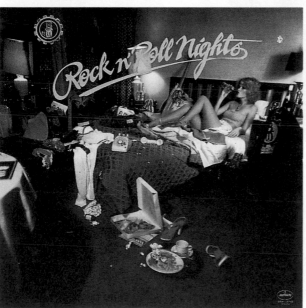

**Bachman Turner Overdrive**
*Rock 'n' Roll Nights*
Mercury, 1979

Concept: BTO
Art Direction & Photo:
James O'Mara

**Dennis Coffey**
*Finger Lickin' Good*
Westbound, 1975

Photo: Joel Brodsky
*Courtesy Atlantic Recording Corp.*

The album cover of Walter Egan (right) created quite a controversy with the obviously under-age girls depicted.

Das Cover von Walter Egan (rechts) war wegen der offensichtlich minderjährigen Mädchen auf dem Foto heftig umstritten.

La pochette d'album de Walter Egan (à droîte) suscita une controverse en raison du trop jeune âge des filles représentées.

**Walter Egan**
*Fundamental Roll*
Columbia, 1977

Design: Ria Lewerke
Photo: Moshe Brakha

**Queen**
*Queen Jazz*
Elektra, 1978

Design: Cream
Concept: Queen
*Courtesy Elektra Entertainment Group*

To illustrate their hit *Fat Bottomed Girls*, Queen included this insert (right) in the album.

Um auf ihren Hit *Fat Bottomed Girls* aufmerksam zu machen, versah Queen das Album mit dieser Beilage (rechts).

Pour illustrer leur hit *Fat Bottomed Girls*, Queen ajouta ce dépliant (à droîte) dans l'album.

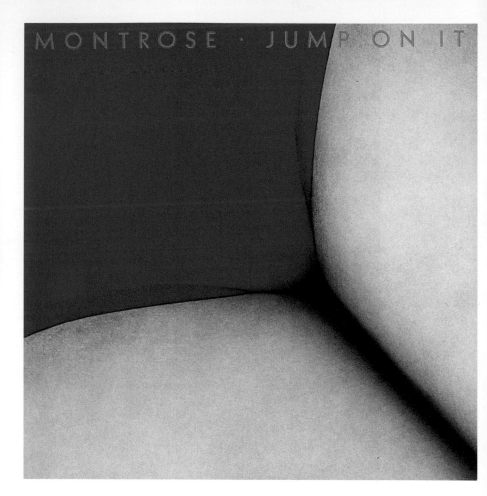

**Montrose**
*Jump On It*
Warner Bros., 1976

Design: Hipgnosis

**Jorge Santana**
*Jorge Santana*
Tomato, 1978

Design: Milton Glaser, Inc.
Painting: John Kacere

**UFO**
*Force It*
Chrysalis, 1975

Design: Hipgnosis

**Godley & Creme**
*Freeze Frame*
Polydor, 1979

Design: Hipgnosis

**Foreigner**
*Head Games*
Atlantic, 1979

Art Direction: Sandi Young
Photo: Chris Callis
*Courtesy Atlantic Recording Corp.*

**Chris De Burgh**
*At The End Of A Perfect Day*
A&M, 1977

Design: Nick Marshall
Art Direction: Fabio Nicolı
Photo: Roger Stowell

**Tom Waits**
*Small Change*
Asylum, 1976

Photo: Joel Brodsky
*Courtesy Elektra Entertainment Group*

**The Scorpions**
*Lovedrive*
Mercury, 1979

Design: Hipgnosis

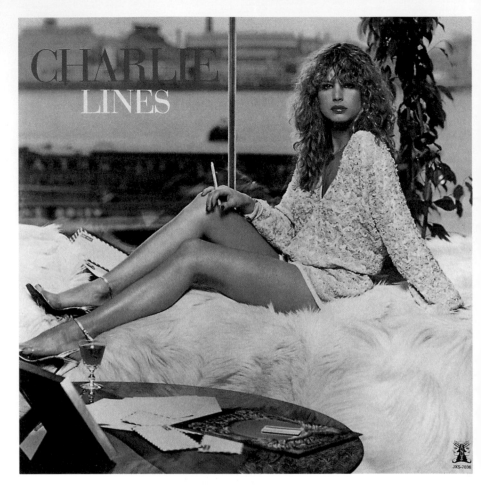

**Charlie**
*Lines*
Janus, 1978

Design: Terry Thomas
Photo: David Darling

Although cocaine is no longer P.C., pharmaceutically correct, note what the model is holding, the mirror and the album title itself.

Kokain ist zwar längst keine Modedroge mehr, aber man beachte, was die Frau in der Hand hält, den Spiegel und den Titel des Albums.

Quoique la cocaïne ne soit plus P.C., pharmaceutiquement correct, remarquez ce que tient le mannequin, le miroir et le titre de l'album lui-même.

**Fresh**
*Feelin' Fresh*
Prodigal, 1978

Design: Wriston Jones
Photo: Oliver Ferrand

**Charlie**
*No Second Chance*
Janus, 1977

Design & Photo: Richard Dilello

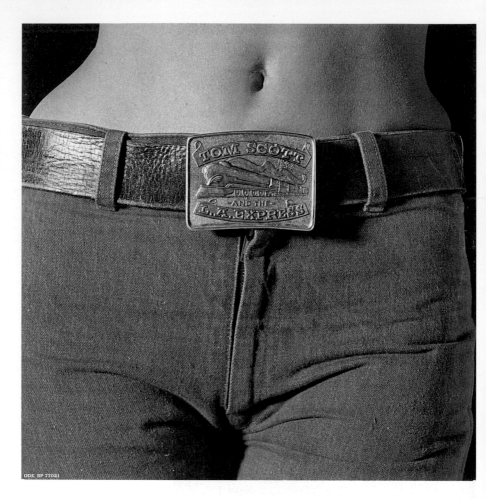

**Tom Scott And The L.A. Express**
*Tom Scott And The L.A. Express*
A&M/Ode, 1974

Graphic Design: Chuck Beeson
Patch & Buckle: Joe Garnett
Photo: Jim McCrary

**Adrian Gurvitz**
*The Way I Feel*
Jet, 1979

Art Direction: Paul Welch/
Acrobat Design
Photo: Keith Ramsden

**Love And Kisses**
*Love And Kisses*
Casablanca, 1977

Photo: Alan Murano

**Roxy Music**
*Country Life*
(Originalcover)
Atco, 1974

Design: Nicholas Deville
Art Direction: Bryan Ferry
Photo: Eric Bowman

**Roxy Music**
*Country Life*
(2. Cover)
Atco, 1974

Design: Nicholas Deville
Art Direction: Bryan Ferry
Photo: Eric Bowman
*Courtesy Atlantic Recording Corp.*

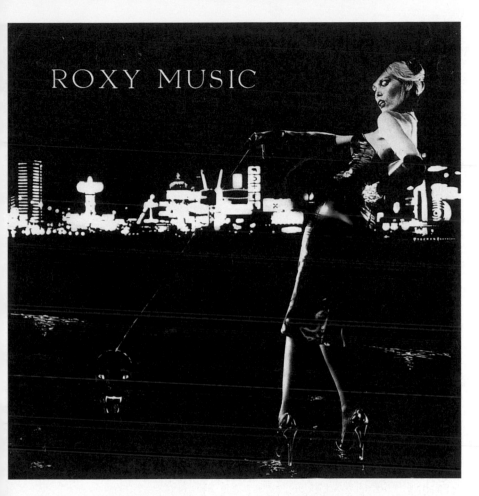

The original cover of Country Life was banned. The subsequent, safe cover is the most complete cover-up noted in rock.

Das Originalcover von Country Life wurde verboten. Das anschließende Cover ist die radikalste Entschärfung eines „anstößigen" Motivs in der Geschichte der Rockmusik.

La pochette originale de Country Life fut interdite. La suivante, pochette de sûreté, est l'emballage le plus complet jamais rencontré dans le rock.

**Roxy Music**
*For Your Pleasure*
Island, 1973

Art Direction: Nicholas DeVille
Artwork: C. C. S.
Photo: Karl Stoeker

**Roxy Music**
*Stranded*
Atco, 1974

Design: Nicholas DeVille
Concept: Bryan Ferry/Bailey/Jennings/Hart
Photo: Karl Stoeker
*Courtesy Atlantic Recording Corp.*

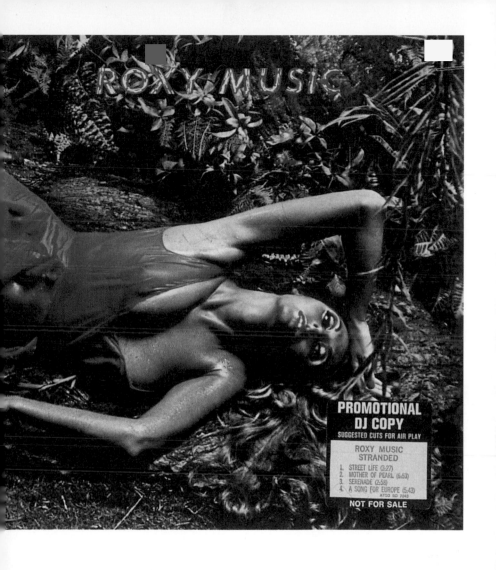

ROXY MUSIC

PROMOTIONAL
DJ COPY
SUGGESTED CUTS FOR AIR PLAY

ROXY MUSIC
STRANDED

1. STREET LIFE (3:27)
2. MOTHER OF PEARL (6:53)
3. SERENADE (2:58)
4. A SONG FOR EUROPE (5:43)
ATCO SD 7045

NOT FOR SALE

**Carole Bayer Sager**
*...Too*
Elektra, 1978

Design: Ron Coro
Photo: Ethan Russell
*Courtesy Elektra Entertainment Group*

**Elkie Brooks**
*Two Days Away*
A&M, 1977

Design: Fabio Nicoli

**Carly Simon**
*Boys In The Trees*
Elektra, 1978

Art Direction: Johnny Lee &
Tony Lane
Photo: Deborah Turberville
*Courtesy Elektra Entertainment Group*

**Cher**
*Take Me Home*
Casablanca, 1979

Photo: Barry Levine

PROMOTIONAL
COPY
NOT FOR SALE

**Elkie Brooks**
*Rich Man's Woman*
A&M, 1975

Design: June Osaki
Art Direction: Roland Young
Lettering: Stan Evenson
Photo: Chris Micoine

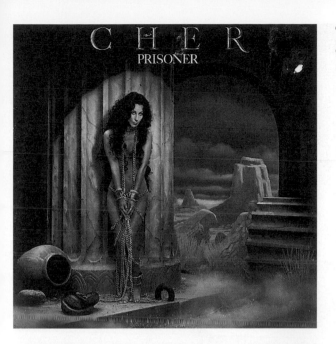

**Cher**
*Prisoner*
Casablanca, 1979

Photo: Harry Langdon

**Rita Coolidge**
*The Lady's Not For Sale*
A&M, 1972

Design: Chuck Beeson
Art Direction: Roland Young
Photo: Bob Jenkins

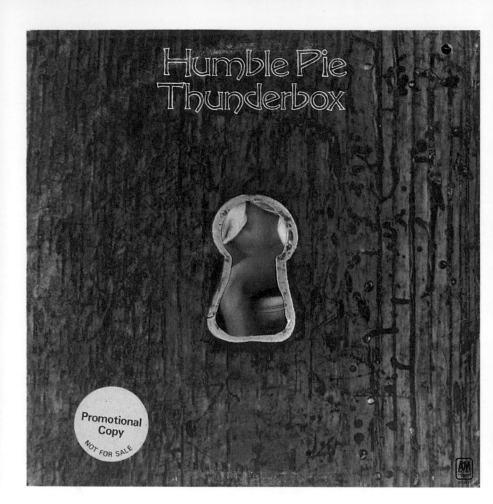

**Humble Pie**
*Thunderbox*
A&M, 1974

Design: Hipgnosis

This group is more famous for the pie on the cover than any music they might have made. With all the attention this cover got, the record sold poorly.

Diese Gruppe ist eher wegen des Kuchens auf dem Cover bekannt als wegen ihrer Musik. Trotz der großen Aufmerksamkeit, die dem Cover zuteil wurde, verkaufte sich das Album schlecht.

Ce groupe est plus célèbre pour la tourte sur la pochette que pour n'importe lequel de leurs morceaux. Malgré le succès de la pochette, ce disque se vendit plutôt mal.

**Mom's Apple Pie**
*Modern Romance*
Brown Bag, 1972

Design: Nick Caruso

**Linda Ronstadt**
*Silk Purse*
Capitol, 1970

Design: Unknown

**Cheryl Ladd**
*Dance Forever*
Capitol, 1979

Art Direction: Roy Kohara
Photo: Harry Langdon

**Lisa Hartman**
*Hold On*
Kirschner, 1979

Design: Rod Dyer, Inc.
Photo: Francesco Scavullo

**Linda Ronstadt**
*Hasten Down The Wind*
Asylum, 1972

Design: Kosh
Photo: Ethan A. Russell/Jim Shea
*Courtesy Elektra Entertainment Group*

**Carly Simon**
*Playing Possum*
Elektra, 1975

Design & Photo: Norman Seef
Art Direction: Glen Christenson
*Courtesy Elektra Entertainment Group*

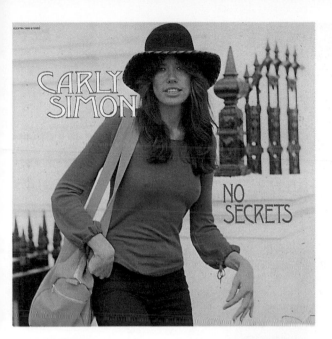

**Carly Simon**
*No Secrets*
Elektra, 1972

Design: Unknown
*Courtesy Elektra Entertainment Group*

**Linda Ronstadt**
*Living In The USA*
Asylum, 1978

Design: Kosh
Photo: Jim Shea
*Courtesy Elektra Entertainment Group*

**Labelle**
*Chameleon*
Epic, 1976

Design: Ed Lee/Andy Engel
Photo: Lock Huey

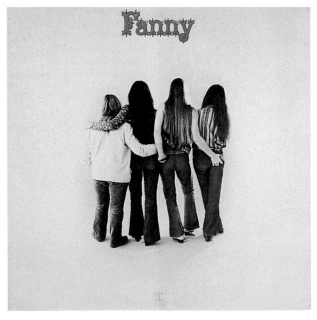

**Fanny**
*Fanny*
Reprise, 1970

Photo: Don Lewis

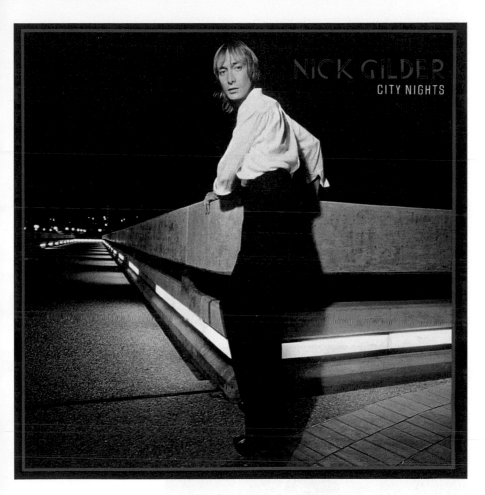

**Nick Gilder**
*City Nights*
Chrysalis, 1978

Design: David Allen
Concept & Photo: Jules Bates

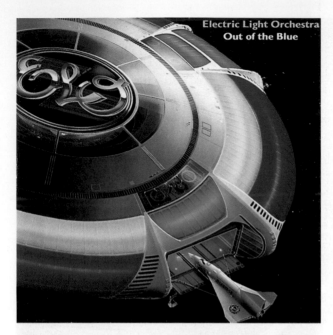

**Electric Light Orchestra**
*Out Of The Blue*
Jet, 1977

Design: Ria Lewerke with Kosh
Illustration: Shusei Nagaoka

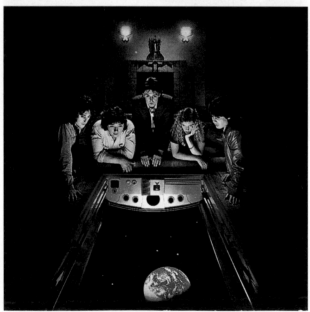

**Wings**
*Back To The Egg*
MPL, 1979

Photo: John Shaw

**UFO**
*Phenomenon*
Chrysalis, 1974

Design: Hipgnosis
Painting: Maurice Tate

**Stray**
*Stand Up And Be Counted*
Pye, 1975

Design: Unknown

**McGuinness Flint**
*McGuinness Flint*
Capitol, 1971

Design: John Kosh
Photo: Ethan A. Russell

**Widow**
*Gone Too Far*
Albatros, 1985

Design: Ken Kinnear &
Rollin Thomas
Photo: Bruce Surber

**Grand Funk Railroad**
*Born To Die*
Capitol, 1975

Painting: Jean-Paul Goude
Art Direction & Photo:
Lynn Goldsmith

**Screamin' Jay Hawkins**
*...What That Is!*
Philips, 1969

Graphics: Greg Irons
Photo: Dunstan Pereira

**Phil Ochs**
*Rehearsals For Retirement*
A&M, 1968

Art Direction & Photo: Tom Wilkes

**Kool And The Gang**
*Ladies' Night*
Delite, 1979

Design: Joe Kotleba
Art Direction: M. Doud
Photo: Raul Vega

**Amii Stewart**
*Knock On Wood*
Ariola, 1979

Design: Cooke-Key
Photo: Brian Aris

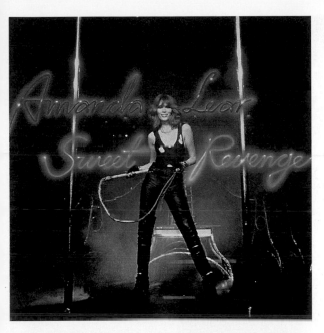

**Amanda Lear**
*Sweet Revenge*
Epic, 1978

Design: Ariola-Eurodisc Studios
Photo: Denis Taranto

**Donna Summer**
*Bad Girls*
Casablanca, 1979

Design: Steve Lumel/
David Fleming/Gribbett
Concept: Donna Summer
Photo: Harry Langdon

**Argent**
*In Deep*
Epic, 1973

Design: Hipgnosis

**Trickster**
*Back To Zero*
Jet, 1979

Art Direction: Martin Poole
Photo: Fin Costello

**Sun**
*Sunburn*
Capitol, 1978

Design: Art Sims
Art Direction: Roy Kohara
Photo: Olivier Ferrand

**Kiss**
*Peter Criss*
Casablanca, 1978

Design: Howard Marks Advertising
Painting: Eraldo Carugati

**Kiss**
*Ace Frehley*
Casablanca, 1978

Design: Howard Marks Advertising
Painting: Eraldo Carugati

**Kiss**
*Gene Simmons*
Casablanca, 1978

Design: Howard Marks Advertising
Painting: Eraldo Carugati

**Kiss**
*Paul Stanley*
Casablanca, 1978

Design: Howard Marks Advertising
Painting: Eraldo Carugati

**Motels**
*Motels*
Capitol, 1979

Art Direction: Roy Kohara/Henry Marquez
Photo: Elliot Gilbert

**Strawbs**
*Deadlines*
A&M, 1978

Design: Hipgnosis

**Supertramp**
*Breakfast In America*
A&M, 1979

Design: Mickey Haggerty
Concept & Art Direction: Mike Doud

**Al Kooper**
*I Stand Alone*
Columbia, 1969

Design: Bob Cato/John Berg/
Al Kooper
"Liberty" by: Sandy Speiser/
Don Hunstein

**Various Artists**
*The People's Record*
Warner Bros., 1976

Art Direction: Michael Hollyfield
Illustration: Ed Scarsbrick

**Sparks**
*Propaganda*
Island, 1974

Design: Monty Coles

**Sparks**
*Indiscreet*
Island, 1975

Photo: Richard Creamer

**Sparks**
*Kimono My House*
Island, 1974

Art Direction: Nicholas DeVille
Concept: Ron Mael/
Nicholas DeVille
Photo: Karl Stoeker

**Supertramp**
*Crisis? What Crisis?*
A&M, 1975

Design: Fabio Nicoli/Paul Wakefield/
Dick Ward
From an Idea by Richard Davies

**Flash And The Pan**
*Flash And The Pan*
Epic, 1979

Design: Janet Perr/Gene Greif
Photo: Ken Ambrose

**Space**
*Deliverance*
Vogue, 1977

Design: Hipgnosis

**10 CC**
*Deceptive Bends*
Mercury, 1977

Design: Hipgnosis

**Black Sabbath**
*Never Say Die!*
Warner Bros., 1978

Design: Hipgnosis

**10 CC**
*How Dare You!*
Mercury, 1976

Design: Hipgnosis with George
Hardie
Photo: Hipgnosis with Howard
Bartop

**Sex Pistols**
*The Mini Album*
Chaos, 1976

Artwork: Satoshi Smash Suginaka

**The Clash**
*The Clash*
CBS, 1977

Photo: Kate Simon

**Slade**
*Slayed?*
Polydor, 1972

Photo: Gered Mankowitz

**New York Dolls**
*New York Dolls*
Mercury, 1973

Photo: Toshi

**The Ramones**
*Ramones*
Sire, 1976

Photo: Roberta Bayley
Courtesy Punk Magazine

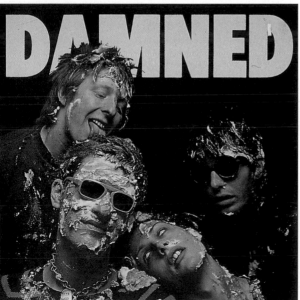

**The Damned**
*Damned, Damned, Damned*
Stiff, 1970s

Design: Big Jobs, Inc.
Courtesy Atlantic Recording Corp.

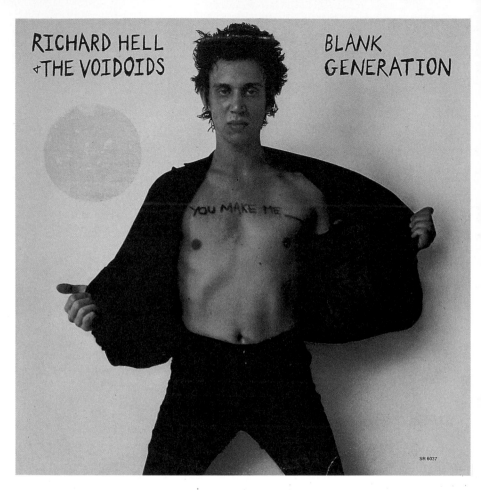

RICHARD HELL
& THE VOIDOIDS

BLANK
GENERATION

SR 6037

**Richard Hell & The Voidoids**
*Blank Generation*
Sire, 1977

Design & Art Direction:
John Gilespie/Richard Hell
Photo: Roberta Bayley

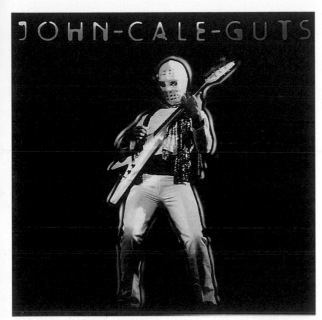

**John Cale**
*Guts*
Island, 1977

Design: Bloomfield/Travis
Art Direction & Photo: Michael Beal

**Elvis Costello**
*My Aim Is True*
Columbia, 1977

Design: Unknown

**The Jam**
*In The City*
Polydor, 1977

Design: Bill Smith
Photo: Martin Goddard

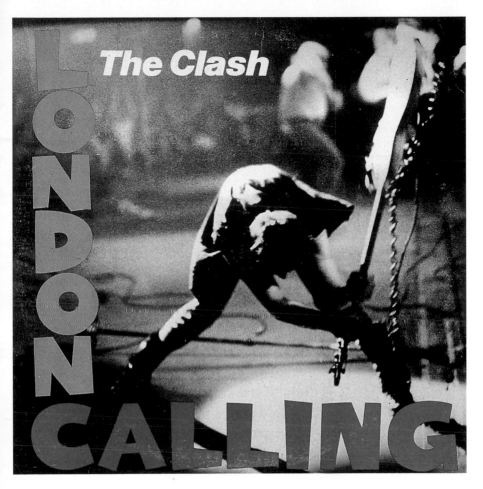

The Clash
*London Calling*
Epic, 1979

Design: Ray Lowry
Photo: Pennie Smith

**The Clash**
*Combat Rock*
Epic, 1982

Design: Unknown

**The Clash**
*Give 'Em Enough Rope*
Epic, 1978

Design: Unknown

**Eddie And The Hotrods**
*Teenage Depression*
Island, 1977

Design: Michael Beal

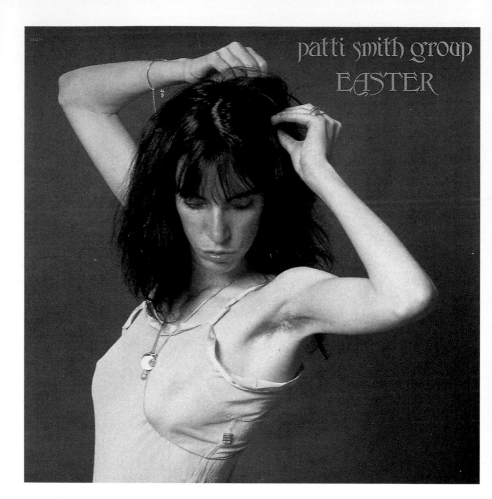

**Patti Smith Group**
*Easter*
Arista, 1978

Design: Unknown

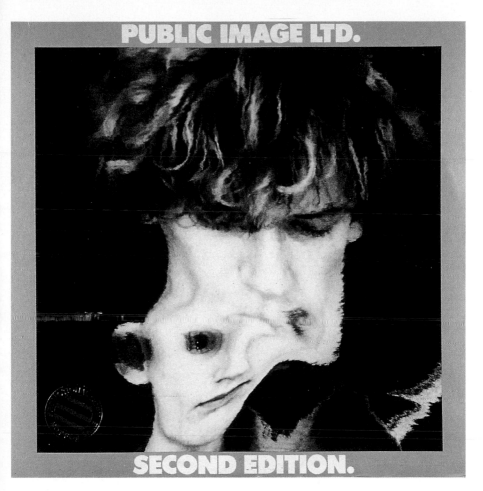

Public Image Ltd.
*Second Edition*
Island, 1979

Photo: Tony McGee

# 1980s–90s

As the eighties began, rock and roll and its faithful followers had reached the second half of their lives. In *My Generation*, The Who sang the lyrics "I hope I die before I get old". Too many rockers lived and died by those lines. In the first three years of the eighties alone, John Lennon, Marvin Gaye, Bob Hite, Bob Marley, John Bonham and Dennis Wilson all died of unnatural causes. Yet rock music, rather then dying or fading away, became bigger than ever.

Part of the reason for the incredible growth of rock was the success of the Sony Walkman cassette machine, which dramatically increased the sound quality and portability of recorded music. In addition, MTV, a total music cable station, was launched in 1981, which brought music videos into homes 24 hours a day. MTV was soon followed by VH-1, an adult music video channel, and TNN, the Nashville video network. Stars could now be made overnight and could just as easily be yesterday's news the following morning. Rather than developing hit acts of their own, the record companies could now buy them fully assembled – batteries included.

The business of music became a billion-dollar industry and needed more megastars to feed the new media machinery. Michael Jackson's

*Thriller* album became the biggest selling album of all time; Madonna sold more records than any other female performer in history; and Whitney Houston had seven consecutive number-one hits, topping The Beatles previous record of six. *Many stars, including Diana Ross and Elton John,* left the record companies that had established them for multi-million-dollar contracts with new labels — only to return to their original labels the same decade, much older, wiser — and richer. The Who, The Doobie Brothers, Yes, The Eagles and Steely Dan all disbanded only to reunite again for another payday.

Perhaps feeling a little guilty about all the money being tossed at them, a number of major music acts started a new trend, charity-rock. Although George Harrison had started the movement with the Bangladesh benefit concert in 1971 , the eighties gave us Band Aid, Farm Aid, Live Aid and the *We Are The World* fund-raising record.

Rock and roll, once anti-establishment, became part of the establishment in its middle age. The biggest rock tours were soon sponsored by beer and soda companies. Eddie Van Halen married Valerie Bertinelli, Ringo Starr married Barbara Bach, Billy Joel married Christie Brinkley and Madonna married Sean Penn. Rock music became so settled down and acceptable that a "Rock and Roll Hall of Fame" was even established in Cleveland. Youthful music movements like rap and hip-hop tried to bring rock back downtown, but most of the multi-millionaire rock stars preferred to stay uptown.

The rebellious punk-rock movement didn't lose its anger but became more musical — with new-wave acts like Graham Parker, Elvis Costello and The Clash. Garage-rock was transformed into grunge rock with Nirvana, Pearl Jam and The Stone Temple Pilots. Reggae not only maintained its popularity but also had a revival with the ska bands Madness and The Specials.

The biggest and most innovative trend in pop music was the development in 1982 of the compact disc. CD sales had expanded enormously by the mid-eighties and, by the end of the decade, the manufacture of vinyl record albums was virtually phased out. Just like the 78 rpm record, the record album became a relic of the past. The room for cover art was reduced from 12 to 5 inches while the price of albums almost doubled. Yet, the public gleefully discarded their record collections and replaced them with CDs. For the first time in rock history, almost everything that had been recorded previously was preserved and reissued. There would be no last waltz.

Anfang der achtziger Jahre hatten der Rock 'n' Roll und seine treuen Anhänger die zweite Lebenshälfte erreicht. In ihrem Song *My Generation* sangen die Who „I hope I die before I get old". Viel zu viele Rockmusiker lebten und starben nach dieser Maxime. Allein zwischen 1980 und 1983 starben John Lennon, Marvin Gaye, Bob Hite, Bob Marley, John Bonham und Dennis Wilson eines unnatürlichen Todes. Aber die Rockmusik war weit davon entfernt, schwächer zu werden oder gar zu sterben, sondern wurde im Gegenteil bedeutender denn je.

Der neuerliche immense Erfolg des Rock war nicht zuletzt dem von Sony entwickelten Walkman zu verdanken, der die Klangqualität enorm verbesserte, und es möglich machte, jederzeit und überall Kassetten abzuspielen. Außerdem wurde 1981 der Musiksender MTV gestartet, der die Menschen zu Hause rund um die Uhr mit Musikvideos versorgte. Kurz darauf folgten VH-1, ein Musikvideosender für Erwachsene, und TNN, die Nashville-Videosendergruppe. Stars konnten nun über Nacht geboren werden und am nächsten Tag schon wieder Schnee von gestern sein. Statt Hits selbst zu entwickeln, konnten die Plattenfirmen sie jetzt fix und fertig kaufen, sozusagen mit eingebauter Batterie.

Die Musikbranche wurde zu einem Milliardengeschäft und brauchte mehr Mega-Stars, um die neue Medienmaschinerie zu füttern. Michael Jacksons *Thriller*-Album wurden zum größten Verkaufsschlager aller Zeiten; Madonna verkaufte mehr Schallplatten als irgendeine andere Popsängerin in der Musikgeschichte, und Whitney Houston landete hintereinander sieben Tophits, womit sie den Rekord der Beatles brach, die es zuvor auf sechs gebracht hatten. Viele Stars, darunter Diana Ross und Elton John verließen ihre Plattenfirmen, die sie berühmt gemacht hatten, und schlossen mit neuen Labels Millionen-Dollar-Verträge ab, nur um noch im selben Jahrzehnt zu ihren ersten Plattenfirmen zurückzukehren – älter, klüger, reicher. The Who, die Doobie Brothers, Yes, The Eagles und Steely Dan lösten sich auf und taten sich dann wieder zusammen, um noch einmal das große Geld zu machen.

Vielleicht, weil sie ob des vielen Geldes, mit dem sie überschüttet wurden, allmählich ein schlechtes Gewissen bekamen, riefen einige Musikstars einen neuen Trend ins Leben: den Benefizrock. George Harrison hatte zwar schon 1971 mit dem Benefizkonzert für Bangladesh ähnliches gemacht, doch erst die achtziger Jahre bescherten uns solche Projekte wie Band Aid, Farm Aid, Live Aid und die Rekordeinnahmen für den Hungerhilfefonds von *We Are The World*.

Der Rock 'n' Roll, einst gegen das Establishment gerichtet, wurde jetzt, in seinen besten Jahren, selbst Teil des Establishments. Die größten Rocktourneen wurden schon bald von Bierbrauereien und Cola-Firmen gesponsert. Eddie Van Halen heiratete Valerie Bertinelli, Ringo Starr heiratete Barbara Bach, Billy Joel heiratete Christie Brinkley und Madonna heiratete Sean Penn. Die Rockmusik hatte sich inzwischen so sehr etabliert, daß in Cleveland sogar eine „Hall of Fame" des Rock 'n' Roll gegründet wurde. Junge Trends wie Rap und Hip Hop versuchten, den Rock zurück in die Innenstädte zu bringen, doch die meisten Rockstars, inzwischen Multimillionäre, blieben lieber in den vornehmen Villenvierteln.

Die rebellische Punk-Rock-Bewegung war zwar zornig wie eh und je, wurde aber durch Vertreter des New Wave wie Graham Parker, Elvis Costello und The Clash musikalischer. Aus dem Garage Rock der Amateur- oder Garagenbands wurde der Grunge-Rock von Gruppen wie Nirvana, Pearl Jam und The Stone Temple Pilots. Reggae war nicht nur nach wie vor populär, sondern erlebte sogar mit den Ska-Bands Madness und The Specials einen neuen Boom.

Der größte und innovativste Schub für die Popmusik kam mit der Entwicklung der Compact Disc im Jahre 1982. Mitte der achtziger Jahre hatte sich die CD auf dem Markt durchgesetzt, und gegen Ende des Jahrzehnts wurde die Herstellung von Vinylschallplatten praktisch eingestellt. Ebenso wie die Schallplatte mit 78 Umdrehungen pro Minute gehörte nun auch die Langspielplatte der Vergangenheit an. Die Fläche für die graphische Gestaltung der Cover reduzierte sich von 30 cm Durchmesser auf knapp 13 cm, während sich der Preis für ein Album fast verdoppelte. Doch die Musikfreunde trennten sich leichten Herzens von ihren Plattensammlungen und ersetzten sie durch CDs. Zum ersten Mal in der Geschichte der Rockmusik wurden sämtliche Aufnahmen der Vergangenheit neu eingespielt und auf den Markt gebracht. Einen letzten Walzer würde es nicht geben.

Quand s'ouvrirent les années quatre-vingt, le rock 'n' roll et ses fidèles entamèrent la seconde moitié de leur vie. *I Hope I die before I get old* («J'espère mourir avant d'être vieux») chantaient les Who dans *My Generation*. Trop de rockers ont vécu et sont morts avec ces mots. Entre 1980 et 1983, John Lennon, Marvin Gaye, Bob Hite, Bob Marley, John Bonham et Dennis Wilson moururent de mort non naturelle. La musique rock, quant à elle, plutôt que de mourir ou de s'évanouir, devenait plus forte que jamais.

Une des explications à cette incroyable croissance du rock est le succès du Walkman Sony qui améliora d'incroyable manière la qualité et la mobilité du son enregistré. En plus de cela, MTV, une chaîne câblée entièrement musicale, fut lancée en 1981, apportant des clips dans les foyers vingt-quatre heures sur vingt-quatre. MTV fut bientôt suivie de VH-1, un chaîne de musique pour adultes et TNN, le réseau de clips de Nashville. Les stars pouvaient désormais être faites pendant la nuit et tout aussi facilement faire partie du passé le lendemain. Plutôt que former des créateurs de hits, les maisons de disques pouvaient désormais les acheter déjà assemblés et les piles fournies avec.

Le marché de la musique devint une industrie milliardaire qui réclamait toujours plus de méga-stars pour nourrir la machinerie des nouveaux médias. L'album *Thriller* de Michael Jackson devint le disque le plus vendu de tous les temps. Madonna a vendu plus de disques que n'importe quelle autre chanteuse dans l'histoire et Whitney Houston a eu sept n°1 consécutifs, battant le précédent record de six détenu par les Beatles. De nombreuses stars, dont Diana Ross et Elton John, quittèrent les maisons de disques qui les avaient lancés pour des contrats faramineux avec de nouvelles compagnies, pour revenir ensuite plus vieux, plus sages et plus riches vers leurs maisons d'origine. Les Who, les Doobie Brothers, Yes, les Eagles et Steely Dan se séparèrent, et se reformèrent ensuite afin de gagner leur vie.

Se sentant peut-être un peu coupables de tout l'argent déversé sur eux, beaucoup de musiciens vedettes ont lancé une nouvelle tendance, le rock de charité. Si George Harrison a été l'initiateur du mouvement avec le concert au profit du Bangladesh en 1971, les années quatre-vingt nous ont donné Band Aid, Farm Aid, Live Aid, et le disque collecteur de fonds *We Are The World*.

Anti-institutionnel à l'origine, le rock 'n' roll devint une institution dans sa maturité. Les plus grandes tournées de rock furent bientôt financées par des marques de bières et de sodas. Eddie Van Halen épousa Valerie Bertinelli, Ringo Starr épousa Barbara Bach, Billy Joel épousa Christie Brinkley et Madonna épousa Sean Penn. La musique rock est devenue tellement acceptable qu'on a ouvert un Rock And Roll Hall of Fame à Cleveland. Des mouvements juvéniles comme le rap et le hip hop ont essayé de ramener le rock au cœur de la ville, mais la plupart des rockstars multimilliardaires ont préféré rester dans les quartiers résidentiels.

Le mouvement de révolte punk n'a pas perdu sa colère mais il est devenu plus musical avec des musiciens new wave comme Graham Parker, Elvis Costello et les Clash. Le garage rock s'est transformé en grunge rock avec Nirvana, Pearl Jam et les Stone Temple Pilots. Le reggae n'a pas seulement conservé sa popularité, il a également connu un renouveau avec les groupes de ska Madness et les Specials.

Le phénomène le plus important et le plus novateur de la musique pop fut le développement du disque compact en 1982. Les ventes de CD augmentèrent considérablement au milieu des années quatre-vingt, et à la fin de la décennie, la fabrication de disques vinyle était pratiquement arrêtée. Tout comme le 78 tours avant lui, l'album 33 tours est devenu une relique du passé. L'espace graphique pour les pochettes s'est réduit d'un carré de 30 cm de côté à un carré de 12 cm de côté, tandis que le prix des albums a pratiquement doublé. Les gens ont allégrement bazardé leurs collections de microsillons et ont remplacé ceux-ci par des disques compacts. Pour la première fois dans l'histoire du rock, presque tout ce qui avait été enregistré a été converti en son digital et réédité. Il n'y aura pas de dernière valse.

**Loverboy**
*Get Lucky*
Columbia, 1981

Design: John Berg
Photo: David Kennedy

**The Marshall Tucker Band**
*Tuckerized*
Warner Bros., 1982

Art Direction: Nancy Greenberg
Photo: Arnold Rosenberg

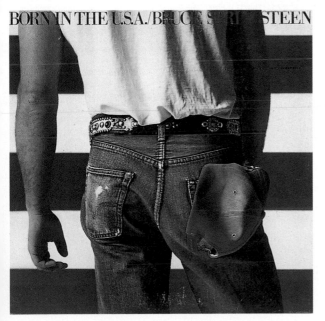

**Bruce Springsteen**
*Born In The U.S.A.*
Columbia, 1984

Design & Art Direction: Andrea Klein
Photo: Annie Leibovitz

**Violent Femmes**
*Violent Femmes*
Slash, 1982

Design: Jeff Price
Photo: Ron Hugo

**Kevin Rowland & Dexy's Midnight Runners**
*"Too-Rye-Ay"*
Mercury, 1982

Design: Peter Barrett
Painting: Andrew Ratcliffe
Photo: Kim Knott

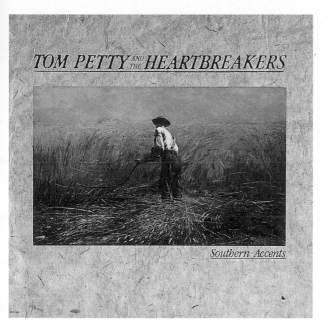

**Tom Petty And The Heartbreakers**
*Southern Accents*
MCA, 1985

Design: Tommy Steele/
Steele Works Design
Painting: Winslow Homer

**Prism**
*Small Change*
Capitol, 1982

Art Direction: Roy Kohara
Illustration: Norman Rockwell

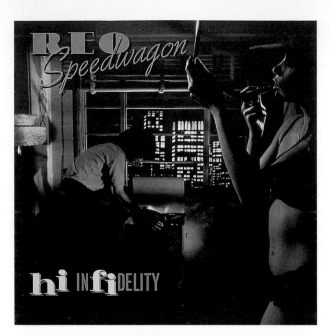

**REO Speedwagon**
*Hi Infidelity*
Epic, 1980

Design: Unknown

**Manhattans**
*After Midnight*
Columbia, 1980

Design: Paula Scher
Illustration: Mark Hess

**Clocks**
*Clocks*
Boulevard, 1982

Illustration: John Lykes

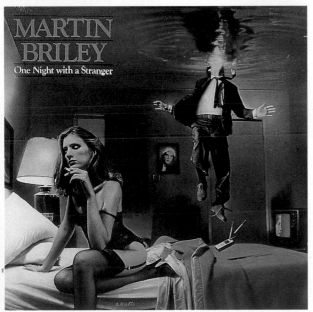

**Martin Briley**
*One Night With A Stranger*
Mercury, 1983

Design: Lumel Whiteman Studio
Art Direction: Bill Levy/
Murry Whiteman
Illustration: Stan Watts

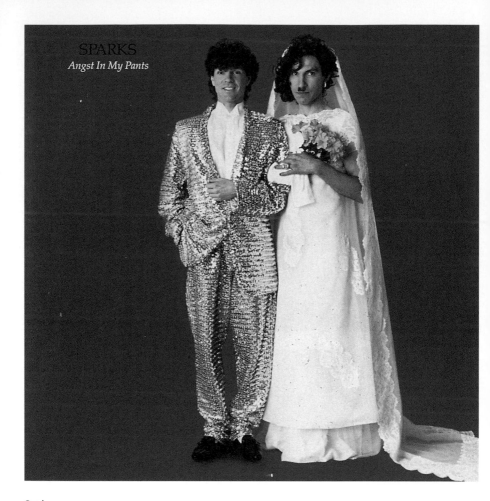

**Sparks**
*Angst In My Pants*
Atlantic, 1982

Design: Larry Vignon
Concept: Ron Mael
Photo: Eric Blum
*Courtesy Atlantic Recording Corp.*

**Depeche Mode**
*A Broken Frame*
Sire, 1982

Design: Unknown

**Midnight Oil**
*Diesel And Dust*
Columbia, 1988

Design: Unknown

**Rush**
*Permanent Waves*
Mercury, 1980

Design: Unknown

**Shooting Star**
*Hang On For Your Life*
Virgin/Epic, 1981

Art Direction: Karen Katz
Photo: Duane Michaels

**Honeymoon Suite**
*Honeymoon Suite*
Warner Bros., 1984

Design: Steve Gerdes/Dean Motter
Photo: Patrick Harbron

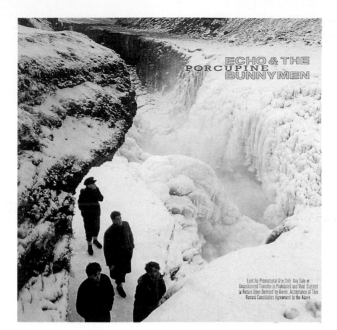

**Echo & The Bunnymen**
*Porcupine*
Sire, 1983

Design: Martyn Atkins
Photo: Brian Griffin

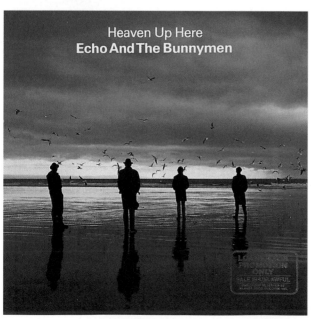

**Echo & The Bunnymen**
*Heaven Up Here*
Sire, 1981

Design: Martyn Atkins
Photo: Brian Griffin

**Echo & The Bunnymen**
*Ocean Rain*
Sire, 1984

Design: Martyn Atkins
Photo: Brian Griffin

**Echo & The Bunnymen**
*Crocodiles*
Korova, 1980

Photo: Brian Griffin

**The Sorrows**
*Love Too Late*
Pavillion, 1981

Art Direction: Karen Katz

**The J. Geils Band**
*Love Stinks*
EMI, 1982

Design: Carin Goldberg/
Mike Handel
Art Direction: Carin Goldberg
Photo: © 1952 Cadence
Industries Corp.

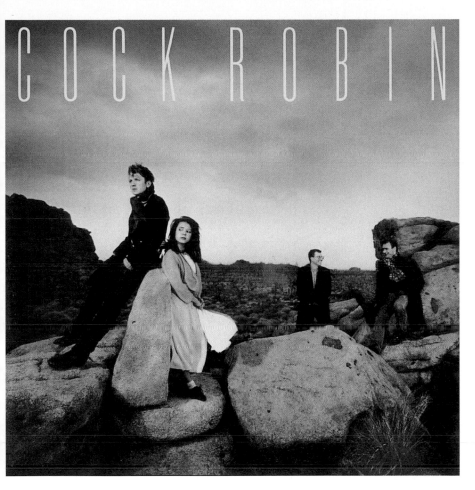

**Cock Robin**
*Cock Robin*
Columbia, 1985

Art Direction: Lane/Donald
Photo: Dennis Keeley

**The Stranglers**
*Dreamtime*
Epic, 1987

Design: Jean-Luke Epstein/Graphyk

**Heaven 17**
*Sunset Now*
Virgin Records Ltd., 1984

Design: Unknown

**Book Of Love**
*Lullaby*
Sire, 1988

Design: Nick Egan & Tracy Veal
Painting: "Cupid Considering" by
Julie Margaret Cameron, 1872

**Church**
*The Church*
Capitol, 1982

Art Direction: Roy Kohara &
Peter Shea
Illustration: Paul Pettie

**Europe**
*Europe*
Epic, 1989

Design: Unknown

**Dead Can Dance**
*Within The Realm Of A Dying Sun*
Cad, 1987

Design: Brendon Perry
Photo: Bernard Oudin

**Visage**
*Visage*
Polydor, 1981

Design: Visage
Artwork: Ian Gillies

**Black Sabbath**
*The Eternal Idol*
Warner Bros., 1987

Design: Shoot That Tiger!
Photo: Cindy Palmano

**The Call**
*Modern Romans*
Mercury, 1983

Design: L&W Design
Concept: Michael Been
Photo: © Paramount Pictures

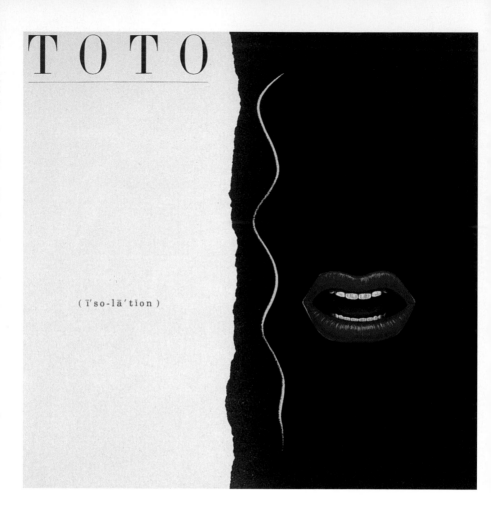

**Toto**
*Isolation*
Columbia, 1984

Design: Bill Murphy, Dyer/Kahn, Inc.
Illustration: Robert Kopecky

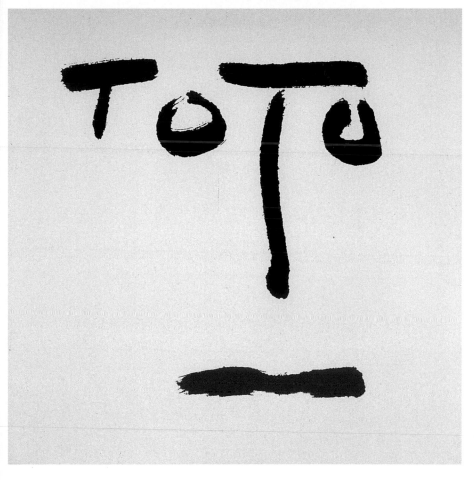

**Toto**
*Turn Back*
Columbia, 1981

Design: Tony Lane

**The Pet Shop Boys**
*Introspective*
EMI-Manhattan, 1988

Design: Mark Farrow/
At Three Associates/
The Pet Shop Boys
Photo: Eric Watson

**Elton John**
*21 At 33*
MCA, 1980

Design & Concept: Norman Moore
Art Direction: George Osaki/
Norman Moore
Photo: Jim Shea

**Le Roux**
*So Fired Up*
RCA, 1983

Design: Mike Doud
Concept, Illustration & Photo:
Paul Maxon

**Elton John**
*The Fox*
Geffen, 1981

Art Direction: Richard Seireeni
Photo: Eric Blum
Photo of Elton John by Terry O'Neil

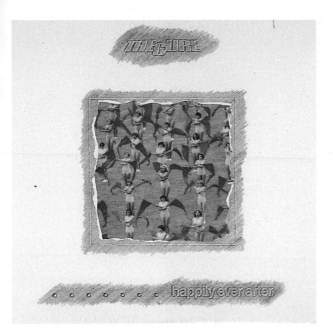

**The Cure**
*...happily ever after*
A&M, 1980

Design: Ben Kelly

**The Hawaiian Pups**
*Split Second Precision*
Portrait, 1983

Concept: The Hawaiian Pups
Art Direction: Chris Austopchuk
Photo: Heinz Kluetmeier/
Sports Illustrated

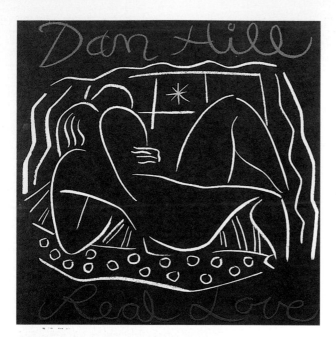

**Dan Hill**
*Real Love*
Columbia, 1989

Art Direction: Stacy Drummond
Illustration: Ann Field

**Joe Jackson**
*Night And Day*
A&M, 1982

Art Direction: Joe Jackson
Artwork: Philip Burke

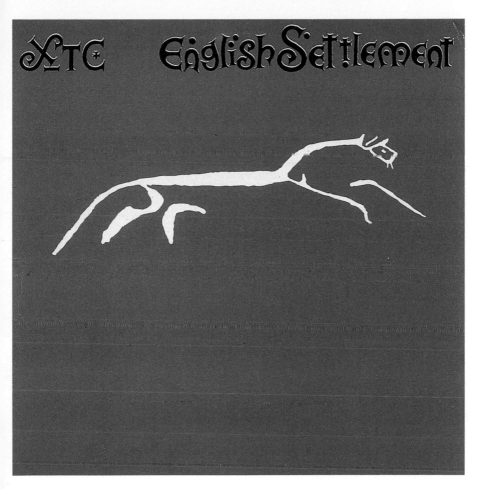

**XTC**
*English Settlement*
Virgin, 1982

Illustration: Art Dragon

**Martin Briley**
*Fear Of The Unknown*
Mercury, 1981

Design & Art Direction: Bob Heimall
Concept: Bill Levy
Illustration: Norman Walker

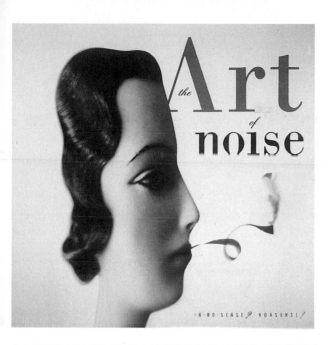

**The Art Of Noise**
*In-No-Sense? Nonsense!*
Chrysalis, 1987

Art Direction: John Pasche
Photo: Alan David-Tu

**Gladys Knight & The Pips**
*Visions*
Columbia, 1983

Design: Nancy Donald
Painting: "Les Memoires d'un Saint"
by René Magritte

**Duran Duran**
*Rio*
Capitol, 1982

Design: Malcolm Garrett/
Assorted iMaGes, London
Illustration: Nagel, Los Angeles

**The Nylons**
*One Size Fits All*
Open Air, 1982

Design: Dean Motter for Diagram
Photo: Patrick Harbron

**Bernadette Peters**
*Now Playing*
MCA, 1981

Art Direction: George Osaki
Painting: Alberto Vargas

**Bernadette Peters**
*Bernadette Peters*
MCA, 1980

Design: Alberto Vargas
Art Direction: George Osaki/Vartan

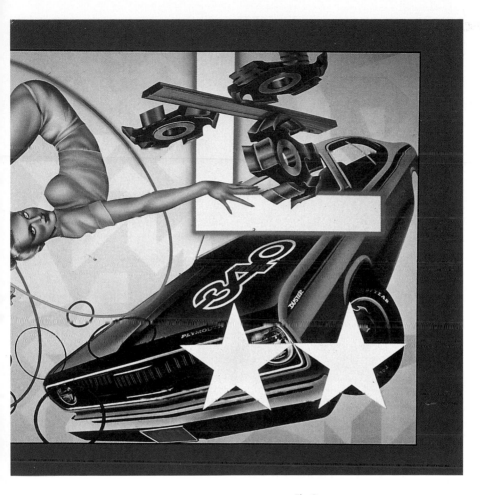

**The Cars**
*Heartbeat Of The City*
Elektra, 1984

Design: David Robinson
Painting: "Art-o-matic Loop
Di Loop" by Peter Phillip
*Courtesy Elektra Entertainment Group*

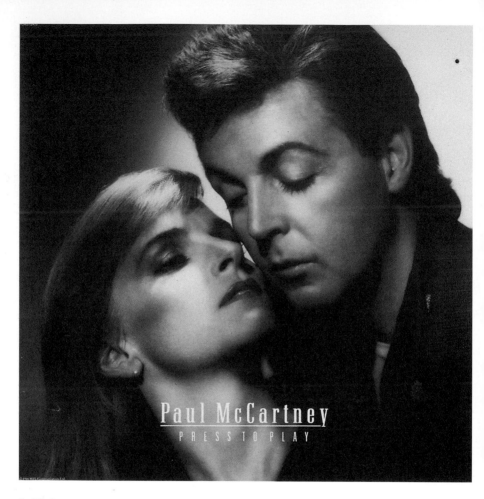

**Paul McCartney**
*Press To Play*
MPL/Capitol, 1986

Photo: George Hurrell

**Midge Ure**
*The Gift*
No Label, 1985

Design: Unknown

**It Bites**
*The Big Lad In The Windmill*
Geffen, 1986

Concept: It Bites
Artwork: Stylorouge
Painting: David O'Connor

**Paul Anka**
*The Painter*
United Artists, 1976

Design & Art Direction: Ria Lewerke
Painting: Andy Warhol

**Talking Heads**
*Speaking In Tongues*
Sire, 1983

Design: Robert Rauschenberg

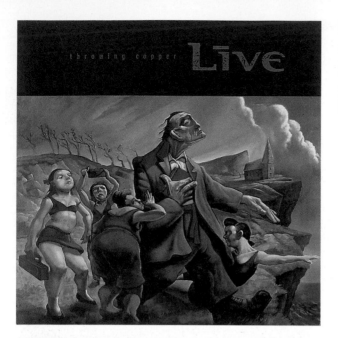

**Live**
*Throwing Copper*
Radioactive, 1994

Design: Tim Steadman/
Todd Gollopo
Art Direction: Tim Steadman
Painting: "Sisters Of Mercy"
by Peter Howson

**Talking Heads**
*Naked*
Fly/Sire, 1988

Design: M & Co., New York
Concept: David Byrne
Painting: Paula Wright

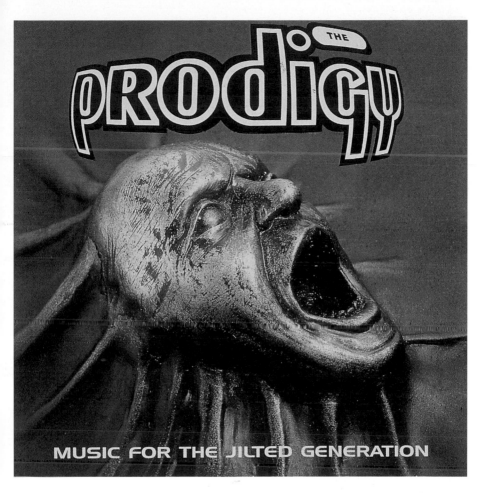

**The Prodigy**
*Music For The Jilted Generation*
XL Recordings, 1994

Photo: Stuart Haygarth

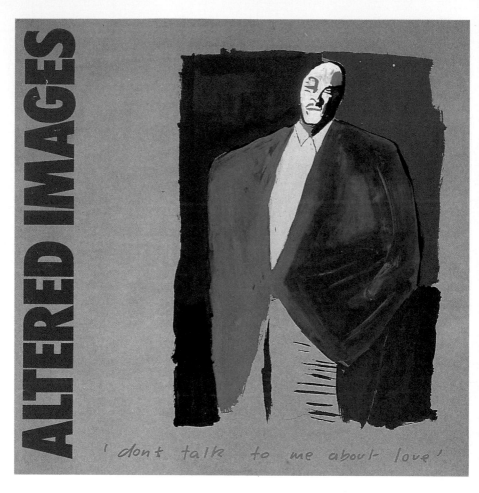

**Altered Images**
*Don't Talk To Me About Love*
Portrait, 1983

Illustration: "Big Joe Turner" by David Band

**Cruel Story Of Youth**
*Cruel Story Of Youth*
Columbia, 1989

Art Direction: Christopher
Austopchuk
Photo: David LaChapelle

**Michael Franks**
*Objects Of Desire*
Warner Bros., 1982

Painting: "Two Tahitian Women"
by Paul Gauguin

**Judas Priest**
*Point Of Entry*
Columbia, 1981

Design: John Berg
Photo: Art Kane

**Simple Minds**
*Life In A Day*
Virgin, 1987

Design: Unknown

**Art In America**
*Art In America*
Pavillion, 1983

Design: Ioannis

**INXS**
*INXS*
Atco, 1980/1984

Design: Art Gecko Graphics
(after Noel Coward)
*Courtesy Atlantic Recording Corp.*

**Manfred Mann's Earth Band**
*Chance*
Warner Bros., 1981

Design: Martin Poole/Ole Kortzau
Photo: "Deck Chairs"/
Courtesy Thumb Gallery, London

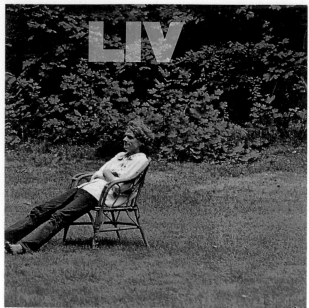

**Livingston Taylor**
*Liv*
Atlantic, 1971

Design: Sam Antupit
Photo: Jim Marshall
*Courtesy Atlantic Recording Corp.*

**Art Garfunkel**
*Watermark*
Columbia, 1978

Design: John Berg
Photo: Laurie Bird

**XTC**
*Black Sea*
Virgin, 1980

Design: Unknown

**Gamma 2**
*Gamma 2*
Elektra, 1980

Design: Mick Haggerty
Photo: Mick Haggerty/
Jeffrey Scales
*Courtesy Elektra Entertainment Group*

**Great White**
*Once Bitten*
Capitol, 1987

Concept: John O'Brien
Photo: Ron Slenzak

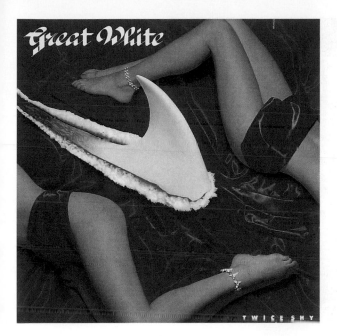

**Great White**
*...Twice Shy*
Capitol, 1989

Design: Bacon/O'Brien Design, Inc.
Concept: Alan Niven
Photo: Doug Hyun

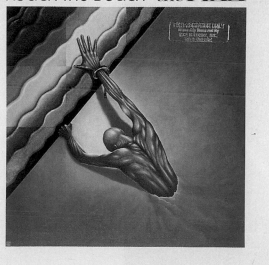

**The Fixx**
*Reach The Beach*
MCA, 1983

Painting: George Underwood

**Def Leppard**
*High 'n' Dry*
Polygram, 1981

Design: Hipgnosis

**The Radiators**
*Law Of The Fish*
Epic, 1987

Art Direction: Christopher
Austopchuk
Photo: Chip Simmons

REO Speedwagon
*You Can Tune A Piano, But You Can't Tuna Fish*
Epic, 1978

Design: Tom Wilkes

**Blur**
*Parklife*
Food, 1994

Photo: Brunskill/Bob Thomas

**Alice In Chains**
*Alice In Chains*
Columbia, 1995

Design: Doug Erb
Art Direction: Mary Maurer

**Mickey Thomas**
*Alive Alone*
Elektra, 1981

Concept: Mickey Thomas
Art Direction: Ron Coro
Illustration: Michael Bryan
Photo: Leon La Cash
*Courtesy Elektra Entertainment Group*

**Gentle Giant**
*Civilian*
Columbia, 1980

Design: Nancy Donald/
Ginger Canzoneri
Photo: David Weiner

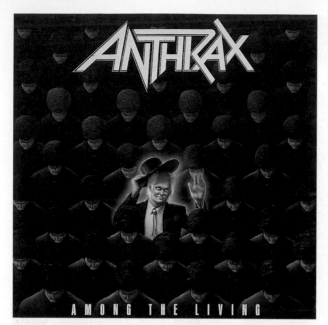

**Anthrax**
*Among The Living*
Megaforce, 1987

Design: Unknown
*Courtesy Zazula Archives*

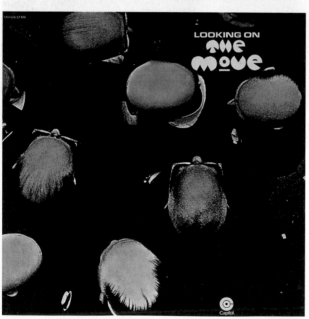

**The Move**
*Looking On*
Capitol, 1971

Design: Graphreaks

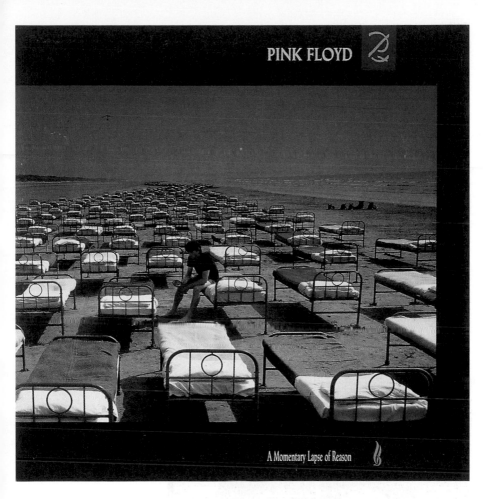

**Pink Floyd**
*A Momentary Lapse Of Reason*
Columbia, 1987

Concept: Storm Thorgerson/Nexus
Art Direction: Storm Thorgerson
Photo: Robert Dowling

**Jane's Addiction**
*Nothing's Shocking*
Warner Bros., 1988

Design: Perry Farrell

**Cold Chisel**
*East*
Elektra, 1980

Concept: Philip Mortlock/
Don Walker
Art Direction: Ken Smith
Photo: Greg Noakes

**Marillion**
*Fugazi*
Capitol, 1984

Design & Illustration:
Mark Wilkinson
Concept: Fish

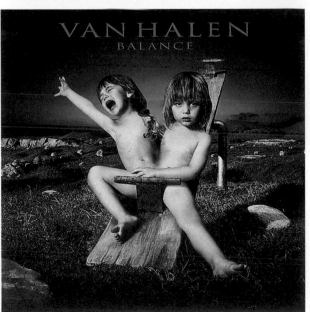

**Van Halen**
*Balance*
Warner Bros., 1995

Art Direction: Jeri Heiden
Photo: Glen Wexler

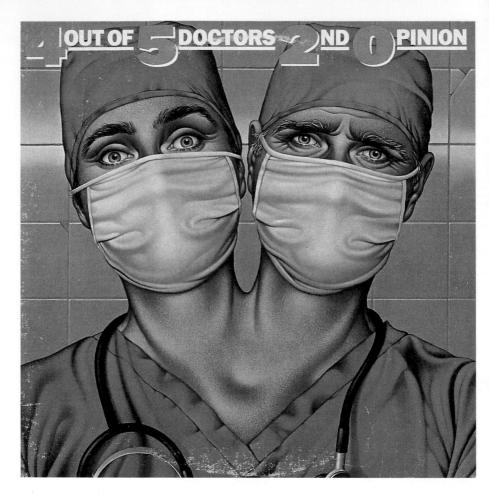

**4 Out Of 5 Doctors**
*2nd Opinion*
Nemperor, 1984

Art Direction: Carin Goldberg
Illustration: Braldt Bralds

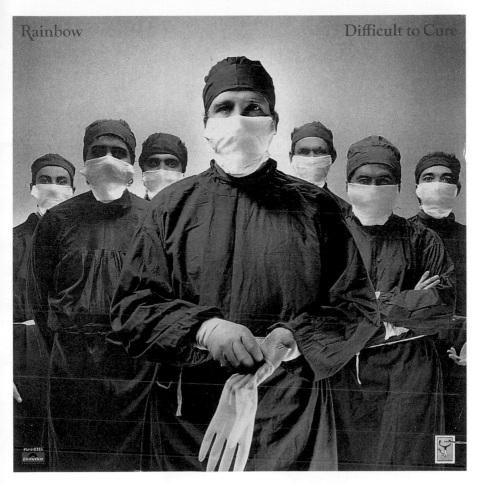

**Rainbow**
*Difficult To Cure*
CBS, 1985

Design: Hipgnosis

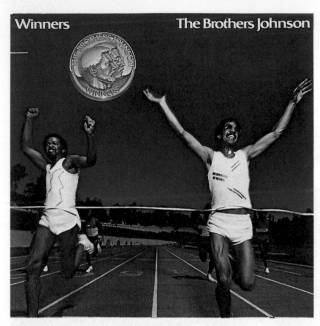

Winners    The Brothers Johnson

**The Brothers Johnson**
*Winners*
A&M, 1981

Design: Chuck Beeson
Art Direction: Chuck Beeson/
Jeff Ayeroff
Photo: Norman Seef

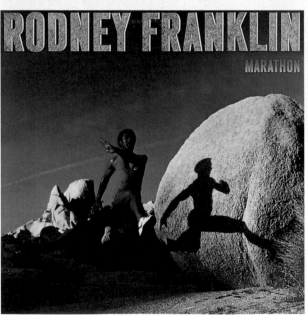

RODNEY FRANKLIN
MARATHON

**Rodney Franklin**
*Marathon*
Columbia, 1984

Design: Lane/Donald
Photo: Weldon Anderson

**Average White Band**
*Put It Where You Want It*
MCA, 1975

Photos: Bruce Cooke

**Ry Cooder**
*Borderline*
Warner Bros., 1980

Design: Unknown

**ABC**
*Beauty Stab*
Mercury, 1988

Design: ABC with Keith Breeden

**The Arrows**
*Stand Back*
A&M, 1984

Art Direction: Dean Motter/
Diagram Studios
Photo: Patrick Harbron

**Roxy Music**
*Flesh + Blood*
Atco, 1980

Design: Bryan Ferry/Antony Price/
Neil Kirk/Simon Puxley/Peter Seville
*Courtesy Atlantic Recording Corp.*

**10,000 Maniacs**
*In My Tribe*
Elektra, 1987

Design: Kosh
*Courtesy Elektra Entertainment Group*

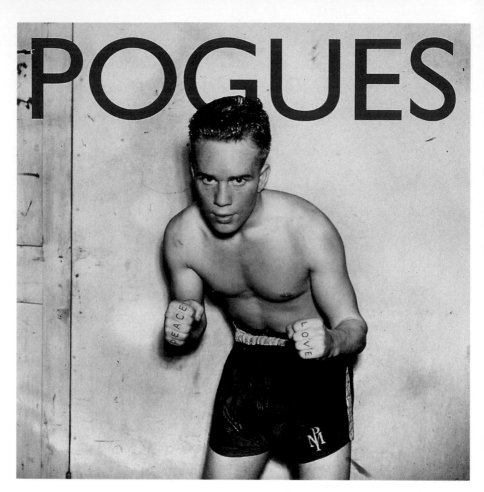

**The Pogues**
*Peace And Love*
Island, 1989

Design: Ryan Art

**Guadalcanal Diary**
*2 x 4*
Elektra, 1988

Concept: Guadalcanal
Photo: Terry Allen
*Courtesy Elektra Entertainment Group*

**Billy Joel**
*Glass Houses*
Columbia, 1980

Photo: Jim Houghton

**Orchestral Manœuvres In The Dark**
*Crush*
Virgin, 1985

Design: XL Design
Illustration: Paul Slater

**Jackson Browne**
*Lawyers In Love*
Asylum, 1983

Design & Art Direction:
Jimmy Watchel/Dawn Patrol
Photo: Matti Klatt
*Courtesy Elektra Entertainment Group*

**Diana Ross**
*Swept Away*
RCA, 1984

Art Direction: Ria Lewerke
Photo: Francesco Scavullo

**Olivia Newton-John**
*Physical*
MCA, 1981

Design & Art Direction:
George Osaki
Photo: Herb Ritts

**Heavy Pettin**
*Heavy Pettin*
Polydor, 1983

Design: Gary Nichamin/
Boom Graphics
Concept: Al Kooper
Photo: Thom Elder

**Tommy Tutone**
*Tommy Tutone-2*
Columbia, 1981

Concept: Tony Lane, A.D./
Paul Cheslaw/David Gales
Photo: Bob Seidemann

**Head East**
*U.S. 1*
A&M, 1980

Design: Williardson & White Studios
Art Direction: Chuck Beeson
Illustration: Robert Bergendorff

**The Hawks**
*30 Seconds Over Otho*
Columbia, 1982

Design: Andrea Kelin
Photo: Gary Jones

**The Red Krayola**
*The Red Krayola*
Drag City, 1994

Design: Unknown

**Dead Kennedys**
*Frankenchrist*
Alternative Tentacles, 1985

Visual Concept: Biafra
Photo: © 1976 Newsweek/
Lester Sloan

**Ian Matthews**
*Spot Of Interference*
RSO, 1980

Design: Bill Smith
Photo: Marilyn Goddard

**Dream Patrol**
*Phoning The Czar*
Pasha, 1988

Art Direction: Hugh Syme
Photo: Mark Sokoc

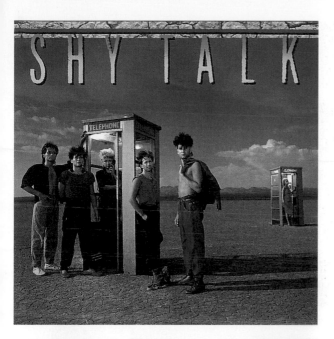

**Shy Talk**
*Shy Talk*
Columbia, 1985

Art Direction: Mark Larsen
Photo: Dorit Lombroso

**Rush**
*Power Windows*
Mercury, 1985

Design, Art Direction,
Graphics & Painting: Hugh Syme

# LOU REED NEW SENSATIONS

**Lou Reed**
*New Sensations*
RCA, 1984

Art Direction & Photo:
Waring Abbott

**Kraftwerk**
*Computer World*
Warner Bros., 1981

Design: Unknown

**Gloria Gaynor**
*I Am Gloria Gaynor*
Silver Blue, 1984

Art Direction: Allen Weinberg
Photo: Art Kane

**Stevie Wonder**
*In Square Circle*
Tamla, 1985

Design & Concept: Renee Hardaway
& Bobby Holland
Art Direction: Renee Hardaway &
Johnny Lee
Photo: Bobby Holland

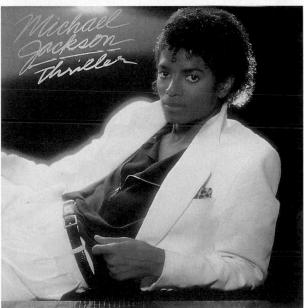

**Michael Jackson**
*Thriller*
Epic, 1982

Photo: Dick Zimmerman

**Kid Flash**
*He's In Effect*
Tabu, 1988

Art Direction: Levine/
Lane Donald/Felsenstein
Photo: Benno Friedman

**The S.O.S. Band**
*S.O.S. Band III*
Tabu, 1982

Design: Jones & Armitage/
Out Of Focus
Photo: Diem Jones/Out Of Focus

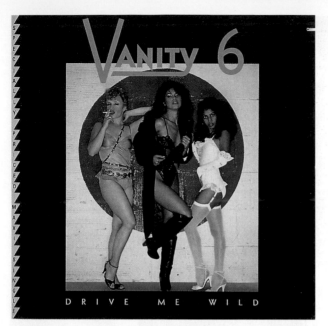

**Vanity 6**
*Drive Me Wild/Bite The Beat*
Warner Bros., 1982

Design: Unknown

**Donna Summer**
*She Works Hard For The Money*
Mercury, 1983

Design: Chris Whorf/Art Hotel
Photo: Harry Langdon

**Morris Day**
*Daydreaming*
Warner Bros., 1987

Design: Janet Levinson
Photo: Jeff Katz

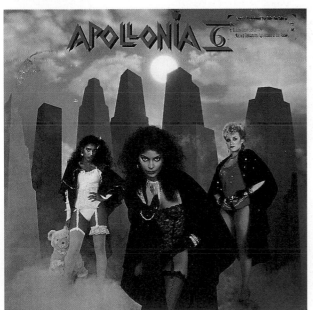

**Apollonia 6**
*Apollonia 6*
Warner Bros., 1984

Art Direction: Jeri McManus &
The Starr Co.
Photo: Larry Williams

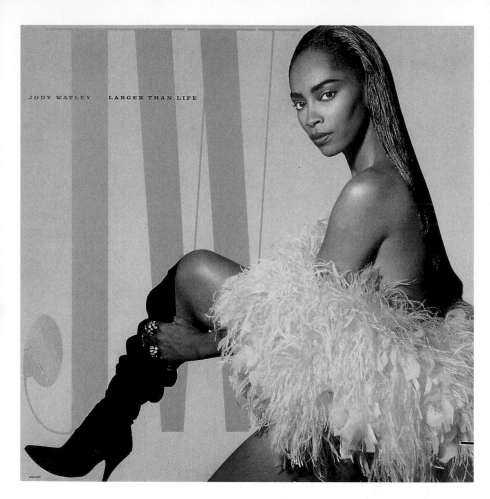

**Jody Watley**
*Larger Than Life*
MCA, 1989

Design: Lynn Robb
Concept: Jody Whatley
Photo: Steven Meisel

**Black Box**
*Dreamland*
RCA, 1990

Photo: Kate Garner

**Cherelle**
*Affair*
Tabu, 1988

Art Direction: Tony Lane/
Nancy Donald
Photo: Alberto Tolot

**Sheila E.**
*Sex Cymbal*
Warner Bros., 1991

Design: Sarajo Frieden
Art Direction: Jeri Heiden
Photo: Philip Dixon

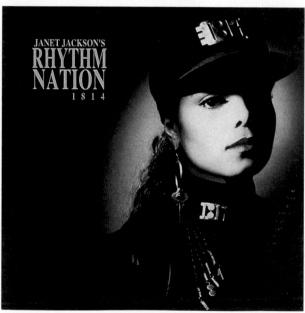

**Janet Jackson**
*Janet Jackson's Rhythm Nation 1814*
A&M, 1989

Design & Art Direction:
Richard Frankel
Photo: Guzman

**George Clinton**
*The Cinderella Theory*
Paisley Park, 1989

Design: Johnny Lee
Photo: Greg Gorman

**Tracy Chapman**
*Tracy Chapman*
Elektra, 1988

Art Direction: Carol Bobolts
Photo: Matt Mahurin
*Courtesy Elektra Entertainment Group*

**Nazareth**
*The Fool Circle*
A&M, 1981

Design: Alan Schmidt & Pat Carroll
Illustration: Chris Moore

**SPK**
*Machine Age Voodoo*
Elektra, 1985

Design: Jodee Stringham
Art Direction: Carol Friedman
*Courtesy Elektra Entertainment Group*

**Al Stewart**
*Past, Present And Future*
Janus, 1974

Design: Hipgnosis

**China Sky**
*China Sky*
Parc, 1988

Art Direction: Tony Lane/
Nancy Donald
Illustration: Jean-Francis Podevin
Photo: Wiley & Flynn

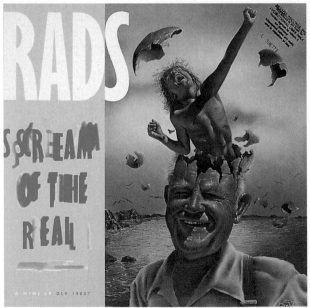

**The Rads**
*Scream Of The Real*
EMI, 1983

Design: Michael Hodgson
Art Direction: Henry Marquez
Illustration: Jim Warren

**Godley & Creme**
*Goodbye Blue Sky*
Polydor, 1988

Design: ICON, London
Art Direction: Richard Evans
Artwork: Mekon
Photo: © 1972 TIMELIFE Books
Ltd. / Ernst Haas

**Briar**
*Crown Of Thorns*
Columbia, 1988

Art Direction: Howard Fritzson
Illustration: Jim Warren
Photo: Pete Cronin

**Stranger**
*Stranger*
Epic, 1982

Design: Nancy Donald
Photo: Robert Peak

**The Brains**
*The Brains*
Mercury, 1980

Design & Art Direction:
Bob Heimall/AGI
Photo: John Paul Endress

**A Flock Of Seagulls**
*Modern Love Is Automatic
Telecommunication*
Jive, 1981

Design: Unknown

**R.A.F.**
*The Heat's On*
A&M, 1981

Art Direction: Michael Ross
Painting: "Le Principe du Plaiser"
by René Magritte, 1937

**Pete Townshend**
*Empty Glass*
Atco, 1980

Design: Bob Carlos Clarke
*Courtesy Atlantic Recording Corp.*

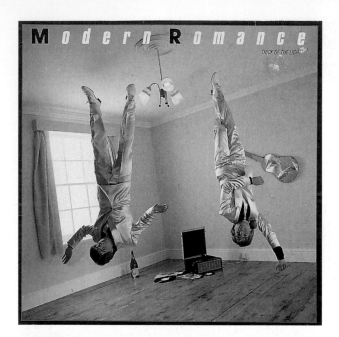

**Modern Romance**
*Trick Of The Light*
Atlantic, 1983

Design: Bill Smith
Photo: Gered Mankowitz
*Courtesy Atlantic Recording Corp.*

**The John Hall Band**
*All Of The Above*
EMI, 1981

Art Direction: Bill Burks/
Peter Corriston
Photo: Brian Hagiwara

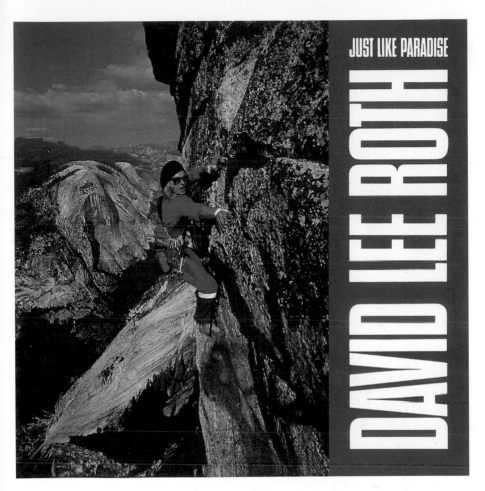

**David Lee Roth**
*Just Like Paradise*
Warner Bros., 1987

Design: Unknown

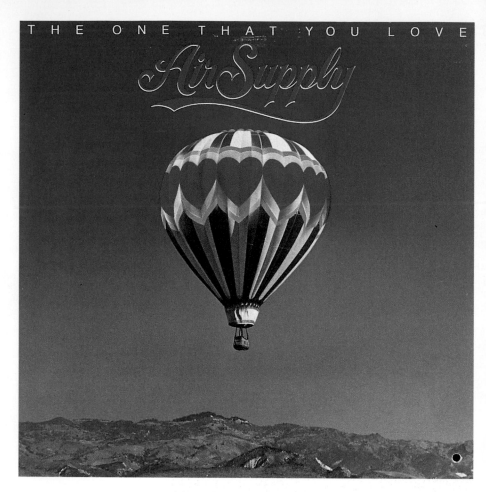

**Air Supply**
*The One That You Love*
Arista, 1981

Photo: G. Maxwell/Alpha

**10 CC**
*Ten Out Of 10*
Warner Bros., 1982

Design: Visible Ink, Ltd.
Photo: John Shaw

**Harlequin**
*One False Move*
Columbia, 1982

Design: Hugh Syme

**Mike Oldfield**
*Five Miles On*
Virgin/Epic, 1982

Design: Mike Oldfield
Painting: Gerald Coulson

**Supertramp**
*...famous last words...*
A&M, 1982

Design: Mike Dowd/
Norman Moore
Concept: Mike Dowd
Photo: Julie Bates/Tom Gibson

**Oingo Boingo**
*Only A Lad*
A&M, 1981

Design: Paul Mussa
Art Direction: Chuck Beeson
Illustration: Chris Hopkins

**Asia**
*Astra*
Geffen, 1985

Design: Roger Dean
© Roger Dean

**Asia**
*Asia*
Geffen, 1985

Design: Roger Dean
© Roger Dean

**Midnight Oil**
*Red Sails In The Sunset*
Columbia, 1985

Artwork: Tsunehisa Kimura

**The Dukes Of Stratosphear**
*Psonic Psunspot*
Geffen, 1987

Design: Unknown

**Beastie Boys**
*Licensed To Ill*
Columbia, 1986

Art Direction: Stephen Byram
Cover Art: World B Omes

**Accept**
*Russian Roulette*
Portrait, 1986

Design: Deaffy
Photo: Didi Zill/Bravo

**Coconuts**
*Don't Take My Coconuts*
EMI, 1983

Design: Mick Haggerty
Photo: Larry Williams

**Spandau Ballet**
*Parade*
Chrysalis, 1984

Design: David Band/Gary Kemp
Photo: John Shaw

**Prince**
*Purple Rain* (Picture Disc)
Warner Bros., 1984

Design: Unknown

**Men Without Hats**
*Safety Dance/Security*
Statik, 1982

Design: Unknown

**Lita Ford**
*Out For Blood*
Mercury, 1983

Art Direction: Glen Christenson
Photo: Herbert Worthington, III.

Although similar covers by Alice Cooper and Ozzy Osbourne had not been censored, this Lita Ford cover was banned and soon changed.

Obwohl ähnliche Cover von Alice Cooper und Ozzy Osbourne nicht zensiert wurden, wurde dieses Lita-Ford-Cover verboten und bald darauf geändert.

Bien que des pochettes semblables d'Alice Cooper et d'Ozzy Osbourne n'aient pas été censurées, celle-ci, de Lita Ford, fut très vite interdite et remplacée.

**Heart**
*Bebe Le Strange*
Epic, 1980

Art Direction: Tony Lane
Photo: Jeff Burger

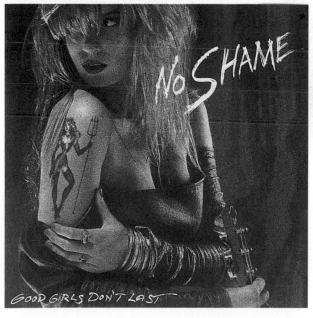

**No Shame**
*Good Girls Don't Last*
Columbia, 1989

Art Direction: Tony Sellari
Photo: Nels

**Fotomaker**
*Fotomaker*
Atlantic, 1978

Design: Dino Danelli
Photo: Thormahlen/Rock
*Courtesy Atlantic Recording Corp.*

**Saxon**
*Innocence Is No Excuse*
Capitol, 1985

Design: Bill Smith Studios
Concept: Nigel Thomas
Photo: Gered Mankowitz

**Melissa Manchester**
*Mathematics*
MCA, 1985

Design: Unknown

**Diana Ross**
*Red Hot Rhythm + Blues*
RCA, 1987

Design: Pietro Alfieri
Art Direction: Ria Lewerke
Photo: Herb Ritts

**Pat Benatar**
*Crimes Of Passion*
Chrysalis, 1980

Design: Unknown

**Twisted Sister**
*Stay Hungry*
Atlantic, 1984

Art Direction: Bob Defrin
Photo: Mark Weiss Studio
*Courtesy Atlantic Recording Corp.*

**Ted Nugent**
*Scream Dream*
Epic, 1980

Design & Art Direction:
Bob Heimall/Stephanie Zuraslagi
Photo: Lynn Goldsmith

**Ozzy Osbourne**
*No Rest For The Wicked*
CBS, 1988

Design: The Leisure Process
Photo: Bob Carlos Clarke

**Blondie**
*Parallel Lines*
Chrysalis, 1978

Design: Ramey Communications
Photo: Edo & Martin Goddard

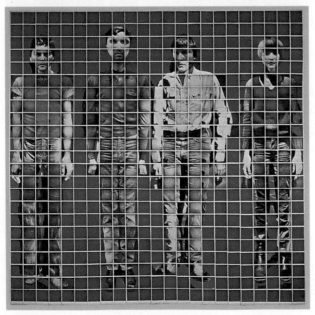

**Talking Heads**
*More Songs About Buildings And Food*
Sire, 1978

Concept: David Byrne
Reproduction: Jimmy DeSana

**Devo**
*Freedom Of Choice*
Warner Bros., 1980

Design: Artrouble

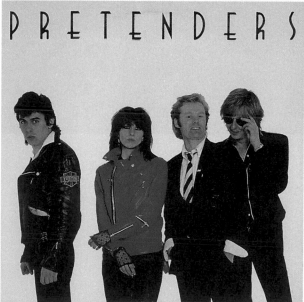

**The Pretenders**
*Pretenders*
Sire, 1980

Design: Kevin Hughes
Photo: Chalkie Davies

**Debbie Harry**
*Rockbird*
Geffen, 1986

Design: Stephen Sprousl
Art Direction: Paula Greif
Background Painting: Andy Warhol
Photo: Guzman

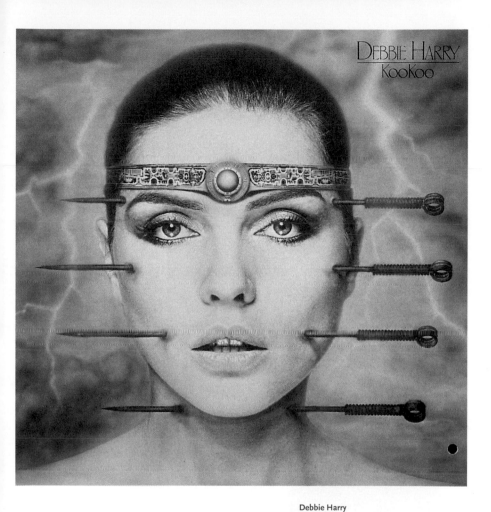

**Debbie Harry**
*Kookoo*
Chrysalis, 1981

Art Direction: Peter Wagg
Concept & Painting: H.R. Giger
from a photo by Brian Aris

**Laurie Anderson**
*Big Science*
Warner Bros., 1982

Design: Cindy Brown
Art Direction: Perry Hoberman
Photo: Greg Shifrin

**Peter Murphy**
*Deep*
Beggar's Banquet, 1989

Design: Peter Murphy
Photo: Paul Cox

**Jennifer Rush**
*Jennifer Rush*
Epic, 1985

Design: Unknown

**Bryan Adams**
*Cuts Like A Knife*
A&M, 1983

Design: Lynn Robb & Mike Fink
Art Direction: Jeffrey Kent Ayeroff
Photo: Jim O'Mara

**Bow Wow Wow**
*Bow Wow Wow*
RCA, 1982

Design: Osamu Nagawaka
Photo: Chris Craymer

**Culture Club**
*The War Song*
Virgin/Epic, 1984

Photo: Stevie Hughes

**Visage**
*Fade To Grey – The Singles Collection*
Polydor, 1983

Design: Green Ink
Art Direction: Alwyn Clayden

**Marianne Faithfull**
*Dangerous Acquaintances*
Island, 1981

Art Direction: Paul Henry
Photo: Clive Arrowsmith

**Bad Company**
*Dangerous Age*
Atlantic, 1988

Design: Anthony Ranieri
Concept: Rich Totoian
Art Direction: Bob Defrin

**Yoko Ono**
*Season Of Glass*
Geffen, 1981

Design: Yoko Ono

**Grace Jones**
*Island Life*
Island, 1986

Design: Greg Porto
Cover Art: Jean-Paul Gorde

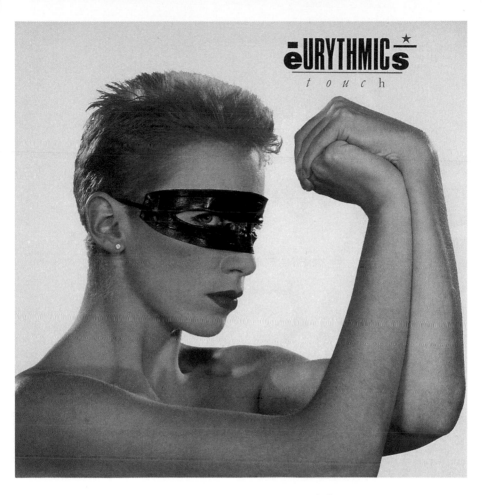

**Eurythmics**
*Touch*
RCA, 1983

Design: Laurence Stevens/
Andrew Christian
Photo: Peter Ashworth

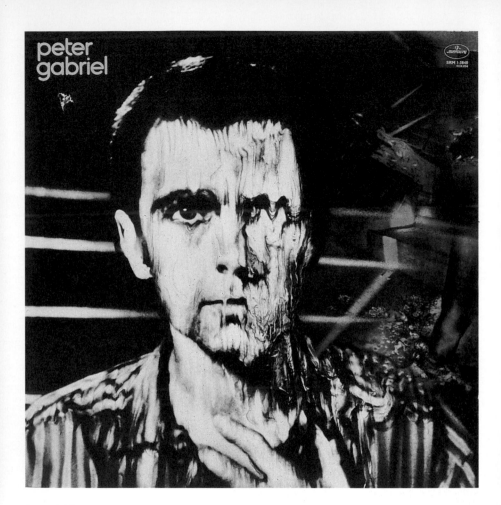

**Peter Gabriel**
*Peter Gabriel*
Mercury, 1980

Design: Hipgnosis

**Peter Wolf**
*Come As You Are*
EMI, 1987

Design: Janet Perr
Art Direction: Henry Marquez/
Janet Perr
Photo: Annie Leibovitz

**Robert Palmer**
*Riptide*
Island, 1985

Design: Robert Palmer
Photo: Guiseppo Pino, Milan

**The B-52's**
*Wild Planet*
Warner Bros., 1980

Art Direction: Robert Waldrop
Photo: Lynn Goldsmith

**Bow Wow Wow**
*The Last Of The Mohicans*
RCA, 1982

Design: Nick Egan
Photo: Andy Earl

**Blondie**
*Autoamerican*
Chrysalis, 1980

Design: Program A

**The The**
*Mind Bomb*
Epic, 1989

Concept: MacPherson/Skinner/Johnson
Photo: Andrew MacPherson

**Tim Finn**
*Tim Finn*
Capitol, 1989

Design: SHEd

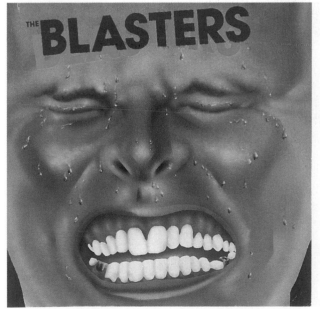

**The Blasters**
*The Blasters*
Slash, 1981

Design: Gustav Alsina
Art Direction: Steve Bartel

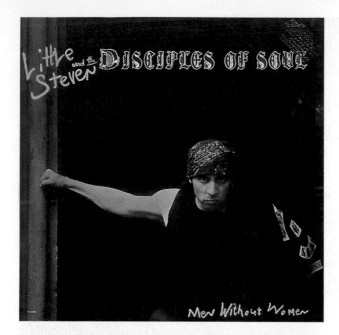

**Little Steven And The Disciples Of Soul**
*Men Without Women*
EMI, 1982

Art Direction: Bill Burks/
Henry Marquez
Photo: Jim Marchese

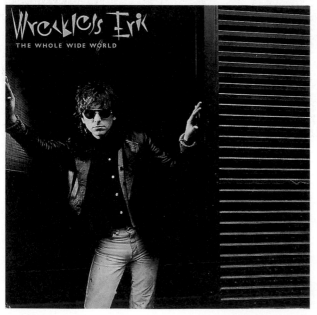

**Wreckless Eric**
*The Whole Wide World*
Stiff, 1970s

Design: Unknown
*Courtesy Atlantic Recording Corp.*

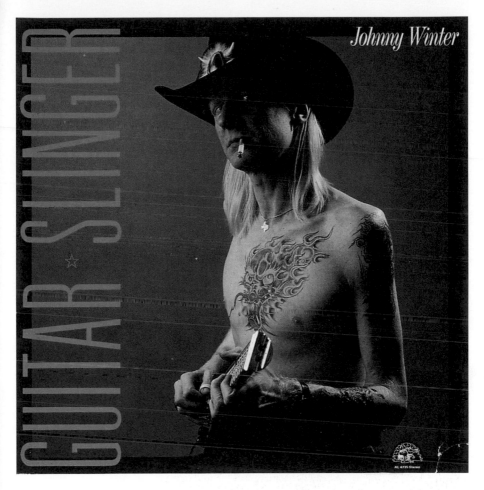

**Johnny Winter**
*Guitar Slinger*
Alligator, 1984

Design: Chris Garland, Xeno
Photo: Paul Natkin/
Photo Reserve, Inc.

**The Call**
*Scene Beyond Dreams*
Mercury, 1984

Design: Ria Lewerke
Photo: Moshe Brakha

**ABC**
*The Lexicon Of Love*
Mercury, 1981

Design: Visible Ink/
Neutron Records
Photo: Gered Mankowitz

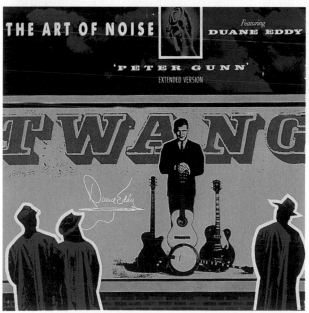

**The Art Of Noise**
(Featuring Duane Eddy)
*Peter Gunn*
Chrysalis, 1986

Design: Unknown

**Cyndi Lauper**
*True Colors*
Portrait, 1986

Art Direction: Cyndi Lauper/
Holland McDonald
Photo: Annie Leibovitz

**Nina Hagen**
*Nina Hagen In Ekstasy*
Columbia, 1985

Design: Marco Paris Design/
Julianna Grigorova Knepler
Photo: Diana Lynn

**The Scorpions**
*Animal Magnetism*
Mercury, 1980

Design: Hipgnosis

**Catholic Girls**
*Catholic Girls*
MCA, 1982

Design: Kathe Schreyer
Concept: Kathe Schreyer
Art Direction: Kathe Schreyer/
George Osaki
Photo: Aaron Rapoport

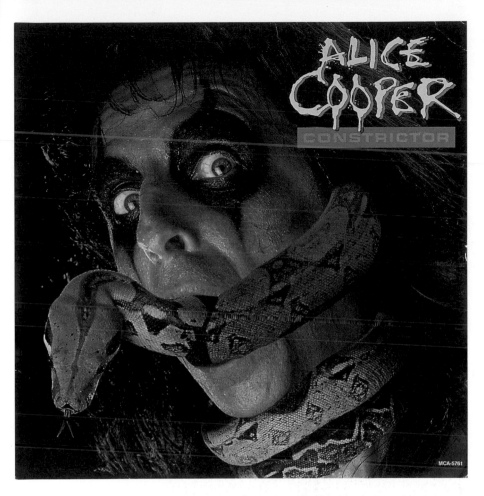

**Alice Cooper**
*Constrictor*
MCA, 1986

Design: David Hale Associates
Photo: Kevin Schill

**The Doors**
*The Best Of The Doors*
Elektra, 1985

Photo: Joel Brodsky
*Courtesy Elektra Entertainment Group*

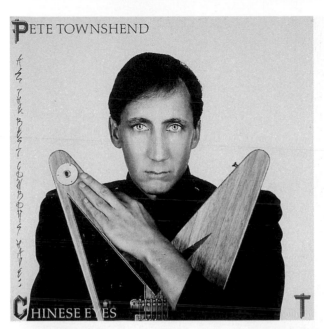

**Pete Townshend**
*All The Best Cowboys Have Chinese Eyes*
Atco, 1982

Design: Davies/Starr
Photo: Chalkie Davies/Carol Starr
*Courtesy Atlantic Recording Corp.*

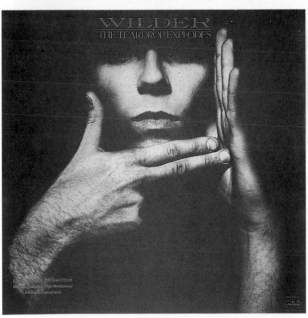

**The Teardrop Explodes**
*Wilder*
Mercury, 1982

Design: Unknown

**Nirvana**
*Nevermind*
Geffen, 1991

Design & Art Direction:
Robert Fisher
Photo: Kirk Weddle

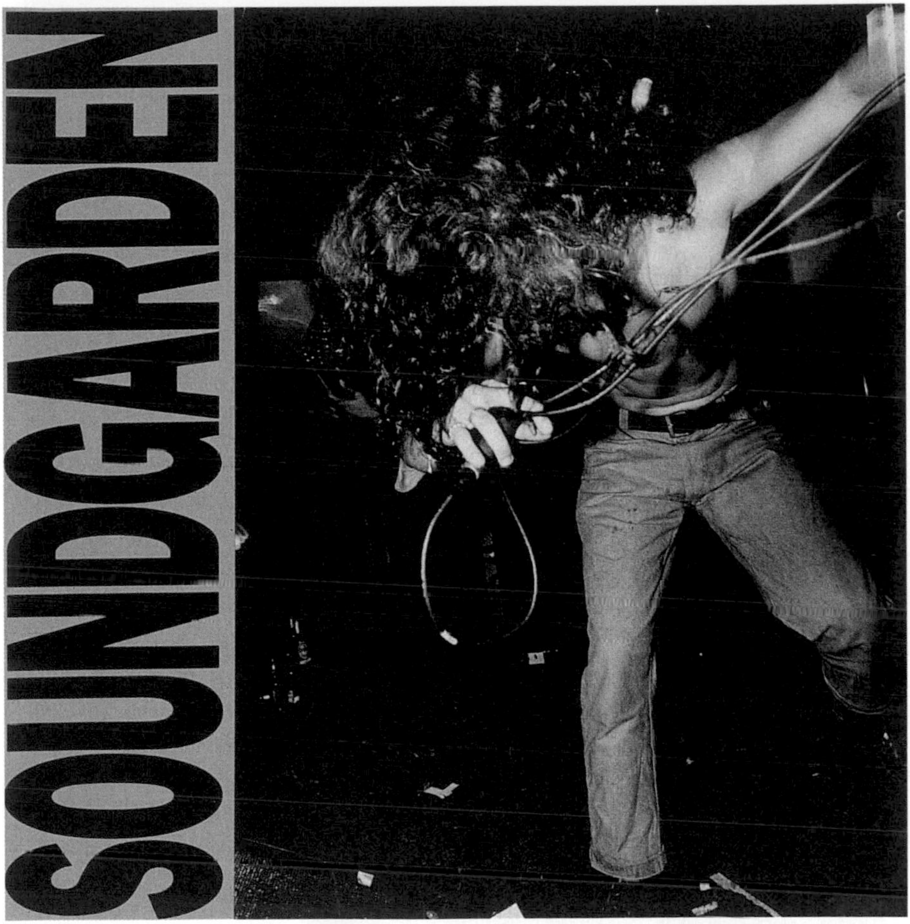

**Soundgarden**
*Louder Than Love*
A&M, 1989

Design: Art Chantry, Third Eye/Bruce Pavitt
Photo: Charles Peterson

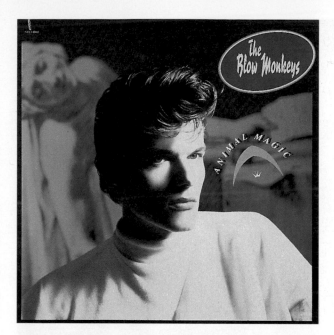

**The Blow Monkeys**
*Animal Magic*
RCA, 1986

Design: Mainartery
Photo: Ian Thomas

**A-Ha**
*Hunting High And Low*
Warner Bros., 1985

Design: Jeri McManus
Art Direction: Jeffrey Kent Ayeroff
with Jeri McManus
Photo: Just Loomis

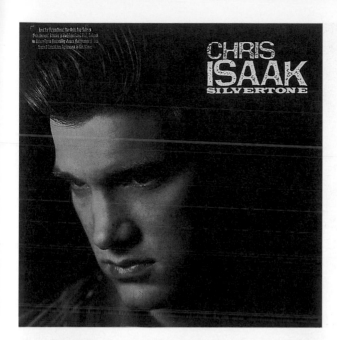

**Chris Isaak**
*Silvertone*
Warner Bros., 1985

Photo: Ric Lopez

**George Michael**
*Faith*
Columbia, 1987

Design: Stylorouge/
George Michael
Photo: Russell Young

**UFO**
*Misdemeanor*
Chrysalis, 1986

Design: Janet Perr
Photo: Marcia Resnick

**Ween**
*Chocolate and Cheese*
Flying Nun Records, 1994

Design: Reiner Design Consultants, Inc.
Photo: John Kuezala

**Sinéad O'Connor**
*The Lion And The Cobra*
Chrysalis, 1987

Cover Art: John Maybury
(Sean Pencil)/Steve Horse
Photo: Kate Garner/Kim Bowen

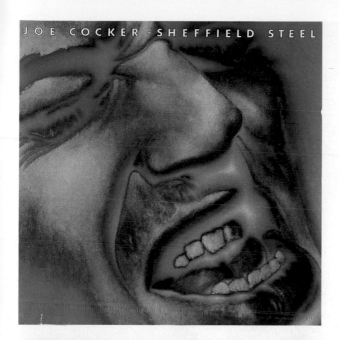

**Joe Cocker**
*Sheffield Steel*
Island, 1982

Painting: David Oxtoby

**Phil Collins**
*Hello, I Must Be Going!*
Atlantic, 1982

Photo: Trevor Key
Courtesy Atlantic Recording Corp

**Björk**
*Post*
One Little Indian, 1995

Design: Me Company
Artwork: © 1995 Me Company,
moral rights reserved
Photo: Stephane Sednaoul

(Back cover)
*Post*

**U2**
*The Joshua Tree*
Island, 1987

Design: Steve Averill
Photo: Anton Corbijn

**The Cranberries**
*No Need To Argue*
Island, 1994

Design: Cally on Art DalkyIsland

Oasis
*Definitely Maybe*
Creation, 1994

Design: Brian Cannon for Microdot
Photo: Michael Specher Jonet

Michael Ochs developed an addiction to rock and roll in the early fifties. To feed his habit, Mr. Ochs headed the publicity departments of Columbia, Shelter and ABC Records in the sixties and seventies. He has also been a disc jockey, taught a rock-history course for UCLA and written for such magazines as *Rock, Melody Maker, Cashbox* and *Crawdaddy*.

Michael Ochs established the Michael Ochs Archives in the mid-seventies. The archives currently house millions of photographs and over 100,000 albums and singles. Photographs from the archives can be found in most rock books and CD reissues.

**Michael Ochs'** Abhängigkeit vom Rock 'n' Roll datiert aus den frühen fünfziger Jahren. Um seine Sucht zu befriedigen, leitete er in den Sechzigern und Siebzigern die Presseabteilungen von Columbia, Shelter und ABC Records. Darüber hinaus war er Diskjockey, gab einen Kurs zur Geschichte der Rockmusik an der UCLA und schrieb für Zeitschriften wie *Rock, Melody Maker, Cashbox* und *Crawdaddy*.

Das Michael Ochs Archives gründete er Mitte der siebziger Jahre. Es umfaßt zur Zeit einige Millionen Fotografien und mehr als 100.000 Alben und Singles. Fotos aus seinem Archiv finden sich in fast allen Büchern über die Rockmusik sowie auf unzähligen Wiederveröffentlichungen von Alben als CDs.

**Michael Ochs** a développé une dépendance au rock 'n roll au début des années cinquante. Afin de satisfaire son irrépressible penchant, M. Ochs a dirigé le département publicitaire des maisons de disques Columbia, Shelter et ABC dans les années soixante et soixante-dix. Il a également été disc-jockey, a enseigné l'histoire du rock à UCLA et écrit pour des journaux et magazines tels que *Rock, Melody Maker, Cashbox* et *Crawaddy*.

M.Ochs a fondé les Michael Ochs Archives au milieu des années soixante-dix. Les Archives abritent aujourd'hui des millions de photographies et plus de 100.000 albums et singles. Des photos extraites de ces archives figurent dans la plupart des livres consacrés au rock et dans des rééditions d'albums en CD.

For more information Michael Ochs can be contacted at
Michael Ochs Archives
524 Victoria Avenue, Venice CA 90921, U.S.A.

# Index

The publishers and Michael Ochs would like to thank

Helen Ashford, Brad Benedict, Dave Booth, Bernd Czogalla,
Laura Dooley, Art Fein, Ursula Fethke, Richard Foos, Arthur
Gorson, Jonathan Hyams, Gary Johnson, Wayne Johnson, Jim
Kennedy, Volkmar Kramarz, Ria Lewerke, Kathrin Marquardt, Ted
Myers, Arlene Ochs, Michele Phillips, Allan Rinde, Fred Siebert,
Rockaway Records, West Coast Photo Lab

without whose help this book would not have been possible.

In addition the publishers would like to thank the following
record companies and license holders for their support:

ABKCO, ACE, Alligator, Alternative Tentacles, Apple, Arista,
Atlantic, Attic, AVI-Excello, Bearsville, Beggar's Banquet, BMG
Ariola, Bug Music, Capitol, Castle Communications, CEMA,
Chancellor, Charly, Evan Cohen, Creation, Crescendo, Roger
Dean, DEL-FI, Disques Vogue, Eastwest, Elektra, Elvis Presley
Enterprises Inc., EMI, Everest, Greensleeves, Gusto, Highland
Music, Intercord, IRS, Jamie, King, Leadclass, LEGRAND, Line
Music, Masters International, MCA, Me Company, Megaforce,
Mercury, Mooncrest, Mushroom, Yoko Ono, Original Sounds,
Overland, Philles, President, PolyGram, Radioactive, RCA, John
Reid Enterprises, Repertoire, Rhino, Gerald H. Sanders, Slash,
Sony, Sun, TKO, Trojan, Vee-Jay, Virgin, Warner Bros., WEA,
Zomba, Zyx.

Special thanks are due to all designers, illustrators, photo-
graphers, painters etc. not mentioned by name, whose work has
made this book what it is.